THE COMPLETE
IDIOT'S
GUIDE® TO

Child & Adolescent Psychology

by Jack C. Westman, M.D., M.S., with Victoria Costello

ALPHA

A member of Penguin Group (USA) Inc.

This book is dedicated to children everywhere and to every adult who makes a lifelong commitment to their care and guidance.

ALPHA BOOKS

Published by the Penguin Group

Penguin Group (USA) Inc., 375 Hudson Street, New York, New York 10014, USA

Penguin Group (Canada), 90 Eglinton Avenue East, Suite 700, Toronto, Ontario M4P 2Y3, Canada (a division of Pearson Penguin Canada Inc.)

Penguin Books Ltd., 80 Strand, London WC2R 0RL, England

Penguin Ireland, 25 St. Stephen's Green, Dublin 2, Ireland (a division of Penguin Books Ltd.)

Penguin Group (Australia), 250 Camberwell Road, Camberwell, Victoria 3124, Australia (a division of Pearson Australia Group Pty. Ltd.)

Penguin Books India Pvt. Ltd., 11 Community Centre, Panchsheel Park, New Delhi—110 017, India

Penguin Group (NZ), 67 Apollo Drive, Rosedale, North Shore, Auckland 1311, New Zealand (a division of Pearson New Zealand Ltd.)

Penguin Books (South Africa) (Pty.) Ltd., 24 Sturdee Avenue, Rosebank, Johannesburg 2196, South Africa

Penguin Books Ltd., Registered Offices: 80 Strand, London WC2R 0RL, England

Copyright © 2011 by Jack C. Westman and Victoria Costello

THE COMPLETE IDIOT'S GUIDE TO and Design are registered trademarks of Penguin Group (USA) Inc.

International Standard Book Number: 978-1-61564-063-8
Library of Congress Catalog Card Number: 2010919309

13 12 11   8 7 6 5 4 3 2

Interpretation of the printing code: The rightmost number of the first series of numbers is the year of the book's printing; the rightmost number of the second series of numbers is the number of the book's printing. For example, a printing code of 11-1 shows that the first printing occurred in 2011.

Printed in the United States of America

Note: This publication contains the opinions and ideas of its authors. It is intended to provide helpful and informative material on the subject matter covered. It is sold with the understanding that the authors and publisher are not engaged in rendering professional services in the book. If the reader requires personal assistance or advice, a competent professional should be consulted.

The authors and publisher specifically disclaim any responsibility for any liability, loss, or risk, personal or otherwise, which is incurred as a consequence, directly or indirectly, of the use and application of any of the contents of this book.

Publisher: *Marie Butler-Knight*
Associate Publisher: *Mike Sanders*
Executive Managing Editor: *Billy Fields*
Senior Acquisitions Editor: *Paul Dinas*
Development Editor: *Megan Douglass*
Senior Production Editor: *Kayla Dugger*

Copy Editor: *Tricia Liebig*
Cover Designer: *Kurt Owens*
Book Designers: *William Thomas, Rebecca Batchelor*
Indexer: *Celia McCoy*
Layout: *Ayanna Lacey*
Senior Proofreader: *Laura Caddell*

Contents

Appendixes

Introduction

From the first time a toddler recognizes her face in a mirror, a question will recurrently arise in her mind: "Who am I?" The answer she comes up with is influenced by traits she inherited and experiences that shape her as she grows. Equally important is the age at which she asks the question. Each stage of a child's growth enables different types of thoughts, emotions, behaviors, and levels of understanding. In this book, you'll find the basic roadmap every child follows to maturity, a journey that is the subject of child and adolescent psychology.

How to Use This Book

The purpose of the chapters that follow is to give you a quick and comprehensive overview of the field of child and adolescent psychology. Whether you are using this book for self-understanding, to better raise a child, as a primer on the field, or as a study aid, here's a quick "trip kit":

Part 1, Discovering Childhood, lays the foundation for child psychology as a field that is now barely a century old. Here you'll find the groundbreaking ideas of the pioneers Freud, Erikson, Watson, and Piaget. Each brought scientific and philosophical ideas from other fields to create this new discipline. How child psychologists applied the scientific method to child behavior and development is key to understanding this burgeoning field.

Part 2, Foundations of Personality, dives into the never-ending dialogue about the relative weight of nature (heredity) and nurture (environment) in shaping personality and behavior. The tools for measuring heritability are presented here. The enormously important role of the child-parent bond in a person's life rounds out this part.

Part 3, A Child Is Part of a Family, presents the evidence to underscore the reality that no child is an island. A child is a part of a child-parent unit. The factors that make someone a "good-enough" parent, as opposed to a "too-good" or incompetent parent are laid out with the accompanying science to back up these conclusions. Child psychologists have spent many years observing functional and dysfunctional families at work. In Chapter 6, you'll find highlights of their results.

Part 4, The Big Picture, takes a chapter to focus on each of the three important growth areas in every child's life: social-emotional, moral, and cognitive development. Here you'll find an overview of the dominant schools of thought that seek to define how a child learns, how he develops empathy and morality, and how he attains "happiness" that accompanies emotional resiliency.

Part 5, Ages and Stages, doubles back and goes into depth on each major stage of a child's life from the womb to young adulthood. In each 2- to 6-year stage, this part focuses on the most important challenge and area of development. For a baby, it's learning to trust and becoming mobile; for a toddler, it's learning language and becoming capable of self-control; for a preschooler, it's developing a self-identity and becoming a social being; for an elementary school child, it's learning how to think logically and becoming a worker; and for an adolescent, it's building a unique self-identity and becoming a young woman or a young man.

Part 6, Issues in Child Psychology, offers in Chapter 16 a comprehensive overview of mental disorders affecting children and teens. Chapter 17 zeroes in on learning disorders, examining their causes and treatments. Child abuse and maltreatment with a focus on recovery are both covered in one chapter. This part then takes a look at the costs and benefits of children growing up in a digital environment.

Part 7, Therapeutic Approaches in Child Psychology, looks first at the history, theory, and practice of psychotherapy for individual children and teenagers. Chapter 21 then focuses on psychotherapy for young people in family and group settings. The dual emphasis in both chapters is on how psychotherapy works to bring about positive behavioral change in children and adolescents and how its effectiveness is measured. Our final chapter returns to the theme of "no child is an island," this time presenting other schools of thought to account for psychological, social, and environmental influences on the "whole child."

A glossary and a list of organizations and online resources for students, parents, and practitioners are included at the end of this book.

Extras

In addition to the narrative for *The Complete Idiot's Guide to Child & Adolescent Psychology,* you'll also find the following other kinds of useful information.

DEFINITION

Key psychological words or phrases explained in a comprehensible way.

FIELD STUDY

Interesting facts from new psychological research.

INSIGHT

The implications of theory and research findings in child psychology.

COMPLICATION

Advice to help you avoid misinterpretations.

Acknowledgments

I am indebted to the children, adolescents, parents, and professionals who have shared their lives with me in my work as a child and adolescent psychiatrist, teacher, and advocate for children and families. My own family has been, and is, the crucible for my own personal development. My tolerant wife Nancy is my supportive life companion. Our sons Daniel, John, and Eric have given us first-hand experience in child rearing and its rewards. They and our daughters-in-law Alison, Jan, and Gretchen have given us our grandchildren Matthew, Laura, Carly, Peter, Megan, Eric, Luke, Clay, and Alexander, who give us hope for the next generation. I am grateful to Victoria Costello for her research on the content of this book and for making it readable.
—Jack Westman, Madison, Wisconsin

I wish to acknowledge my sons Brendan and Devin for the insights they've inspired and the joys they've given me as a parent.
—Victoria Costello, San Francisco, California

Trademarks

All terms mentioned in this book that are known to be or are suspected of being trademarks or service marks have been appropriately capitalized. Alpha Books and Penguin Group (USA) Inc. cannot attest to the accuracy of this information. Use of a term in this book should not be regarded as affecting the validity of any trademark or service mark.

Discovering Childhood

Part

1

The pioneers Freud, Erikson, Piaget, and Skinner gave us a variety of perspectives on the most essential aspects of a child's development. After a hundred years, theirs are still the primary schools of thought that govern research and practice in child psychology. When can an association between any two variables be labeled cause and effect? For this relatively new science, methodologies and standards for new studies and experiments have emerged to pave the way to the future.

Pioneers and New Perspectives

In This Chapter

- The roots of child psychology come from the fields of philosophy, medicine, and zoology
- The building blocks of personality: sex, love, and learning
- The conditioned responses that shape human behavior
- The origins of identity crisis lay in childhood

We can thank some fancy footwork by two professors of philosophy in the 1870s for the birth of psychology as an academic discipline. One German, Wilhelm Wundt of the University of Lepzig, the other American, Henry James of Harvard, were not content to cast about for answers to big questions like "What is consciousness?" or "Why are we here?" Instead, they got practical and asked "How can adults shape a child's personality?" and "How does someone learn a new skill?" By applying the scientific method and moving their students from the library to the laboratory, these learned men and pioneers inaugurated the science of psychology.

It didn't take long after that for the field of child psychology (also called developmental psychology) to take form. It was a Vienna neurologist turned psychiatrist named Sigmund Freud who got the ball rolling in the 1890s, although children were not Dr. Freud's first patients. Although he treated adults, Freud zeroed in on childhood as the primary source of adults' psychological ills. From there, visionaries from philosophy, biology, and linguistics added to a growing body of research and writings. Sometimes agreeing but more often at odds with each other, they spent the next 50 years developing the *theories*, research methodologies, and clinical practices which have become today's child psychology.

The Birth of a New Science

Prior to the nineteenth century, the conventional wisdom about childhood reflected more about the morality of a time period than any particular scientific theory. Children were viewed as property to be exploited, or as savages to tame and mold into small adults. Current unquestioned assumptions, such as the modern understanding that children's minds take years to develop an adult faculty for reason, were unknown.

Babies—Blank Slates or Barbarians?

In the seventeenth century, British philosopher John Locke (1632–1704) famously called the mind of a newborn a "tabula rasa"—a blank slate. Not intended as a putdown, Locke viewed children as passive recipients of knowledge and called for their proper moral and intellectual training.

The romantic view of children as gentle savages with an innate purity who—if not tampered with—would grow up naturally into good and moral adults, is ascribed to the French philosopher Jean Jacques Rousseau (1712–1778). Those since Rousseau's time who view biology as destiny use Charles Darwin's theory of *evolution* as a primary filter for their observations and studies of children. Unlike the "tabula rasa" contingent, these scientists see children as active participants in their own learning, endowed with innate traits to point them in the right direction as they mature.

Divergent Perspectives

Throughout this book, you'll see two different perspectives or biases reappearing frequently in psychological research and practice. One emphasizes nature or biology in a child's development. The other emphasizes nurture or environmental influences. You'll notice that the pendulum often swings from decade to decade, one period favoring the evolutionary perspective and the other veering toward the environmental explanation. Today it is understood that neither perspective suffices alone to account for a child's development of *cognitive*, motor, emotional, and social abilities. In mainstream psychology, intelligence and temperament, for example, are viewed as innate traits that are malleable in that they can be shaped by a child's schooling and parenting.

> **DEFINITION**
>
> The word **cognitive** in psychology pertains to mental processes used in perception, problem solving, recall, thinking, and sensation. Cognitive development is the process by which a baby becomes an intelligent person, acquiring knowledge as he grows and gradually improving his ability to think, learn, reason, and abstract.

The First Child Psychologists

The first scientists studying childhood did not necessarily treat children. Still, they each wanted to identify when and how children develop the ability to think, speak, learn, and love. For the most part, these theorists were also reformers. They wanted to make children's lives better by applying their insights to contemporary child-raising practices and education.

Three general perspectives on child development emerged in the first half of the twentieth century. They are listed here separately, although ideas and results of studies from one often impacted the others, sometimes significantly.

It's Biological

Biological theorists often came to psychology from other biological sciences. They based their assumptions about children on behaviors they studied in the field of ethology (the scientific study of animal behavior) or human biology. They viewed biological maturation as a gradual process that enabled a child's emotional and cognitive growth. As baby ducks instinctively knew to follow the large bird closest to them after climbing out of the egg, so, too, would a human newborn "follow" the adult human in closest proximity to them after making their way through the birth canal. Key concepts from the evolutionary view of child development were influential on two important developmental theorists, Jean Piaget and John Bowlby.

Live and Learn

Learning theorists viewed human behaviors as learned, although many in this school also believed that children had "sensitive periods." At these times in their maturation, children were best equipped to learn different skills. Those whose work fits into this diverse category are united by a belief that experience and learning trump a child's innate tendencies. The first learning theory proponent was William James. Later, the strict behaviorists James Watson and B. F. Skinner built upon the original principle of tabula rasa. Later this perspective was greatly expanded by the most well-known developmental theorist, Jean Piaget.

Unconscious Urges

The third main body of theory at the beginning of the field of psychology belonged to the *psychodynamic* theorists, beginning with Sigmund Freud and followed by Erik Erikson. The idea that personalities are shaped by early unconscious life experiences came from Freud's pioneering work. Freud and Erikson shared a common belief that human development is a conflictual process where the resolution of one age-related crisis leads to another new and necessary challenge—shaping the individual in the process.

DEFINITION

Psychodynamics is the study and theory of the psychological forces that underlie human behavior, emphasizing the interplay between unconscious and conscious motivation.

The Psychodynamics of Childhood

Before Freud created the psychodynamic approach, the fields of medicine and psychology largely discounted the importance of unconscious motivations on an individual's personality or behavior. Nor was there an appreciation for the significance of childhood experiences in a person's development. Before Freud, the mind was viewed largely as a thinking machine, and there was little comprehension of the importance of the emotional side of one's life. All that changed in Vienna, right before and after the turn of the last century.

A Theory of Personality

Sigmund Freud (1856–1939) came to his "theory of personality" as a medical doctor treating "hysterical" females for a wide range of nervous conditions. Using a novel talk therapy process called psychoanalysis, Freud looked back at the first years of his patients' lives for clues to their later personality dysfunctions. From this work, he determined there were three components to personality:

- **Id**—The part of the person that is present at birth, and which exists solely to satisfy inborn biological instincts, largely sexual and aggressive in nature.

- **Ego**—The conscious and unconscious mind, which works to find reasonable, realistic, and socially acceptable ways to satisfy the urges of the Id.

- **Superego**—The seat of conscience, which emerges between the ages of 3 and 6 as children internalize the values of their parents.

As one can infer from just this kernel of Freud's theory, these components of personality were often in discord, if not in a state of war with each other. The central causes of this conflict, Freud believed, were the biological urges that arose in normal maturation. At each stage of growth, these sexual/aggressive urges manifested in a different erogenous zone of the child or adolescent. When manifested, an urge precipitated a need to be met. But, Freud warned, this should not be overly indulged, or the individual's maturation might be delayed.

Here are Freud's five stages of normal emotional maturation from birth to adulthood:

- Oral, from birth to 1 year; involving the mouth and feeding

- Anal, from 1 to 3 years; involving urination and defecation

- Phallic, from 3 to 6 years; brought on by the child's need to identify with the same-sex parent while experiencing strong emotions for the opposite sex parent (referred to as the Oedipal or Electra complex)

- Latency, from 6 to 12 years; when earlier sexual conflicts are repressed and attention turns to school work

- Genital, from 12 years to adulthood; the reawakening of earlier sexual urges

Inadequate resolution of one of these stages explained a later personality problem for the adult, Freud said. Someone with a food or smoking fixation may have been severely punished for thumb-sucking in her first year, during the oral stage. In the process of growing up, this girl may have repressed her feelings about the conflict she experienced as an infant, but it would still be unconsciously driving the behaviors troubling her as a grown woman.

Although many aspects of Freud's work have been rethought and revised since his time, his contributions to psychology are considered fundamental. Beyond his revolutionary ideas, Freud trained a new generation of practitioners in psychological theory and practice. His daughter, Anna Freud (1895–1982), established child psychoanalysis as the foundation for child psychotherapy with her book *Ego and the Mechanism of Defense*.

Love Is All You Need

Born in Germany, Erik Erikson (1902–1994) moved to the United States in 1933 and taught at Harvard and Yale. One of Freud's theoretical heirs, Erikson placed less emphasis on children as passive slaves to their psychosexual urges. Instead, he saw them as active explorers interacting with their environment and cultural influences.

Erikson was in accord with Freud on the basic psychodynamic tenets of personality and the unconscious, and he was the first to apply these to his study of children. As with any Freudian worth his salt, Erikson believed that in their earliest years children develop patterns that regulate, or at least influence, actions and interactions for the rest of their lives.

In his seminal work *Childhood and Society*, Erikson elaborated on how children develop the foundation for mental health in distinct stages. But he didn't stop with childhood. Erikson identified eight distinct stages of maturation from birth through the end of a person's life. From this work, Erikson coined the term "identity crisis" to refer to the conflict and resolution that occurs in each stage of life. Like Freud, Erikson emphasized the benefits of successfully resolving the conflict presented in one stage as preparation for the next one.

In each of his stages, Erikson identified the central conflict a person confronts as a struggle between two opposites. He also pointed to the strength that came from successfully navigating each of these crises.

Erikson's Stages of Psychosocial Development

Age	Stage	Strengths Developed
0–1 year	Trust vs. Mistrust	Hope
2–3 years	Autonomy vs. Shame and Doubt	Self-control and willpower
4–5 years	Initiative vs. Guilt	Purpose
6–12 years	Industry vs. Inferiority	Competence
Adolescence	Identity vs. Role Confusion	Fidelity and devotion
Young adulthood	Intimacy vs. Isolation	Love and commitment
Middle age	Generativity vs. Stagnation	Production and care
Old age	Integrity vs. Despair	Wisdom

Erikson said the main challenge of a newborn baby's first year is the struggle to trust. With this idea, Erikson laid the foundation for the concept of attachment (see Chapter 4). This special bond between the baby and the significant adults in her life begins with the mother and, as Erikson pointed out, has lifelong implications. Some of Erikson's writings at mid-century on this subject proved prophetic, especially his observation that children lacking a basic sense of trust are incapable of developing higher levels of social functioning, such as the capability to form meaningful personal connections with others.

Erikson's observations on the challenges that occur in later periods of a child's emotional development are included in the upcoming chapters devoted to the ages and stages of child development, Chapters 11 to 14.

The Learning Theorists

In contrast to the psychodynamic theorists' focus on the unconscious motivations that propel a child's maturation, the learning perspective—especially the behavioral school of thought within it—can be summarized as "what you see is what you get." To the original "behaviorists" there was nothing invisible about child behavior. There were only overt observations and well-learned associations between actions and rewards or punishments. These associations, the theorists insisted, and not a child's innate abilities, form the real building blocks of development.

The First Behaviorist

Pioneering behaviorist John B. Watson (1878–1958) wanted to prove that he could mold an infant's actions and feelings at will. In a 1920 experiment, he placed a gentle white rat next to a 9-month-old boy, and watched as the boy happily played with the rat. Two months later, Watson reintroduced the same boy to the rat, but added a loud bang whenever the boy reached for the furry creature. Eventually he associated the bang with rats and developed an intense fear for them. This proved that children easily learned fears. (Note: Such an experiment would be deemed unethical today.)

In this experiment, the "unconditioned" or naturally occurring behavior occurred when the child initially played calmly with the rat. It was replaced with the "conditioned response" of fear.

Reinforcements and Punishers

Through his experimental work with animals, B. F. Skinner (1904–1990) put flesh on the bones of behavioral learning theory. He came up with a series of insights and demonstrated how children learn positive behaviors. He also came up with a variety of techniques using conditioned responses to get children (and adults) to "unlearn" negative behaviors.

Key components found in Skinner's concept of behavioral learning included:

- **Operant**—The act, at first voluntary, that is repeated or stopped depending on the consequence it brings about.

- **Reinforcer**—The consequence of an act (positive or negative) that increases the possibility that the act will be repeated. To a child, a positive reinforcer is simple praise. For a love-sick teenage boy, the possibility of getting dumped by his girlfriend is a negative reinforcer, demonstrating that the idea of something bad happening can be enough reinforcement to produce the desired behavior. It may prompt him to bring his girlfriend flowers on Valentine's Day—a nice thing to do, but it's still the negative reinforcer of getting dumped that's motivating him.

- **Punisher**—Any consequence of an act that decreases the probability that it will occur. Getting "grounded" for staying out after curfew is a punisher. Ignoring, isolating, or taking away privileges are common punishers used by parents and teachers with children and adolescents.

- **Operant learning**—A form of learning where voluntary acts (operants) become either more or less likely to occur, depending on the consequences they produce.

COMPLICATION

All punishers are not equal. Behaviorists found that ignoring an attention-seeking, misbehaving child can be a much more effective means to "extinguish" his unwanted behavior than raising your voice or otherwise punishing the child.

With this operant learning theory, Skinner made the claim that there are no innate aggressive or cooperative instincts or stages in children's lives. Rather, behavior is shaped by a child's experiences to be aggressive or cooperative toward others. The best way for a child to learn a big new task, Skinner showed, was to break it down into smaller steps and reinforce each of those steps with a reward.

INSIGHT

Turn down the praise machine. In laboratory tests, behaviorists demonstrated that children are more likely to learn and repeat a new desired behavior if they receive occasional, intermittent, authentic praise. It works better than a constant stream of "that's brilliant" or "you're so smart" every time a child does the "right" thing.

The major contribution of Skinner's operant learning research was its practical blueprint for "behavior modification." This approach has been widely adopted by parents, teachers, therapists, and others as a tool for managing and training children (and adults). Using behavior modification, a problem classroom behavior such as speaking out of turn can be addressed by a teacher using a simple two-step process:

1. The adult/teacher identifies the reinforcers that sustain the student's negative behavior and eliminates them. A reinforcer for speaking out of turn would be allowing the student to ask his question even though he did not raise his hand and was not called on.

2. The teacher models and reinforces the desired behavior by allowing the student to speak only when he raises his hand and is given permission to speak.

Children as Active Explorers

As just discussed, pure behavioral psychologists attempt to elicit specific responses but do not attempt to understand or change the person's underlying emotions or thoughts. They call for the use of reinforcers and punishers to change behavior, never mind how the student feels or what he thinks before, during, or after the response. The learning theorists who followed Skinner embraced his concept of operant learning. But they added new ideas of their own about how a child's built-in cognitive learning abilities make operant learning possible.

Learning theorist Albert Bandura (1925–) took behavioral psychology's core concepts in a new direction when he insisted that young children are not the same as Skinner's animals who responded in rote fashion to reinforcers such as bells or food. Rather, Bandura believed that children are active information processors who learn by observing and imitating others in their environment. They use their thinking and interpretative abilities to understand what they see. They selectively mimic the modeled behavior of others, and it was this ability to select and imitate that constituted the "social" part of the "cognitive social" learning theory that Bandura advanced.

How Thinking Changes

Cognitive developmental theory which, like the psychodynamic, behavioral, and social learning theories, evolved during the first quarter of the twentieth century, focused on how a child's thinking changes over time. The man whose name became synonymous with this perspective was Swiss zoologist and philosopher turned child development theorist Jean Piaget (1896–1980).

Piaget believed children have no inborn knowledge about reality. But he insisted that they have innate cognitive abilities that allow them to naturally make sense of their world by "constructing" a reality. Comparing a child to a scientist, Piaget taught that a child weaves his experience into "theories," which he is then capable of revising when he receives new data, depending on his age. The major points of change in a child's cognitive development, Piaget said, occur at the ages of 2, 7, and 11 or 12.

Piaget brought an evolutionary scientist's perspective to his work with children. He combined knowledge of animal behavior with meticulous observations of his own three children to refine his theoretical work.

Cognitive Development Theory

Here in brief are the major precepts of Piaget's cognitive development theory, which we will return to in greater detail in later chapters:

- **Scheme**—Piaget's notion of a scheme is an organized pattern of thought or action, also called a "cognitive structure" that a child constructs to make sense of an experience. Example: newborn babies have a built-in template for recognizing human faces.

- **Assimilation**—This is Piaget's term for the process by which children interpret new experiences by incorporating them into their existing schemes.

- **Disequilibrium**—This is what happens when children have an experience that causes an imbalance or presents a contradiction between the new experience and an existing scheme.

• **Accommodation**—This occurs when children change their scheme to incorporate or adapt the new experience. Equilibrium returns when the new scheme is constructed to fit the new experience.

Theory in Action

Let's put Piaget's cognitive development principles into action. Consider Zoe, a 2-year-old, who is learning the names of animals at a farm with her mother.

1. Zoe sees her first cow and says, "Look, there's a doggie." This is Zoe attempting assimilation, as she tries to fit her new experience of seeing a cow into the existing scheme she has for dogs.

2. But then her mother points out, "But it's bigger than a dog, and it gives milk." Hmmmm, thinks Zoe. It must be something else. This is Zoe encountering disequilibrium.

3. Zoe makes the leap that Piaget called accommodation when, after hearing new information supplied by her mother, when her mother says the word "cow," she comes up with a new scheme for cows.

4. Zoe is pleased with her ability to organize the world around her. She has returned to cognitive equilibrium.

From his observations, Piaget concluded that as their brains and nervous systems matured, children were able to construct increasingly complex schemes to understand their worlds. He then plotted four stages for a child's normal cognitive maturation from birth to adolescence.

Ages and Stages

Piaget divided the development of a child's ability to learn into four distinct stages.

Sensorimotor Stage (Birth–2 Years)

In this stage, babies only know what they see, touch, smell, taste, and hear. Using their senses, they learn through their physical interactions with the environment around them. They are not yet capable of representational (or symbolic) thought.

This is the ability to recognize that things (a word or image) can represent (or stand in for) other things. For example, when a baby drops a rattle to the floor, it no longer exists because he can't see it. Nor can he conjure a symbolic image of this thing he no longer sees, because that would require representational thought.

Preoperational Stage (2–7 Years)

In the stage of preoperational thought, a child regularly uses mental representations or symbols in play and language. This is the heyday of a child's fantasy or pretend play. Children of this age also possess a basic logic based only on their personal experience, a reasoning capability that Piaget called "intuitive."

It's sometimes easier to understand the cognitive capabilities of children in the period of preoperational thought by looking at what they don't yet understand. For example, children in this age group don't yet perceive that other people might think or see things differently than they do. This is what Piaget referred to as egocentrism.

Preoperational stage children often give inanimate objects life and feelings, a concept called animism. They're also prone to artificialism, the tendency to believe that superhuman agents can move mountains, cause a hurricane, or make the sun rise or fall. It's no wonder why superheroes appeal so strongly to preschoolers.

Piaget observed that the preoperational logic of a child of this age lacks what he called "conservation." This means they don't understand how something or someone can be the same when it or that person looks different. They don't understand, for example, that Dad is still Dad even if he's sporting a beard. Or that a glass of milk is still the same amount if it's poured into a different size glass.

Concrete Operations (7–11 Years)

To a child of 7 to 11 years, this principle of conservation is no longer a problem. Elementary school–age children comprehend how things work (operate), which allows them to think more objectively about themselves and their world. Unlike their 2-year-old siblings, they are no longer the center of the universe. Their logical ability is much more advanced. Their one area of lack, Piaget observed, concerns the same concreteness that gives them such a better grasp of the world. The problem is that their mental processes are still tied to direct sensory experience—to what they can personally see, hear, taste, touch, and smell.

Formal Operations (12 Years–Adulthood)

It is only after children reach the age of 12 or so that they're capable of abstract thought. That is the ability to think about things that cannot be perceived using their senses—things which are not tangible or material. Children of this age can also use deductive reasoning, the process of going from the general to the specific facts.

Piaget's most significant contribution to child psychology was his insight that children do not think like adults. He insisted that children need hands-on experience to learn. Only then can they create their own schemes and change them when necessary. This was a very different approach to teaching children than what came before him. Piaget's strongest impact as a theoretician was on children's education.

Building On the Big Four Theorists

New discoveries and theories about how children's minds and personalities develop did not stop with Freud, Erikson, Skinner, and Piaget. In the last half of the twentieth century to the present, child psychologists have continued to build on and diverge from the foundation created by these pioneers. With the help of long-term family and twin studies, new brain imaging technologies, and discoveries in genetics, many of the pioneers' ideas have been revised or refined, and in a few cases discarded. And yet the same knotty issues that caused rifts between the first child psychologists are still fueling debate in the field today.

Active questions today include the following:

- How much of a child's development is attributable to heredity and how much results from the environment in which he grows up? (Can either be reversed, quantified, or predicted?)

- How active or passive is the child in his own development?

- How much impact do all of the cultural, educational, and other social forces together have on a person's development? (Do child psychologists sufficiently take into account the "whole child"?)

- Should child psychologists study psychologically healthy or unhealthy children and adults? (Should there be a science of "happiness"?)

New technologies that allow researchers to peer into a living brain and decode the human gene have fertilized the work of those attempting to answer these and other questions about children. Snapshots of this new research, along with novel theories and implications, will be included throughout this book.

The Least You Need to Know

- The field of child psychology emerged from inquiries into the origins of adult personality problems in childhood.
- Those who saw children as empty vessels to be filled with the "right" information and behaviors became today's behaviorists.
- Learning theorists differed from strict behaviorists in their belief that children are active explorers who construct their own realities.
- The first theoretical perspectives explaining how the brain and personality of a child develop remain the principal directions guiding today's psychological research.
- Piaget was the first to map out the stages of a child's cognitive development that determine when a child can learn specific knowledge and skills.

Researching Child Behavior

In This Chapter

- Why an association between two variables doesn't prove cause and effect
- What makes "the scientific method" scientific
- How good psychological research is like a good recipe
- When a variable confounds a research outcome
- What the unbreakable rules are for research with children

In news reports you often hear the phrase, "A recent study shows …" These are usually trend or lifestyle stories offering insights about why children and adults behave the way they do. A common source for these stories is a child development study like the ones that populate this book. When reported in the media, the headlines may sound more like common sense than breaking news. But if the information comes from a credible psychological study, the results have been vetted to meet accepted scientific standards. The methods discussed in this chapter demonstrate how psychological research meets the standard of "scientifically sound" and, in the process, becomes news.

The Scientific Method

In science, a new untested idea is called a hypothesis. The notion that the earth revolved around the sun was as old as classical Greece but remained an untested hypothesis in the 1600s when Galileo set out to prove it with the help of a telescope. The hypothesis that a newborn baby's failure to form a secure attachment can hinder his physical, emotional, and cognitive growth remained an unproven hypothesis until a child psychologist first studied the lagging development of motherless monkeys. The *scientific method* fills the gap between a hunch and a theory.

> **DEFINITION**
>
> The **scientific method** calls for the use of objective (measurable) data, not subjective (opinions) data. It requires researchers to allow their data to decide the merits of their thinking—not the other way around.

From Question to Theory

From every hypothesis a central question emerges. Does the earth revolve around the sun? Is a baby who doesn't experience a secure attachment in the first year at risk for retarded growth?

To answer the question, a psychological researcher gathers data using study designs and methods that are outlined in this chapter. With the data she collects, a researcher forms a theory to account for it. Her theory should answer the original question and assist in making accurate and specific predictions about the future.

The last step for a researcher doing a formal study is to disseminate the results of that work in a report shared with peers who work in the same discipline. This is done through a network of scientific journals. Prior to a study being printed in one of these journals, it goes through a vigorous peer review.

The Must-Haves

A scientific article in a journal details the process a researcher used to arrive at the results cited. In many ways, a research report works like a recipe in a cookbook. Both are clear in their intentions and results. They are methodical and replicable. One sponge cake should resemble another. The same is true of two experiments testing the same hypothesis. But how is this achieved? What are the components of replication?

COMPLICATION

Validity and reliability rule! Research cannot be valid unless the results obtained provide an answer to the specific question posed by researchers. Reliability assesses whether the same outcome will be produced by other researchers who repeat the experiment.

Here are the key components you'll find in good recipes and in reliable research:

- **Introduction: What's the Point?**—In the introductory paragraph, the researcher must introduce her study by describing its expected result.

- **Participants**—The people who share certain characteristics (for example, age, sex, or geographic location). They individually agree to undergo the tests, interviews, or other procedures that the researcher will use to produce data for her study.

- **Method**—The researcher details the method(s) she used in a research study. She must explain how she measured a participant's behavior before a new stimulus is introduced so there is a "base level" to compare against any changes in that behavior.

- **Results**—The results of a psychological study must be discussed in detail.

Statistics will often be used to assess data. These will then be interpreted and analyzed. A research article in a scientific journal will conclude with the investigator's reflections and suggestions. These are directed at other researchers working in the same field, citing avenues for investigation to fill remaining gaps in knowledge.

Several chroniclers of the approximately 100-year history of child psychology believe that of the tens of thousands of studies done by researchers during this time, a mere 20 or so have shaped the major tenets of the field as it now exists. As you'll see in upcoming chapters, many subsequent studies have been done to elaborate and apply these formative theories to new populations and situations.

If A, Then B?

Descriptive methods for studying children's behavior permit researchers to objectively record how children with certain characteristics or histories behave and respond under specific conditions. This approach has been used to answer research questions such as: "Are children who watch violent television programming more aggressive with their peers than children who don't regularly watch violent TV?" The primary steps to carry out such a study include the following:

- A researcher obtains detailed data on the violent TV watching habits of all children participating in the study with a comparable number of children who fit into each of several different categories of violent TV watching time.

- The children are observed as they interact with their peers on the playground during recess on multiple occasions.

- Observers record the number of instances of aggressive behavior displayed by each child, using clear criteria to separate aggressive acts from nonaggressive play.

At the end of such a study, there may or may not be an association made between watching violent television and aggressive behavior on the school playground.

When Seeing Is Believing

An advantage of naturalistic observation, especially with babies and younger children, is that it gets researchers past the hurdle of working with participants who possess limited verbal and cognitive skills. It can also provide a unique perspective on real-life behaviors. On the negative side, naturalistic observations can be undermined by the sheer number of behaviors and interactions occurring in a naturalistic setting.

Another approach to descriptive research that addresses the difficulty of isolating one behavior from others in real-life settings is to bring study participants into structured "laboratory" environments created specifically for observational purposes. For example, if researchers want to determine how often a 3-year-old at play will pick up and look at a picture book and engage in "prereading activity," then where the child is placed during the observation will make a large difference in the results. A child playing in a family room filled with a dozen other play choices may never pick up a picture book. However, the same 3-year-old placed in front of only two play choices, one a toy truck and the other a picture book, can be observed making a clear choice between two options.

Another factor affecting the validity of these research studies is "observer influence." This raises the question of whether children are acting naturally in front of an observer who is a stranger to them. Will they show off, or become shy? Researchers try to minimize such possibilities by spending time in the environment with the children before they begin making formal observations. Two-way mirrors and videotaping are two other techniques used to overcome any unwanted observer influences in naturalistic or structured observations.

FIELD STUDY

In one large-scale study, researchers wanted to see if and how mother-child interactions differed in babies who were exposed to cocaine during pregnancy compared to those who were not. Researchers brought 695 mothers and their 4-month-old babies (236 who had the prenatal exposure to cocaine) into a structured observation setting. In three two-minute periods, the exposed babies' facial reactions (recorded on video) revealed them to be less positively engaged with their mothers than the nonexposed babies. According to the study results, mothers who'd used cocaine appeared to be less "synchronized" with their babies than non-cocaine-using mothers. The size and controlled conditions used in this study permitted researchers to make informed statements about the association being investigated, but it did not distinguish between the contribution of either the mother or the baby to the diminished "synchronization."

Keeping It Objective

Do you think your expectations shape what you see and hear in a situation? Another important ground rule for those observing children for research purposes in naturalistic or structured environments is to remove "observer bias" as much as possible. The best way to do this is to make sure the person doing the actual observing and recording of behaviors does not know the expected results of his observations beforehand. For example, the observer looking for aggressive actions on the playground should not know which participants watch violent television and which don't. This minimizes the risk that an observer's expectations will influence the flavor of his observations and potentially change the outcome of the research.

In addition to making direct observations of children there are two other interactive processes used in descriptive psychological research.

Just Ask: Self-Reports

To find out if a 3-year-old likes picture books, he can be asked the question directly. His answer or the answer given by his parent about the child's reading habits is considered a self-report. Self-reported information can be obtained either in face-to-face interviews or through written questionnaires.

One potential disadvantage of self-reporting is the possible inaccuracy of the child's or parent's memory when answering questions. Respondents (both children and adults) will sometimes give the answer they believe their interviewer wants to hear, not the actual answer. Interviewers must be extremely careful not to lead children to give a particular answer through the type of questions asked or by displaying certain body language during the interview (head nodding, leaning forward, etc.).

With some research questions, an in-depth "case study" concerning one or a few children is done to assemble descriptive research. Often the subjects of these child case studies are exceptional in some way, for example the child is a prodigy or a victim of abuse. Case studies usually include naturalistic and structured observations, as well as self-reports and other assessment methods.

In summary, descriptive research with children can produce voluminous data on participants' behaviors and responses under controlled and uncontrolled conditions. A researcher can quantify and qualify aspects of behavior such as aggression, attention, and favored activities. He can look for associations between things. For example the results of playground observations may establish an association between the quantities of aggressive acts observed on the playground with more hours of watching violent television.

But these methods cannot give researchers a certain finding about the strength of that association or about cause and effect. They cannot say that TV violence caused the children's aggressive behaviors on the playground, or whether aggressive behavior led the child to watch more violent TV. Perhaps other factors were more important, for example, a child witnessing conflicts involving adults in the home environment. These questions require different types of research methods to make a definitive correlation between one factor and others.

The Body Speaks

Unlike other fields of medicine, psychologists traditionally have not had the benefit of physiological tests—blood tests, x-rays, pulse rate, temperature reading—to make diagnoses and determine paths of treatment. Instead they have largely relied on interviews and observations conducted with their adult and child patients. In recent years, child psychologists have increasingly turned to physiological techniques to probe the biological underpinnings of children's perceptual, cognitive, and emotional responses.

Heart Rate and Novelty

Physiological techniques can be particularly useful with younger nonverbal subjects in a research study. Heart rate, for example, is a very sensitive reading of a baby's psychological state. A baby who is very interested in a new stimulus will usually have a decreased heart rate. An uninterested baby will show no change in his heart rate. A baby who is frightened by a novelty will have a quickened heart rate.

Brain function in children can also be measured using electroencephalographical (EEG) readings of brain wave activity through electrodes unobtrusively attached to a child's scalp. In other studies, saliva tests for hormonal changes have proved to be effective in capturing an emotional response of fear in controlled settings. Disadvantages in psycho-physiological measures of children can stem from the unknown influence of other factors which could be affecting a child's reactions. Among these are mood swings, fatigue, or hunger.

Picturing the Brain

The refinement of two recent technologies gives psychologists access to their patients' brains in ways unimaginable to their colleagues only a quarter century ago:

- Positron emission tomography (PET) is a brain imaging technique that produces a three-dimensional image of functional processes in the body. It can be used to study the area of the brain activated by a particular task. Because the radioactivity decays rapidly, it is limited to monitoring short tasks.

- Functional magnetic resonance imaging (fMRI) measures changes in blood flow related to neural activity in the brain. fMRI dominates the brain mapping field because of its relatively low invasiveness, absence of radiation exposure, and relatively wide availability. It can be used to reveal brain structures and processes associated with perception, thought, and action.

Correlating and Computing

A correlational design is a type of research that, while it cannot solve the question of cause and effect, it can indicate the strength of an association between two variables. The statistical process used to figure out if there is a causal relationship between two variables produces its answer in the form of a *correlation coefficient*.

DEFINITION

A **correlation coefficient** (symbolized in an equation by an *r*) is a numerical index, ranging from –1.00 to +1.00, of the strength and direction (negative or positive) of the relationship between two variables. The more extreme the value in either direction (–.70 or lower; +.70 or higher) makes a stronger association between the two variables, either negatively or positively.

Positive or Negative Relationships

Negative correlations indicate an "inverse" relationship: as one variable increases, the other decreases. Among grade school children, aggressive behavior and popularity are inversely related. The more aggressive the child, the less popular he will be. A researcher might describe the outcome of a study documenting this association as producing a –.80 correlation between aggressive behavior and popularity.

Positive correlations demonstrate that as one variable increases, the other variable does also. For children, height and weight are usually positively correlated. When a child grows taller, she also weighs more. Researchers of a study updating the association between schoolchildren's heights and weights might report a +.90 correlation between the two.

Interpretations—Take Care!

A correlation between two variables can be put into the form of an equation using the r symbol for the correlation coefficient:

- When $r = 0$, the two variables are completely unrelated.

- When $r > 0$, the variables are positively related; when one increases the other does also, as in the children's height and weight example.

- When $r < 0$, the variables are inversely related; when one increases the other decreases, as in the example of children's aggression and popularity.

Thus, a relationship between the two variables is established, but still without assigning cause and effect. Why not? Let's look at the pitfall of jumping too quickly to causation using a hypothetical correlation involving children's traits and behaviors.

After studying 100 children and rating two variables, their sports performance and popularity, the correlation coefficient between children who are good at sports and social popularity is .70. This means that children who are good sports performers are more popular. But what is the cause and effect relationship between these two variables? There are at least two possibilities:

- Participating in school sports makes kids more popular.
- Popular kids are more likely to participate in school sports.

But what if both of these two cause and effect relationships are invalid? What if a third variable, not yet accounted for, is the real cause of both of the other two variables?

- Parents who provide a secure and supportive family environment produce children who are more popular *and* more likely to participate in school sports.

Bottom line: Cause and effect cannot be determined in a correlation study.

Measuring Cause and Effect

An experimental research method is designed to solve the type of causation question presented by the TV violence/playground aggression and the sports participation/popularity correlation studies. This method can enable researchers to figure out which variable is the cause of a particular behavior and which is the response. There are some new factors involved.

Independent and Dependent Variables

With the experimental method, researchers systematically manipulate the factor/ behavior or variable that they think is the cause of a particular behavior so that they can prove their hypothesis:

- The key factor/behavior which is believed to be causative is called the "independent variable."

- The other factor/behavior which is believed to be the behavior that is caused by the independent variable is called the "dependent variable."

- Children are assigned randomly to different treatment groups. Any differences between the groups can then be attributed to the treatment each receives.

Put It to a Test

Let's apply this experimental approach to a research hypothesis. Suppose researchers wish to test whether students learn better in a classroom with windows letting in light and fresh air than in a windowless classroom with fluorescent lighting and vented air. Here's how they would go about it.

Tenth grade students come to a testing site with two different classrooms, one with windows (independent variable) and the other windowless (also an independent variable) to see how they perform on a test (the dependent variable in both cases). The students are randomly assigned to one or the other classroom where they would receive an identical reading assignment. Both groups have the same amount of time to read the assigned story and take a comprehension test afterward. If students perform significantly and consistently better on the test in the classroom with open windows, the researcher can say with confidence that this independent variable has a positive effect on student performance.

To recap, the steps for this experimental study are ...

1. Assigning participants to two different conditions—open windows and no windows.

2. Creating a standardized setting—room in a school.

3. Manipulating an independent variable—study with windows and study without windows.

4. Measuring a dependent variable—scores on a test.

5. Comparing results—students with open windows scored higher.

6. Conclusion—open windows enhance studying.

Confounding Variables

But what if there was an unknown factor contributing to the better performance of the students tested in the classroom with windows? Let's say, for example, several of the participants had come from gym class where they'd run around the track four times. Might the fact that they'd exercised in the fresh air have affected their better performance?

This is then a "confounding variable" in the experimental design. To prevent any confounding variables from interfering with a test of the independent variable (the influence of open windows on test scores), researchers must use "experimental controls." These are steps taken by an experimenter to ensure that all extraneous factors that could influence the independent variable are roughly equivalent in each experimental condition. In the case of the open window test experiment, researchers can make sure all participants came from an equivalent setting for the hour before exam time. This process of making sure no other factors interfere with the outcome of an experiment is referred to as "controlling for" any confounding variables.

In summary, correlational and experimental methods both have strengths and weaknesses. Correlations establish the strength of a relationship between two or more variables but not causation. The experimental method can establish causation but is not always appropriate with every age group and question. Whenever possible, researchers prefer to use both methods to test a hypothesis.

Designs and Timelines

After all that, an investigator's process of planning a course of research is still not over! With both correlational and experimental studies, the investigator must choose a "design" for her study. Many times, when studying children, researchers want to monitor changes in their behavior over a certain length of time. Often they aim to measure behavioral changes and assign relationships and causes among different variables. There are two types of designs to deal with how children's behaviors change over time: these are called cross-sectional and longitudinal designs.

Cross-Sectional Design

Sometimes, researchers wish to map out the possible reasons for a behavior change by testing children of different ages. In this design, researchers compare groups of children of different ages against one another at the same point in time. For example, three groups of children (each age group is called a "cohort") ages 5, 7, and 11 years old might be given a test to measure their problem-solving skills in language and thought. Or the same age groups might be monitored for their preferences in friendships—whether they prefer same sex or opposite sex friends.

INSIGHT

One pitfall of cross-sectional studies is called the "cohort effect," meaning the differences between the tested age groups may result from certain isolated environmental events as much as from the normal developmental process being examined. What if, for example, you are testing for problem-solving skills and one group of 7-year-olds had the benefit of a particular new curriculum addressing that area of problem solving at age 6 while another group of 7-year-olds did not?

Longitudinal Design

In a longitudinal study, the same participants are observed and tested repeatedly at different points in their lives. This approach can be used with virtually any aspect of children's development: social, cognitive, emotional, and physical. It is the only way to answer questions about whether a specific behavior identified in a 5-year-old child, for example aggression or inhibition, will continue or be discontinued as that youngster reaches ages 7, 11, or 16.

Disadvantages of longitudinal designs include the higher administrative requirements and costs involved in tracking a cohort over a long period of time. Dropouts among participants are common. Even if the majority of children remain in the study, another pitfall is that they may become test-savvy, thus altering results over the course of time.

COMPLICATION

There are a number of different ways used by researchers to measure the statistical significance of their study results. For example, in the commonly used "Chi square method," a .05 level is interpreted as statistically significant. This means that there are 5 chances in 100 that a result is false, or 95 chances in 100 that it is true.

Cross-Cultural Design

When a developmental study has involved a large number of participants, it's often tempting to generalize from its finding(s) and declare a trait or behavioral pattern a "universal" truth about children. Before publishing such a new finding, researchers will often attempt to find out whether their study results might differ when using participants from different cultures or groups. For example, children from a wealthy suburb may test differently on language or math than those living in a working-class urban neighborhood. White and minority students might test differently as well, regardless of their economic class.

FIELD STUDY

In one study, researchers sought to compare two sets of children and adolescents in Brazil who had been diagnosed with attention deficit hyperactivity disorder (ADHD). One group lived in a rural area, the other in an urban setting. The research question was whether the same emotional disorders (depression, anxiety) seen in American youth with ADHD also accompanied participants with ADHD in one or both Brazilian locations. Results showed that the same disorders were "stable in" (common to) youth with ADHD in all three locations, thus removing the issue of cultural differences.

In cross-cultural studies, researchers determine whether any of the differences they find represent a confounding variable that could affect their measurement of the independent variable in their study. In general, child psychologists have concluded that the environmental context in which a child grows up often does have a direct bearing on many aspects of his development.

Ethics of Research on Children

There are well-established rules for any psychology professional seeking to measure child behavior in a research setting. Ethical research minimizes risk and deception to participants, allows individuals to freely decide if they wish to participate, and keeps individual results confidential.

Protection from Harm

At all times, research must minimize a child's stress as a result of the types of procedures used or tests given. If a research procedure results in any negative consequences for a child, the researcher must do whatever is necessary to correct the situation. If information is collected that affects the child's well-being, it should be given to the child's parents and to an appropriate expert.

Informed Consent

Researchers must explain the purpose, procedures, and all known risks and benefits of their studies to participants. With minors, they must obtain informed consent from both children older than 6 years of age and their parents.

Privacy

Researchers must keep all information obtained from participants confidential. They may not reveal participants' names or other identifying information to anyone and may not include this information in written reports or articles without prior consent. Most reports give only group results or averages, not individual results. Results from individuals must remain anonymous.

Benefit to Risk Ratio

Research designs and procedures must be sound enough that the information to be gained has sufficient value to outweigh any harm, stress, or inconvenience for participants. In some cases, participants may receive compensation for their participation in a study.

Research Implications

If results of research may be of concern to a particular group, researchers should be sensitive to how, when, and where that information is disseminated.

Making Interpretations

When interpreting a psychological study, one must take great care to first find out the type of research method or study designs used. By knowing whether the end result comes from a correlational or an experimental study, you can determine whether or not it's appropriate to extrapolate a cause/effect relationship from that study.

As the earlier examples illustrate, a correlational study on the relationship between TV violence and children's aggression can rate the strength of an association but cannot assign cause and effect. An experimental study that controls for any confounding variables, such as the degree of conflict a child witnesses in his home environment, can make a stronger association. Such a study could theoretically come up with a finding of cause and effect between TV violence and a child's level of aggression on the school playground.

Similarly, when digesting a cross-sectional study of children in different age groups, it's important to find out whether researchers have accounted for any major environmental differences (divorce, urban/rural, family move, family size) that may affect the participating children and change the study results.

A result is regarded as statistically significant if it is unlikely to have occurred by chance; but significant does not mean important. For example, a study of people in two different countries might show that there is a statistically significant difference of 1 point between the average IQs of the two countries. The difference is significant but unimportant.

In order to determine if a statistically significant result is important, a variety of methods are used to measure "effect size." These methods are too complicated to be described here. Suffice it to say that measurements of effect size are used in evaluating the importance of statistically significant results.

The Least You Need to Know

- An association can show the strength of a relationship between two variables—such as watching violent TV and aggressive behavior—but can't definitively prove cause and effect.
- In order to be accepted by the scientific community, research findings must be replicated by other independently conducted studies.
- Long-term studies offer the advantage of tracking behavior in the same children over time, but pose the risk of losing participants who move away or lose interest.
- Experimental designs eliminate many confounding variables of naturalistic observations with a structured environment.
- Cultural differences can throw a wrench into even a large-scale study's claims of universality.
- Scientific evidence needs to be taken with a grain of salt.

Foundations of Personality

This part provides a back-to-back look at the two most important factors shaping a child's personality: his genetic inheritance and the quality of his attachment bonding. Inheritance is broken down into the language of chromosomes, genes, and DNA. The biological process of passing on genes for body, temperament, and intelligence is portrayed. To figure out the relative importance of genes and environment for a variety of traits, you'll find here the latest tools for quantifying heritability.

The many ways that a consistent bond of warmth and affection positively impact a child's growth will fill in the nurture side of the child development equation in this part. The research on attachment chemistry will amaze along with the negative effects on a child's developing brain when a secure attachment is missing from his early life.

Nature and Nurture

In This Chapter

- The biological moment when you become "you"
- The genetic traits that influence a child's personality
- The understanding of when heredity is and isn't destiny
- The importance of using neurons

A research psychologist was once asked which aspect of a child's development is more important, nature or nurture. His answer: That's like asking a mathematician which is more important, the length or the width of a rectangle. Of course, both are equally important! In this chapter, we see the mechanisms of nature that produce a unique human child. We also learn how child psychologists track the process of nurturing a child's growth.

The Biology of Heredity

Each of the trillions of cells in your body has one thing in common: your unique genetic blueprint. Imagine looking through a powerful microscope into a single cell and going right to the nucleus at its center. Inside the nucleus, you see 23 pairs of chromosomes. What is a chromosome? It's DNA (deoxyribonucleic acid), your hereditary material, wrapped around a protein in a double spiral (helix) pattern. A sequence of DNA encodes a gene, meaning it contains the directions that a gene will express or follow. A gene can make a cell become a part of an arm or a lung. It can also regulate other genes or simply be what is called "junk DNA." In people, genes vary in size from a few hundred DNA segments (base pair molecules) to more than two million segments. The Human Genome Project has estimated that humans have a total of between 20,000 and 25,000 genes. In this chapter, the key aspects of genetics for a child's psychological growth are discussed.

How You Become "You"

Each of your parents bequeathed to you half of your original 46 chromosomes. It happened when your father's sperm joined with your mother's ovum and became a single fertilized egg cell called a zygote. In that moment, DNA came from each parent to form your unique genetic blueprint. In the transfer of a mother and father's genes to the new zygote, the chromosome from the mother has one version of a gene and the chromosome from the father has another version of the same gene. These versions are called the *alleles* of a particular gene.

Small differences in the sequence of DNA base pair molecules in the allele from both parents contribute to their child's unique physical and psychological features. Most genes are the same in all people, but a small number of genes (less than 1 percent of the total) are slightly different between individuals. This is why your DNA is unlike anyone else's on the planet. The exceptions, of course, are identical twins, because they are the result of splitting the same fertilized zygote into two zygotes. And even their genes differ over time through a process called *gene mutation*.

What Genes Do

As mentioned previously, a gene is the basic biological unit of heredity. The DNA in your genes contain "instructions" dictating a particular structure, function, or trait to be *expressed*.

> **DEFINITION**
>
> Gene **expression** is what happens to the surrounding cell when DNA is activated at any point before or after birth. It's what gives each cell a purpose.

How are genes expressed in the body?

- Genes promote cell growth by dictating the production of amino acids, enzymes, and other proteins essential to the formation of other cells.

- Genes regulate cell differentiation during mitosis. A particular cell might become part of a hand or stomach.

- Genes regulate the pace and timing of human growth and development by turning on and off other genes. When it's time for a growth spurt during early childhood, certain genes will signal the cells of bones, muscles, and other organs. Genes also are regulated by surrounding proteins.

Genetic scientists have now counted and named each of the 46 chromosomes and many of the estimated 25,000 human genes, calling them by numbers and letters or a combination of the two. They've also attempted to count the number of DNA (genetic material) bases on each chromosome with the objective of associating genes, DNA bases, and chromosomal locations with specific human traits.

There are four patterns of genetic expression in human reproduction: simple dominant-recessive inheritance, sex-linked inheritance, co-dominant inheritance, and polygenetic or multiple gene inheritance.

Single Gene Inheritance

Thousands of human traits are determined by a single pair of genes (alleles). In each pair, one gene and the trait associated with it tend to dominate. This is then the dominant gene. The other is recessive. When these two different genes occur in a single fertilized egg cell, only one dominates. Here are some examples:

Dominant Traits	Recessive Traits
Dark hair	Blond hair
Curly hair	Straight hair
Normal vision	Color blindness
Normal vision	Nearsightedness
Normal blood clotting	Hemophilia
Normal blood cells	Sickle-cell anemia
Huntington's disease	Normal brain
Pigmented skins	Albinism

Let's look at the trait of nearsightedness. About three quarters of all people have normal vision, while the remaining quarter are nearsighted. The gene that bestows normal vision is dominant, and the nearsighted gene is a weaker, recessive allele. This means that someone can be born nearsighted only when they inherit two recessive, nearsighted alleles. People of this *genotype* will then pass a nearsighted gene to their children who will display a nearsighted *phenotype*. But can two normal-sighted people produce a nearsighted child? Yes. If the mother and father both carry one normal vision allele and one nearsighted allele, they both can pass on the recessive allele and produce a nearsighted child.

DEFINITION

A **genotype** is your genetic blueprint. A **phenotype** is the physiological expression or result of your genes in combination with environmental factors you experience.

Huntington's disease, which causes a gradual degeneration of the nervous system, is a genetically inherited disease linked to a dominant rather than recessive gene. If a parent carries the gene for Huntington's disease, his offspring have a 50 percent chance of inheriting it. If that gene is inherited, the individual will get the disease, which usually strikes after the age of 40. Fortunately, it is a rare disease.

Sex-Linked Traits

Some single gene, inherited characteristics are determined by genes located on the sex chromosomes. Males have XY sex chromosomes and females have XX sex chromosomes. The vast majority of sex-linked attributes are produced by recessive genes that are found only on X chromosomes, most often affecting males. Why is that? With XY sex chromosomes, males are more susceptible to sex-linked traits because they don't have an additional X chromosome to carry an alternative version of the gene. Of the more than 100 sex-linked characteristics, many are disabling. These include hemophilia, two kinds of muscular dystrophy, and certain forms of deafness.

COMPLICATION

Despite centuries of the persecution of queens whose fate depended on producing a male heir, it turns out that it was the king's chromosomes all along that dictated the sex of the new prince or princess.

Polygenetic Inheritance

Most human traits are influenced by many pairs of gene alleles, not just one set. Polygenetic traits include height and weight, intelligence, skin color, susceptibility to cancer, and temperament. Most personality traits are also of this type, with the result that a child is never exactly like her mother or father. More often each of us inherits some of both of our parents' personalities.

Is Heredity Destiny?

The answer in a word is "no," with a caveat ... unless an individual is the recipient of a gene for a fatal congenital disease or condition for which there is no known cure. Two such diseases are Huntington's disease and cystic fibrosis. In the vast majority of people heredity is not destiny. Genes are involved in creating susceptibilities to a disease, and environmental influences can either moderate or trigger such a genital vulnerability. For most of us, heredity is only part of the larger picture.

Given the fact that so many inherited illnesses are believed to be polygenetic in origin, it has been difficult for researchers to isolate the primary genes that give someone a higher risk to a particular disease. Since the monumental decoding of the human genome in 2003, molecular geneticists have been working feverishly around the world to make these definitive links. The goal of this research is to find new avenues of treatment for diseases by intervening at the site of the gene's expression. Progress has occurred, but no major breakthroughs in terms of genetic information leading to a cure have yet been made.

Children's Genetic Disorders

Some children are affected by heredity early in life in ways that disrupt their normal development. Sometimes eggs or sperm have more or fewer than the usual 23 pairs of chromosomes. The best example is Down's syndrome. Babies with this condition have distinctive facial features including a fold over the eyelid and a smaller head. They appear to develop normally during their first few months, but their mental and behavioral growth soon lags behind their peers. Mental retardation is the usual outcome. Babies with Down's syndrome typically have an extra twenty-first chromosome that is usually provided by an egg with the abnormality.

An older mother's eggs which have been in her ovaries since her adolescence may have deteriorated over time, causing a higher incidence of Down's syndrome for mothers giving birth after age 40.

Behavioral Genetics

This is where nature meets nurture. Behavioral genetics is a relatively new scientific field that aims to trace the *hereditability* of different traits and illnesses. To do that, researchers study the relative weights of inherited and environmental influences on a person. But behavioral geneticists' interests go beyond inherited illnesses or disabilities. They also want to quantify the nature/nurture balance in "normal" human intelligence, personality, and mental health. Researchers come to behavioral genetics from many other fields including genetics, zoology, biology, psychiatry, and psychology.

DEFINITION

Hereditability is a mathematical estimate of the degree of genetic influence on a specific trait, illness, or behavior.

Hereditability estimates for a given trait can range from 0.00 to 1.00. The higher values mean there is a stronger genetic influence on a particular trait. Height is estimated at .90, meaning your height is highly dictated by how tall your parents are and the heights of their genetic lineages.

Any heritability value higher than .50 is considered significant. Here are some examples of more complex human behaviors and their hereditability estimates:

- General intelligence: .52
- Verbal fluency: .30
- Sociability: .64
- Extroversion: .51
- Anxiety: .70
- Aggression: .40
- Belief in God: .22
- Hyperactivity: .75

- Obesity (body mass index): .50 to .90

- Alcoholism: .50 to .70

- Schizophrenia: .70

Researchers have found that someone's cognitive ability (learning aptitude) has a lot to do with heredity. Personality, too, has a big inherited component, particularly temperament—your dominant mood and style of behavior from birth.

INSIGHT

Several studies have shown that, contrary to researchers' original expectations, heritability values for cognitive (intellectual) skills actually increase with age. That means, as you get older, the relative influence of your parents' intellectual strengths and weaknesses is greater than when you were a child. Wrap your head around that one!

In contrast to our cognitive abilities, when it comes to personality traits where heredity plays a significant role—extroversion, emotionality, and activity level—hereditability appears to diminish as a child matures into adulthood. Perhaps this is simply the teenager settling into his own identity and responding to new environmental influences—college, profession, close relationships—that continue to shape him.

So how do behavioral geneticists come up with these heritability values? There are two methods used.

Twin Studies

In twin studies, researchers compare the genetic contribution to a given trait by comparing measurements from identical and nonidentical twins. Remember, identical twins shared a fertilized egg, so they're genetically identical, too. Nonidentical twins each had their own fertilized egg (thus sperm and egg) and are no more genetically alike than any two siblings—50 percent, on average. But both types of twins are usually raised in the same or similar environments. So the major difference between each twin is the amount of genetic material they have in common (plus any nonshared aspect of their environments).

Here's how they do it, using IQ as an example:

1. Take a measurement of each twin's IQ.

2. Correlate the measurements between the members of each pair of twins. Remember from Chapter 2 that a correlation measures the strength of an association between two variables, with a higher number correlation demonstrating a stronger association.

3. Compare the correlations for identical twins (.80) to the correlations for nonidentical twins (.52).

If there is an important genetic contribution to IQ, the identical twin correlation would be much higher than the correlation for the nonidentical twins—as it is in this case.

A heritability estimate is then arrived at by doubling the difference between the two correlations:

Difference = .28

Heritability estimate = .28 × 2 = .56

Adoption Studies

The other method for computing heritability uses adoption studies. Adopted children share 50 percent of their genetic material with their biological parents and siblings and 0 percent of their genetic material with their adopted families, with whom they share 100 percent of their environment. Adoption studies compare correlations between both biological and adopted children. If there is an important genetic influence on a particular trait, the correlation with the biological family members should be considerably higher than the correlation with the adopted family members.

What About Environment?

Some typical questions about the degree to which genes shape the individual over time include these head scratchers:

- Wouldn't a child with a predisposition to solitary and quiet activities tend to choose solitary activities, which would then reinforce this personality type as he grows up?

- Because extroversion and introversion have a significant heritability factor, if a child has an introverted parent(s) or sibling(s), wouldn't this tend to shape the family environment and reinforce his behavior?

Each question raises an important point about the interaction between genes and environment. Life is a constant interplay between the two.

Nature and Nurture at Work

There are two more advanced concepts to help track how nature and nurture work together to create the person you are.

Reaction Range

Reaction range refers to the fact that the same genotype can manifest as a variety of phenotypes, depending on the different environmental factors to which you are exposed. Let's apply this principle to IQ. As you just learned, IQ has a significant heritability value of .52. This leaves plenty of room (theoretically a value of .48) for other environmental factors to impact a child's eventual, manifested intelligence: schools and tutors, educated parents who spend a great deal of time discussing scholastic matters with their child, and others. Reaction range in this context defines the number of possible manifestations given the inherited trait. For example, the higher a child's inherited IQ, the wider her possible range of IQ manifestations. Essentially this child has more to work with. A child who inherits a lower IQ has a narrower range of possible outcomes, but his IQ can still be favorably influenced.

Niche-Picking

Another useful concept, niche-picking is seen to be taking place when a young person deliberately seeks out an environment to fit his heredity. In an ongoing feedback loop, he receives positive signals when he's in an appropriate environment for his temperament, IQ, or any other inherited trait. When given a choice, even an extroverted 4-year-old can at least express a preference between a preschool that puts more emphasis on early reading versus one that provides more outside play. He picks the niche that feels right for him.

Neuroscience and Child Psychology

When it comes to the growth of the brain, beginning in the womb and then every day after, the neurons (conducting in contrast with structural brain cells) are where most of the action takes place. Every newborn baby has billions of neurons, each shaped like a tree. The neuron's body or trunk is called the axon. Each cell contains a nucleus that controls the neuron's basic metabolic functions. The axon can be seen as sending out information to other neurons. Every mature neuron also has a root system called dendrites. These dendrites receive chemical messages—in the form of a neurotransmitter—from other neurons, which travel across a gap called the synapse. Special receptors on the dendrites bind to the arriving neurotransmitter, triggering an electrical response in the receiving neuron.

A Time of Rapid Growth

New neurons are generated at an astonishing rate throughout pregnancy. For neurons to grow, and thus the brain to enlarge, synapse formation is of crucial importance, with 1.8 million new synapses per second produced from the time a fetus is 2 months of age until the child reaches age 2. Because the synapse is the place where two neurons communicate with each other, to allow this phenomenal growth to take place, the dendrites of each neuron must develop larger surfaces. This process has been compared to the unfettered growth of a forest.

Thinning the Forest

One of the jobs of genes is to direct the growth of neuron axons and dendrites to their correct locations in the brain. And that doesn't only mean getting each neuron to its own right location. Every neuron must also be connected to the other neurons with which they must maintain communication. For example, a neuron in the retina of the eye needs to have a direct communication "line" to the visual area of the thalamus. How does this occur? Neuroscientists aren't sure.

One important piece of the process they have identified is the producing and pruning of synapses that goes on during gestation and early childhood. In fact, children are thought to produce twice as many synapses as they will eventually need. But this overgrowth of neural synapses is just nature doing its job.

After overgrowth, neuroscientists say, nurture steps in to help the brain sort out and keep the neurons, synapses, and neural connections that are most useful to the developing child. Only the neurons and connections that the child's brain uses are kept. The rest are thinned or pruned away from lack of use.

Use Them or Lose Them

The peak period for synaptic growth in children occurs between the age of 1 and 6 years. By age 14, dramatic pruning of those synapses has taken place. This fact of neurobiology has enormous implications for parents and others who interact with young children. A young brain is shaped by the child's earliest experiences. Everything a child sees, touches, hears, tastes, and smells is translated into specific electrical brain circuits, which then tend to dominate the child's brain.

INSIGHT

Those brain circuits and structures that wire up earliest are thought to set the "organizing template" for future development. The brain's emotional circuits are among the earliest to develop.

If a child experiences many fearful experiences early in life, fear and mistrust get hardwired in her emotional brain circuit. If she gets lots of love and cuddling, her brain reflects that instead. The key factors that make the difference between which responses and behaviors are kept and which fall away are repetition and reinforcement. Your individual pattern of (neural) connections forms the basis of all your movements, thoughts, memories, and feelings. In a word, *you*.

How Plastic Is a Child's Brain?

The neuroscience of child development does not say that the case is closed for a child's emotional and cognitive brain growth by age 3, 6, or late adolescence. In fact, research increasingly provides more and more evidence that the brain never stops growing and changing, throughout adolescence and well into adulthood and old age. The term *plastic* is used to describe the brain's lifelong ability to reorganize itself in response to input received from the environment.

> **DEFINITION**
>
> Neural **plasticity** involves both increases in the number of connections between neurons and physical changes in the shape and structure of those connections. It accounts for learning, memory, and recovery from traumatic head injuries throughout one's lifespan.

Interventions

The caveat to this neural plasticity is that as you age, the rewiring of your neural connections gets harder and takes longer. Interventions with children and teens in response to emotional and psychological problems or learning disabilities are now routinely and effectively done as early as possible. These interventions may include psychotherapy for disorders such as depression or OCD. There are also methods for the retraining of vision and other sense perceptions for learning problems such as dyslexia. The advantage of doing any of these interventions earlier rather than later in a child's life is to intervene and help the brain rewire before its connections are "set in their ways."

The Blossoming Brain

There is a fixed sequence to the development of a child's brain. This makes knowing which abilities and functions mature first and last, beginning at birth, fundamental to child psychology. Here is a rough guide to this sequential process of brain wiring, starting from the earliest brain areas to mature and ending with those that take the longest.

1. Basic autonomic functions in the brain stem, including breathing, heartbeat, and temperature control.

2. Emotional learning in the brain's central limbic system controls the processing of incoming sensory information and memory storage, and tags it for further processing in the frontal cortex.

3. Vision and hearing in the rear occipital lobe and the temporal lobes above the ears.

4. Speech and language production in the temporal lobes.

5. Planning and abstract reasoning, as well as emotional and motor control in the frontal lobes behind the forehead.

The brain's neural wiring process is cumulative. This means that in order for the thinking part of the frontal cortex to function properly, its limbic "feeling center" has to develop first.

The Least You Need to Know

- Although the heritability of some traits such as height are high, many more human characteristics such as intelligence are only moderately heritable.
- Twin studies provide a valuable way to assess the relative weight of nature or nurture in that a larger number of traits are the same or similar in twin siblings.
- The brain is plastic, to a point. Cells are constantly regrowing or being pruned for lack of use.
- Sensitive periods of brain growth favor learning certain skills at these times.

Attachment Theory

In This Chapter

- The survival instincts of human babies
- When anxiety is a healthy sign in babies
- The chemistry of parent-child bonds
- The long-term implications of your first attachment

A child's attachment to a significant caregiver is the single most influential event in the development of his personality. It's the source of the child's sense of security, self-esteem, and self-control. But the impact of a first attachment goes far beyond emotions. It shapes how well he remembers and learns, and how he gets along with others. A secure attachment (as with its weakness or absence) wires a child's brain in a set pattern. How can one aspect of early childhood hold so much power for the span of a lifetime? And how do child psychologists know what they know about attachment? In this chapter, both questions are answered.

Theory and Practice

John Bowlby (1907–1990) did his naturalistic observations of children more than a half century ago, but subsequent research has only fortified adherence to his perspective among psychologists. Bowlby was a British physician and a trained psychoanalyst who accepted Freud's central tenet of the importance of a person's early childhood experiences in the formation of personality. To Freudianism, Bowlby added a detailed analysis of the specific interactions that create a secure versus insecure early attachment between a mother and her child. And he drew on *ethology* to make evolution the organizing principle to account for how these interactions spring from the survival instincts of both mother and child.

> **DEFINITION**
>
> **Ethology** is a branch of biology concerned with the adaptive behaviors of different animal species. In his attachment theory, Bowlby said that children who form a bond to a primary adult are more likely to survive, so when babies practice the instinctive behaviors that help create attachment, they are acting out an important adaptation made early in human history when mothers carried their babies on their bodies while foraging for food.

It's In Their Smile

How can anyone resist such a face? A baby's smile and kewpie pie cheeks are indeed irresistible to most adults. Bowlby pointed out how this visual charm operates as a brilliant adaptation (not unlike baby cubs, kittens, or birds), nearly guaranteeing essential affection, comfort, and food will come a baby's way. Meanwhile, a mother's innate drives to succor and protect her newborn are usually enough to make her play her part in this highly reciprocal relationship.

In what Bowlby called the "human attachment system," babies have a large repertoire of highly effective signals to ensure they receive what they need to survive and thrive. When they're not smiling, they cry and fuss, or they coo and grab at their mother's face, hair, and breasts. They also track her every move around the house just like a duckling follows its mother through tall grass.

Babies are sociable by the age of 3 months, but they usually save their biggest smiles for the significant caregiver in their lives; adults mirror these smiles right back. By calling these behaviors adaptive, Bowlby made the point that they are inborn. The baby's purpose, he said, is to stay physically close to the most important source of his independent survival.

Bowlby noted that newly hatched geese and ducklings develop a preference for the first moving object they see, a process called "imprinting." Similar to these birds, human newborns prefer moving objects and often recognize their mothers within days of birth. However, full bonding on the part of a human baby takes much longer than other animal species, at least six months longer than a duckling. Fortunately, human parents usually pick up any slack in the bonding process.

After only a few minutes with a newborn, mothers and fathers typically say they're goners, already "in love." Sounds pretty adaptive, doesn't it?

> **INSIGHT**
>
> Neuroscientists say babies take longer than their parents to fully bond because their limbic systems, and the frontal cortex of a baby's brain which processes emotions, take from six to nine months to develop the capacity for bonding.

Attachment and Locomotion

In a baby's sixth or seventh month, she has reached prime time to solidify her attachment with a primary adult, usually mother. In another bow to ethology, Bowlby noticed that this timing coincides with the start of a baby's crawling. This suggested to him a link between independent locomotion and the completion of the baby's process of attachment which began at birth. Of course, it takes a baby a lot longer to climb out of his crib than it does for a chick to hop out of the nest. Before chicks and toddlers go wandering too far away, instinct makes sure that they know where "home base" can be found.

> **INSIGHT**
>
> Safety and exploration are the two competing goals in a baby's earliest years. A child who stays safe survives; a child who explores develops the intelligence and skills needed to successfully grow. These two needs often oppose each other. This is why Bowlby and his successors believe that a child develops an internal "thermostat" to monitor his level of safety in the environment. When he gets too far from home base, an internal alarm bell sounds.

It's a familiar dynamic where a child ventures away from mother (either by crawling or "toddling") until some impulse prompts him to turn around and check to see whether mother is still close by. If she's still where he left her, he may keep going. Or he may come back to touch base before restarting his exploration. The attachment bonding process permits children to regulate their urges to explore or to cling to that special adult by internalizing what Bowlby called "working models" of their caregivers. One such working model in the previous situation is "It's okay. Mom will be there if I crawl farther." Another might be "I can't go too far, she may leave me … it's too scary." Babies form one or another model based on their mothers' behaviors over time.

The Rhesus Monkey Experiments

Striking images of some very unhappy, even self-destructive monkeys convinced many doubters about the importance of early animal and human mother-child bonding in the 1950s. These photos came from Harry Harlow's (1905–1981) famous series of Rhesus monkey experiments. Harlow separated a group of infant monkeys from their mothers and raised them with two types of substitute mother figures. One was made of bare wire; the other had a soft cloth cover over a wire form. Harlow's research questions were …

- Would infant monkeys form attachments to the inanimate mother substitutes?

- Would they receive any observable emotional comfort from either kind of substitute mother?

The infant monkeys did form an attachment, but only with the cloth-covered wire mother surrogates, not the uncovered wire forms. Interestingly, both types of surrogates provided food by way of a bottle attached to the wire. This told researchers that the bonding they observed between the infant monkeys and the cloth-covered surrogates was not solely based on nourishment. Something else was behind the bonding.

FIELD STUDY

Harlow's Rhesus monkey experiments strongly inferred that serious negative consequences occur when a human baby is deprived of a strong bond with a mother figure in the first year of life. Bowlby then confirmed this hypothesis with his observations of children in post–World War II orphanages.

The baby monkeys in Harlow's experiments habitually clung to the cloth-covered wire "mothers" in a manner strikingly similar to how they would hold on to a real monkey mother. The experiment provided a convincing demonstration that the critical ingredient in attachment formation is not food but "contact comfort." Because they were gentler to touch, these softer surrogates were the next best thing to a mother monkey.

Harlow's results altered the psychoanalytic view of how the mother-child bond is formed, making skin-to-skin physical contact as important as the oral gratification received by newborn babies while being nursed or bottle-fed by their mothers. Harlow's study also went against the position of the behavioral theorists who emphasized food itself as the primary reinforcer of a baby's behavior.

Other insights gleaned from these experiments concerned the long-term negative impact on the monkeys' emotional and physical health as a result of this deprivation. To compensate for a missing mother, these monkeys would suck obsessively on their own bodies. They remained huddled in corners, rocking themselves, with distant looks in their eyes. Later, when placed with other monkeys, they became hostile, aggressive, and rarely mated.

Later experiments with other monkeys helped clarify the importance of timing for human mother-baby attachment patterns. Monkeys who spent at least three months with their mothers before being separated showed less severe behavioral abnormalities than those separated from birth. Monkeys separated from their mothers at the age of 6 months showed no long-term negative behaviors. Researchers concluded that there is a sensitive or critical period for bonding between monkey mothers and infants which lasts for six months. In humans, this critical period is believed to last three years, with any deprivation suffered in the first year of life considered the most harmful.

Making a Secure Attachment

Even with mother and child instincts and parental awe to move things along, attachment is not an instantaneous process that begins and ends in the delivery room. It's more like a dance which begins before birth and continues throughout a baby's first year. Although the mother usually is the primary object of a baby's attachment, the likelihood is equally strong that whoever provides consistent and affectionate care of a baby—whether father, grandparent, or an adoptive parent— can form the same secure attachment with that baby.

Factors that increase a secure attachment include …

- A single primary, regular caregiver for the baby's first six months, rather than a series of irregular caregivers.

- Synchronized routines for eating, sleeping, and stimulation with that caregiver, especially during a baby's first few months.

- Consistent smiling, touching, and affection by the primary caregiver.

- Acting consistently in response to the baby's distress with comfort, warmth, and competency.

COMPLICATION

A caregiver's sensitivity to a baby's distress is important, but too much of a good thing is counterproductive. Research shows that when super-attentive mothers responded instantly to their baby's every gurgle, cry, and hiccup, their children became less securely attached. The lesson: children react poorly to smothering. It hampers their independence and inhibits the process of learning to self-soothe.

Chemistry of Maternal Attachment

Another perspective on attachment is revealed by the biochemistry behind parent-baby bonding drives and behaviors. Using brain scans and tests of hormone levels and heart rates, researchers can now see the biochemical results when a secure attachment is made and when it fails to take place.

A Mother's Chemistry

A woman's hormones prepare her for giving birth, and then ready her for feeding and nurturing a newborn baby. During pregnancy, her brain circuits are literally rewired, and her senses attuned to the extra physical and emotional demands of caring for a newborn. As a result of her evolutionary instincts that manifest in this intense chemical preparation for childbirth, she will focus nearly all of her attention and energy on this tiny person until its survival is assured.

For humans, and throughout the animal kingdom, the hormone oxytocin is fundamental to the first mother-child bonding that occurs after a baby is born. Much of what is known about the role of this hormone in creating and maintaining human bonds comes from animal experiments. Female rats and sheep (ewes) given injections of oxytocin will even take care of young rats and young lambs they've never seen before.

In human labor and childbirth, a mother's uterine contractions trigger the brain to release a flood of oxytocin and the neurotransmitter dopamine. The pain-suppressing effects of these hormones are essential after a woman has experienced anywhere from 6 to 36 hours of labor. When the baby is born, they create a residue of euphoria as chemical flooding peaks in the first minutes following birth—often coinciding with the first time the newborn is put to his mother's breast for suckling.

> **INSIGHT**
>
> It is well-known that a mother who has decided to have her baby adopted should not touch the infant, because the act of touching and smelling the baby causes her to release oxytocin. This causes many mothers to reconsider their decision to make an adoption plan.

During the last month of pregnancy a mother-to-be starts producing the hormone that prepares her for nurturing and lactation: prolactin. This hormone causes milk to be secreted from her breast. Oxytocin assists by enabling the milk let-down response in a woman's breasts and sensitizing the new mother to her infant's touch. In fact, the baby's touching of his mother's breast with his hand or lips causes oxytocin to be released. During nursing, oxytocin surges, bringing pleasure and relaxation to the mother and deepening the mother-baby bond.

A Father's Chemistry

The latest studies have shown that when a man becomes a father, his brain goes through changes, too. Soon after hearing the news that he's about to be a father, a man starts to produce cortisol, a stress hormone. Cortisol levels tend to spike around four to six weeks after a man hears the big news, and then they decrease as the pregnancy progresses. Then, about three weeks before the baby arrives, his testosterone levels fall by about 30 percent, making him more cooperative, less competitive, and more likely to show his softer side.

For men, the hormone vasopressin plays a key role in preparing for a baby's birth, helping them make the emotional connections required by new fatherhood. Also, during the last few weeks of his mate's pregnancy, a man's prolactin level rises by 20 percent. It's not clear what effect prolactin has in a man, but it is thought to have an indirect impact on his falling testosterone levels. After his child's birth, his estrogen level, a nurturing influence which is normally very low in a man, increases. The point of these changes appears to be to make fathers more mater-nal in their behaviors, at least more than their normally high levels of testosterone will allow. About six weeks after birth, a man's hormone levels begin to return to normal. Higher estrogen, along with lots of skin contact with his baby, triggers the release of oxytocin in a man. All this chemistry helps reinforce a father's newfound cuddling and cooing behaviors.

At the same time, fathers interact with babies and toddlers in different ways than mothers. A father is more likely to jiggle or rock babies in a playful, rhythmic fashion, while women use firm or light touching to soothe and contain them. As children grow older, a father tends to take a more rough-and-tumble approach to their physical care, and to be more challenging and less sympathetic than a mother. Research shows that both approaches are good and necessary for developing children. When the primary attachment is made between mother and baby in her baby's first six months, research has shown that they both typically begin to form much closer relationships with fathers and siblings soon thereafter.

Chemistry of Insecure Attachment

Like her mother, when a baby receives affection and loving attention, she enjoys the calming effects of oxytocin. A lack of nurturing touch early in her life can create a negative neurochemical pattern in her brain, based on those early disappointments. With negative expectations brought to future attachments, this child may react to the increase of oxytocin caused by physical or emotional intimacy with fear, not with an anticipation of pleasure.

Instead of the warm and fuzzy feelings activated by oxytocin, stress chemicals are triggered. Cortisol, the chemical that keeps us alert and helps us deal with stress, seems to be the main culprit at work here. Sometimes cortisol is necessary, for example, in the morning when its concentration is highest to help us wake up. But cortisol's dampening effect on oxytocin is a less positive thing when you wish to be calm and open to human connection. Either of these lifelong positive and negative biochemical patterns begins in baby's first year.

Attachment Styles

In the 1970s, psychologist Mary Ainsworth built on Bowlby's theory of attachment by creating a now famous series of controlled laboratory experiments with mothers and babies, called the "strange situation" experiment. The goal of these experiments was to figure out the detailed patterns and styles of behavior that cause either a secure or insecure parent-child bond.

Two concepts are central to these experiments:

- **Stranger anxiety**—Wariness or fear of unfamiliar adults, shown by most infants between the ages of 6 and 24 months

- **Separation anxiety**—Distress that infants between 6 and 24 months experience when separated from their primary caregivers

Normally anxiety is not viewed as a positive experience. But in the case of children younger than 3, fears toward strangers and separation from a mother are healthy and appropriate responses. In fact, they provide evidence of a child's positive, secure relationship with a mother or other primary caregiver.

To closely observe attachment behaviors between mothers and babies in a more controlled setting, Ainsworth scripted eight episodes to test mothers' and babies' responses to certain stresses. The dual focus throughout is on the baby's response to the mother's absence and the presence of a stranger, and on the mother's responses to her baby. Ainsworth's now-famous and commonly used "strange situation experiment" involves 1-year-old babies and mothers from a variety of backgrounds and ages.

The Strange Situation Experiment

There were eight stages in Mary Ainsworth's strange situation procedure. After each stage listed next, the behavior of a securely attached baby is noted. Stages two through eight last about three minutes each:

1. Introduction—An assistant introduces mother and baby to the room while mother holds her baby. 30 seconds.

   A calm baby is held by mother.

2. Unfamiliar room—Baby is on the floor with toys available to play with, mother sits nearby.

   Baby may be wary of the new room, but uses mother as a base of security, maintaining eye contact with her while playing with toys.

3. Stranger enters—An unfamiliar female knocks, enters the room, speaks with mother, and then goes to play with baby.

   Baby may show "stranger anxiety" and clearly prefers mother to playing with stranger. While mother is present, baby may allow stranger to approach and play nearby.

4. Mother leaves quietly, leaving baby with stranger who goes and sits in mother's chair.

   Baby shows "separation anxiety" and renewed stranger anxiety. May accept some comfort from stranger but clearly wants mother back.

5. Reunion of mother and baby; stranger exits. Mother comforts baby. And if baby wants to continue playing with toys, does so.

   Baby seeks contact and comfort from mother. Baby clings to mother. Baby may continue to play after receiving comfort.

6. Mother leaves again, saying "bye-bye" on her way out, leaving baby alone.

   Baby shows renewed separation anxiety and distress.

7. Stranger enters again, joining baby who is still alone, sits in mother's chair, then calls or goes to baby.

   Baby may show more anxiety toward the stranger and clearly prefers that mother returns.

8. Reunion of mother and baby, with mother picking up baby and stranger leaving.

   There's joy for baby upon reuniting with mother. Baby wants to hang on to mother.

Observing Attachments

Ainsworth found that secure attachment relationships tend to be associated with mothers who hold their babies frequently, and with mothers who hold their children long enough so that they appear satisfied when they're put back down. Securely attached babies are aware of their mother's whereabouts and confident that she will return after leaving the room. If they're distressed, securely attached babies usually obtain quick comfort after being held by their mothers. Other qualities of a secure mother-baby attachment include …

- The mother is sensitive to calls and signals of distress from the baby and responds quickly.

- The mother goes along with the interactions and games that are initiated by the baby.

- The mother adjusts the baby's feeding and sleeping schedules according to the baby's rhythms.

- The relationship is mutual, not dominated by the needs and moods of the mother.

Based on her observations, Ainsworth concluded that "indifferent parenting" led to insecure attachments between mothers and babies. Other researchers have subsequently added data from observational studies to show that obtrusive and overstimulating parenting styles can also lead to insecurely attached babies.

Mothers of insecurely attached babies were found to frequently be anxious and irritable. The most extreme of these mothers showed little interest in their children, handling them in a mechanical fashion, and behaving otherwise resentfully toward their babies.

Four Attachment Styles

From thousands of controlled observations of mothers and children, Ainsworth formalized a system for rating attachments, using four categories.

Types of Attachment/ Percentage Who Fit This Category	Baby Behaviors
Secure/65 percent	Uses mother as home base; prefers her to stranger; may show distress at her leaving; seeks physical contact when reunited with mother

continues

continued

Types of Attachment/ Percentage Who Fit This Category	Baby Behaviors
Insecure-avoidant/ 20 percent	Doesn't prefer mother to stranger; avoids contact with mother when reunited
Insecure-resistant/ 10 percent	Shows ambivalence toward mother; seeks contact, then resists it; doesn't avoid contact with mother; some show anger; some are passive
Insecure-disorganized/ 5 percent	Acts confused or dazed; may be calm, then angry; often will remain motionless; shows apprehension; sometimes is resistant or avoidant

Whether avoidant or resistant, insecurely attached babies learn that their caregivers will not respond sensitively to their needs. As a result, in times of stress they may reject their mothers' attempts to comfort them by looking away or showing anger and frustration.

Babies who exhibit insecure-disorganized attachments sometimes have parents who are neglectful or abusive. Often, researchers found that these parents had unresolved difficulties with their own parents and may have been abused as children. Their pregnancies were often unplanned and unwanted. In less severe cases, disoriented insecure behavior can occur when a mother displays anxiety or sends mixed signals to her baby.

Obstacles to Attachment

The most often-cited obstacles when developing a secure attachment are the quality of the mother's care-giving and the compatibility of the baby's temperament with the mother's temperament.

Maternal Depression

Depressed mothers often miss and ignore a baby's signals of distress. They also have a harder time entering into a synchronous relationship with their child. With depressed mothers, babies first become angry at their mothers' lack of attention and responsiveness, perhaps crying harder and for longer periods. But over time, these babies begin to match the mothers' depressive symptoms. As mentioned earlier, by the age of 6 months, babies internalize a specific working model of their mothers as either responsive or nonresponsive, and their brains rewire to reflect this experience.

FIELD STUDY

In a pioneering study at Columbia University, psychiatric epidemiologist Myrna Weissman showed that when mothers of grade school children were successfully treated for depression, the depressive symptoms in a significant percentage of the children also dramatically improved. The study's key finding is that depressed children's improvement came without direct treatment of the children.

It is estimated that 13 percent of pregnant women and new mothers develop situational depression as a result of new motherhood. Any existing low level depression or susceptibility to it can be aggravated by the hormonal shifts, added stress, and sleeplessness that accompany having a baby. Post-partum depression is an insufficiently recognized factor that can inhibit the development of a secure attachment in a baby's first six months.

Mismatched Temperaments

It takes two people—an adult and a baby—to form a secure attachment. Stella Chess described three different expressions of temperament: easy, slow to warm up, and difficult. A friendly "easy" baby who is more likely to approach than withdraw from novelty in her environment has been found to have an easier time becoming "securely attached." A "slow to warm up" baby requires more induce-ment to draw into a relationship. A "difficult" baby requires more time.

Some recent research has leant a more integrative approach to the question of which factor is most likely to inhibit attachment: the quality of a mother or other primary figure's care-giving, or the baby's possibly difficult temperament. The major finding was that the quality of care-giving a baby receives is most predictive of whether the child forms a secure or avoidant attachment as measured in a strange situation test. However, the baby's temperament appears to be decisive in determining which type of insecure attachment is formed. Temperamentally fearful children tended to form insecure-resistant attachments, where they kept their distance from mother but protested strongly. More outgoing babies with unresponsive mothers formed insecure-avoidant attachments where they protest less but were content to ignore the mother in favor of a stranger.

FIELD STUDY

Babies are just as likely to form secure attachments with fathers as mothers if the father is the primary caregiver. Summing up the data from studying 710 babies in 11 studies, the percentage of secure versus insecure attachments was 65/35 for fathers and 65/35 for mothers. The type of attachment formed also tended to be alike from one parent to the other.

Is Early Attachment Destiny?

The existing research shows that babies who form secure primary attachments to their mothers in the first year turn out better, meaning they display more favorable development outcomes later in childhood. Here's a sampling of that research.

Securely attached children at age 12 to 18 months when measured at 2 years of age were found to …

- Be better problem solvers.
- Be more complex and creative in their symbolic play.
- Display more positive and fewer negative emotions.
- Be more popular with their playmates.

Each of these findings was made in a controlled setting comparing 2-year-olds who had the benefit of secure attachments to those found to be insecurely attached to their primary caregivers.

Longer-term studies paint a similar picture. Children who were securely attached to their caregivers at 15 months of age were re-examined in follow-up studies at ages 11 to 12 and ages 15 to 16. Among the findings were the following:

- Those who had been securely attached as toddlers were described at the older ages as socially more popular, more curious, and self-directed.

- Those insecurely attached at 15 months were socially and emotionally withdrawn, and less interested in learning. They also tended to be unenthused about surmounting challenges.

These studies showed that the type of secure or insecure attachment that exists between parent and child in the first few years tends to be the same in the child's grade school and high school years. Other research has shown that a secure relationship with another person—father, grandparent, adoptive parent, or daycare provider—can somewhat offset the negative consequences of a poor attachment with a mother.

One reason why John Bowlby used the term "working models" to describe how young children internalize their earliest relationships was to emphasize that a child's working models could change. They could improve (or deteriorate) as a result of later relationships with teachers, romantic partners, or close friends. But even with these caveats, don't fail to understand the importance of a baby beginning life with a secure bond to a significant adult.

Attachment and Working Mothers

Although many people would like to hear a definitive statement about the positive or negative effect of daycare on young children, there are few absolute or simple answers to this question. However, there is evidence for parents to consider when making individual decisions.

From the research …

- Separations from working mothers and placement in daycare generally do not prevent babies from establishing a secure primary attachment. This is true if the mother and father are sensitive and responsive caregivers when they are home with their child.

- Babies younger than 6 months placed in full-time daycare face an elevated risk of forming an insecure attachment, and, in one study, they had lower scores on school readiness at 36 months.

- One large nationwide study found that time spent in daycare added to the risk of a child's forming insecure attachments only when it was combined with mothering that was less sensitive and less responsive.

- High-quality daycare helps buffer young children from the negative effects of being separated from their parents.

- Even when daycare is less than optimal, a child's outcome depends more on the quality of care received at home.

- A mother's attitudes toward working outside the home and placing her baby in daycare are extremely important in shaping the attachment she forms with her child. Any sort of resentment negatively affects the mother-child bond.

If there's any ideal scenario to be garnered from the existing data it is this: a mother with a positive attitude who spends the first six to seven months as a full-time, stay-at-home mother stands the best chance of forming a secure attachment with her baby.

Of course, public policy and business practices are not as supportive of mothers making this choice in the United States compared to other Western countries. Using the same measurements discussed in this chapter, those societies which provide longer paid maternal and paternal leave and supply subsidized childcare, have higher rates of securely attached children. In Great Britain and Sweden, 75 percent and 74 percent of infants respectively were securely attached, compared to 64 percent in the United States. For low-income Americans, the number of securely attached babies is 50 percent.

The Least You Need to Know

- Attachment between babies and a significant adult is an instinctual process with life-long implications.
- Within a secure attachment, a baby finds safety and the will to explore her world, developing an internal thermostat to keep both in balance.

- Babies and mothers in "strange situation" research studies are rated on four different styles of attachment that range from a secure attachment to avoidant, resistant, or disorganized insecure attachments.
- Babies younger than 6 months in full-time daycare are at a higher risk for developing an insecure attachment compared to babies with at-home mothers.

A Child Is Part of a Family

Part

3

In this part, the lens is widened. No child grows up alone. So in Chapter 5 we define parental competency in light of child development research. There's surprising new information to share about the impact of siblings and being the only child. Then, because more than half of children younger than 18 in the United States live with a single parent for at least five years, we look at the short- and long-term psychological impact of single parenthood and divorce on children.

Within every family there is a unique culture and rules that shape a child's sense of self, as well as her morality, and the degrees of self-discipline and emotional resilience she carries into young adulthood. Different avenues of research in child psychology provide important new perspectives on these topics in Chapter 6.

The Parent-Child Relationship

In This Chapter

- The three essentials of parenthood: consistency, communication, and constraints
- The measures of parental competency
- The real reason behind sibling rivalries
- The immediate and delayed impacts of divorce on children

Every family has a unique culture and power sharing system. During the past three decades, scientists have examined the impact of different parenting styles, and the importance of sibling relationships on a child's personality formation. They've also assessed the impact of divorce on children. In this chapter, we discuss these findings and include author Jack Westman's insights from his clinical experience and advocacy for children and families.

Attachment Parenting

Childrearing theories and practices in popular culture tend to be cyclical, even faddish. During the past century the pendulum has swung between greater emphases on love in certain periods and limits in others. In the 1920s, John Watson, the first behavioral psychologist, advocated strictness to the point of warning mothers against the dangers of expressing love to their children. In the 1960s, Benjamin Spock brought a balanced approach between love and discipline. In the late 1970s, the battle between diametrically opposed views returned. Parent Effectiveness Training told parents to "talk to your children" and warned against harsh discipline. James Dobson, in *Dare to Discipline*, took the opposite perspective, viewing corporal punishment as "a purifier of rebellion."

Where are we now? "Attachment parenting," a hands-on approach based on John Bowlby's theory of parent-child bonding and popularized by pediatrician T. Berry Brazelton, has become the central theory guiding today's parental advice. A large and growing body of *outcomes-based* psychological evidence has now accumulated to support its main tenets.

> **DEFINITION**
>
> **Outcomes-based** evidence does not rely on ideology, anecdotes, or popularity to determine the effectiveness of a childrearing practice or clinical intervention. Instead it uses empirical, often quantitative data about whether and how a particular method or practice "works." Research methods used to obtain outcomes-based evidence can be experimental or correlational; a long-term study design can be cross-sectional or longitudinal.

Applying attachment theory to the practices and challenges of parenthood requires placing the child in the context of a family. Then that child must be seen as part of a larger community, bringing social and cultural forces to bear on her development.

Consistency

Parents, like babies, form working models of their children as the parent-child attachment style emerges gradually over time. A child with any temperament does everything in her capacity to signal the need for nurturance. A mother with a particular temperament responds, or does not respond, based on her mood, how many children she has, and how overworked she is—or what childrearing expert she's been reading lately.

Children with sunny dispositions and happy mothers are most likely to develop secure attachment bonding. But it's still possible for a dedicated mother to overcome her own temperamental difficulties or her child's less-pleasant disposition and foster a secure attachment.

A parent's capacity to respond to the emotional and mental states of a newborn baby is the foundation of secure attachment bonding. A baby's working model of a sensitive, responsive parent creates an internal sense of cohesion and interpersonal connection for the growing child. After forming, this bond generally lasts and fortifies the older child for challenges to come. This allows her to learn to control her emotions, behaviors, and responses to get the nurturance she needs from her family and from other important people in her growing circle. It's this ability to self-organize that gives the child a sense of security when a mother or other primary caregiver is not present.

Communication

Talk is cheap, and that's a good thing for a growing child. The development of a child's brain and personality depends upon continuous communication between a child and her parents. What begins nonverbally through touch expands into a two-way conversation built on observation and interaction. It then becomes the invisible umbilical cord uniting parent and child through the ups and downs of family life.

Talking is a parent's easiest way to help build a child's cognitive and emotional IQ. Research has shown that it's *not* what is said that matters. It's the quantity of words spoken in a positive tone that improve a child's brain power.

FIELD STUDY

In the mid-1990s Betty Hart, Ph.D., and Todd Risley, Ph.D., at the University of Kansas followed 41 families of various socio-economic backgrounds for two and a half years. The children were 7 to 9 months old at the beginning of this study. Graduate students observed interactions between parents and babies, noting the number of words spoken and the tone used by parents. Later, this data was correlated with the children's IQ scores. The outcome: the more words spoken in a positive tone at home, the higher the children's IQ scores at age 3, regardless of the family's socio-economic status.

Many studies have emphasized the importance of parents listening to their children. Although verbal interactions between parents and children are priceless, parents also shape their children's minds when they "speak with their feet."

Constraints

As the baby becomes a toddler, she learns to regulate her emotional states in response to parental boundaries or constraints, especially when and how often the parent says or signals "no." Over time, a child learns that her wishes are not automatically gratified and that her mind and a parent's mind are separate. This separation is a necessary prerequisite for the child to learn self-control so that she can modulate her own behavior and emotional states in pro-social ways. So a certain amount of struggle between parent and child is a good thing. In fact, this clash of separate minds and wills is an essential element in her mental and social development.

Throughout childhood, there are many times when a parent leads a child and other times when a child leads a parent. The challenge for parents is learning how to appropriately shift back and forth between leader and follower roles with their children. For example, during infancy a child actually wields great power and leads a parent by setting the feeding-sleep cycle. Parental power is introduced later around limit setting. Many parents do not realize how important it is to set limits, even for toddlers. It is easy to give in to their demands. The more difficult but rewarding course is to help them learn the limits of their power. Parents who show empathy to their children and to others, and who set firm limits for their children especially as they reach grade school age, raise children who show high levels of self-discipline and compassionate behaviors.

There's more on the research regarding the impact of different parental authority styles on all aspects of a child's development in Chapter 6.

Measuring Parental Competency

The vast majority of parents are competent. They love their children and want only what's best for them. Their natural nurturing instincts and cultural models lead them to do their best, which is more often than not "good enough." A trademark sign of a competent parent is their overall confidence in their own parenting abilities. Such parents' concern for their children leads them to question and doubt themselves at times and seek the advice of other parents, relatives, or experts.

An Incompetent Parent

Incompetent childrearing practices often produce maladjusted, unhappy children who have serious trouble learning and getting along with their peers. In adverse environments, such as a chaotic family life, child maltreatment, and parental mental illness, children may become frightened or angry and lash out or turn away from others. In steeling themselves against their own emotional pain, they become inured to the pain of others. From such troubled childhoods often come unproductive, anti-social young adults who are a drain rather than a positive force in the larger community.

At any given time, about 4 percent of parents can be defined as incompetent, as conservatively inferred from substantiated child neglect and abuse cases. This breaks down to 8 percent of one-parent and 3 percent of two-parent homes. Although small in percentage, the number of incompetent parents is significant, almost three million. At least twice as many have not been ruled as incompetent yet. Most people do not appreciate the enormous impact this comparatively small number of incompetent parents has on society. Incompetent parents cost the economy an average of $2.8 million for each child they raise who becomes a criminal or welfare dependent.

Unlike "good-enough" parents who may be concerned about their effectiveness as parents, most incompetent parents minimize or deny their incompetence. Incompetent parents are unable to handle responsibility for their own lives, much less for their children's lives. Because incompetent parents have difficulty controlling their own impulses, they are vulnerable to substance abuse and alcoholism. They are insensitive to the needs of others and are unreliable. They do not form dependable attachment bonds with their children. They alternately neglect or overreact to their children's behavior with unpredictable and inconsistent sequences of indifference, idle threats, and severe punishment.

Impact on Children

The children of incompetent parents are confused when what happens to them seems to bear little relationship to what they do. Their children's consequent erratic behaviors aggravate the parents' inconsistent childrearing practices. As a result, their children lack sensitivity to the needs of other people and behave unpredictably just like their parents. Their children often become adults who do not control their impulses and who are insensitive to the effects of their behavior on other people.

The "Good-Enough" Parent

British pediatric psychiatrist Donald Winnicott (1896–1971) recognized that, because all parents are imperfect, they should strive to be "good-enough" parents. In simple terms, good-enough parents are adults committed to parenthood. Their behavior shows they care about what happens to their children. They can restrain themselves from harming them. They do not neglect or abuse their children in a legal sense. This definition of good-enough parents flows from our cultural expectations of parents. Good-enough parents are parents who …

- Assume responsibility for their own lives.

- Sacrifice some of their own interests for their children.

- Provide limits for their children's behavior.

- Give their children hope for the future.

- Want their children to become responsible, self-sufficient, and ethical adults.

- Know that their children will inevitably face hurts and difficult times in their lives.

- Help their children learn to delay the gratification of immediate urges and tolerate frustration.

- Teach them the value of work and avoiding harming others.

- Give love and support while their children grow through the stages of childhood and adolescence into successful and responsible adults.

As every parent eventually learns, the life lessons that provide opportunities for a child or teenager to acquire positive qualities often arise as problems or crises. They result from a fight on the school playground; a failed test; lack of money for a desired object; or rejection from a sweetheart, job, or a college. These are the "teachable moments" in a child's life, and although none can be planned or scheduled, all require a parent's patient guidance.

Can a Parent Be "Too Good"?

Carolyn Warnemuende in her book, *The Good-Enough Parent*, differentiates between good-enough and "too-good" parents who try to shield their children from unhappiness and disappointments and place them at the center of the family's life. Their children do not learn the lessons necessary in mastering life or the skills of being a member of a group.

"Too-good" parents ...

- Do for their children what they are capable of doing for themselves.
- Give children the message that they are more important than the parents are.
- Give their children too many opportunities.
- Fail to take a leadership role in the family.
- Develop mutual dependency with their children instead of interdependency.

The parent-child bond at its best is a buoyant springboard to launch a child as a positive, contributing member of his community. And yet parents receive no special training for the increasingly complicated task of parenthood.

Parenthood Certification

Jack Westman and the advocacy organization Wisconsin Cares, Inc., have proposed a "parenthood pledge" as a step toward ensuring that all children have competent parents. This pledge would be made by mothers and fathers who, in order to be eligible, must not be under the legal and physical custody or guardianship of other persons or the state. Minors and developmentally disabled or incarcerated adults and their families would receive Parenthood Planning Counseling when their pregnancies are diagnosed in order to help them make decisions and choices regarding guardianship. If willing and able, the mother and/or father's custodians or guardians would assume legal and physical custody of the newborn babies until the mother and/or father become self-sufficient. Newborns without legal and physical custodians would come under the custody of the state, and an adoption plan would be made effective at childbirth. A *modified birth certificate* would become a parenthood certificate as well.

> **DEFINITION**
>
> A **modified birth certificate** would certify both the birth of a child and the signing of a parenthood pledge by the baby's mother and/or father if she or he is eligible, able, and willing to do so.

According to Wisconsin Cares, Inc., a parenthood pledge and the modified birth certificate as defined above would set the standard that to assume responsibility for raising children parents should be able to assume responsibility for their own lives first. It also would provide an opportunity to inform parents about parenting resources. Parent education also would be available based on outcomes-based evidence of what works and what doesn't.

Family as a Social System

As the single most important environmental influence on a child, the family unit is where almost 50 percent of the child's intelligence and personality are forged (with the other 50 percent of both generally accepted to be of genetic origin). The family also is the primary force shaping a child's moral character. While today's parents value their time with their children as much as any generation before them, the family as a social unit is under more stress than ever before. This was the conclusion of a video study by psychological researchers at UCLA who recorded 800 hours of naturalistic observations of local families during the afterschool and after work hours. Among the 2008 study's specific observations:

- A total of 46 percent of households with children had two parents working outside the home (up from 36 percent in 1975).

- The entire family gathers in one room of the home 14 percent of the time.

- Children do only 3 percent of the household chores (giving children an allowance did not change this).

- Parents are generally disorganized about dividing up chores and childcare responsibilities, leading to continual negotiations and additional stress between parents and parents and children.

- After food preparation, cleaning activities, and basic childcare activities, parents spend most of their time with their children: shuttling them to and from extracurricular activities, helping with homework and enforcing homework deadlines, planning children's activities, and spending leisure or "free" time—such as watching TV—together.

- Mothers spend more time after work and/or at home with children than fathers, and they bear a heavier "second shift" as parents than do fathers. Mothers spend 34 percent of their time at home in solo activities with children; fathers spend 25 percent of theirs.

> **INSIGHT**
>
> Culture and child development are inextricably linked. Take sleeping arrangements, for example. In the United States, most babies and toddlers sleep alone in cribs, with the exception of 20 percent of U.S. Hispanic households. For these and two thirds of the rest of the world's families, children sleep in their parent(s)' bed. In Japan, co-sleeping is the custom until a child reaches age 5.

In a recent survey reported in the publication *Zero to Three*, 37 percent of parents said they don't spend as much time as they would like with their children. The impact of shrinking family time on children, as well as on schools and the broader community, has become an area of concern and further research for child psychologists and sociologists.

The Irreducible Needs of Children

Dr. Westman has distilled a list of the most commonly agreed upon principles for successfully meeting the irreducible needs of children that have emerged from child development research:

- A parent's self-confidence as a parent comes from the attachment bond maintained with a child, not from the child's expressed gratitude, which will come later.

- Physical expressions of love are essential from birth on, diminishing in openness and frequency as these gestures become awkward for older children.

- The amount of time spent with a child is more important than the amount of money spent on that child.

- Parents should provide a limited number of toys and games that have lasting value. Cups and blocks are just as much fun as expensive toys for young children.

- Two-way communication between parent and child is central to a child's positive growth. Talking, singing, reading, and playing are important ways to engage a child.

- Every child is different. A parent should identify and encourage each child's individual interests.

- Children need constraints. Parents should maintain their legitimate authority. They are needed more as parents than as pals.

- Parents should build their child's self-esteem by acknowledging realistic accomplishments, not unearned praise.

- Parents need to avoid treating their child as a possession or as an extension of themselves.

- Parents should balance the need to adjust their lifestyle to meet the demands of childrearing with their concurrent need to maintain adult relationships and interests.

- Parents should not be seduced by the convenience of an "independent child" and encourage a child to grow up too fast too soon.

Sibling Relationships

Although families are getting smaller, most American children are growing up with at least one sibling. Birth order is a subject of curiosity for psychologists and lay people alike. Parents assume that it's better to space their children closer together so that they'll grow up to be "friends" with interests in common. Another common belief is that same sex siblings will be emotionally closer. Well, it turns out that something else better predicts the quality of relationship that two brothers, two sisters, or a brother and a sister (of any ages) may have with each other: the quality of the oldest sibling's friendships outside the family. One researcher concluded that while siblings are a given, a friendship is something a child needs to work for. If you have close friendships, apparently you are also more likely to enjoy your siblings.

Sibling relationships, research has found, are remarkably stable over time. If you're close to a brother or sister when you're 5, you're likely to be at 9 and 15, too. The key apparently is not whether or not you fight. Fighting between siblings is a given and not necessarily harmful as long as it doesn't turn into bullying. The determining factor of your future emotional tie is whether (in addition to fighting) you also have fun together. It's the glue that binds siblings over the long haul.

Sibling Rivalry

Siblings fought, it was once believed, primarily to get the largest share of their parents' attention and affection. But when a psychologist got around to thoroughly researching this behavior, it turned out that being Mom and Dad's favorite child was the very last reason why siblings really fought. The top contentious issue found in one survey of 108 sibling pairs was, in fact, toys: who got to play with what first. This was true according to 80 percent of the older children and 75 percent of the younger siblings surveyed. The study investigators concluded that siblings of all ages have plenty of their own reasons for fighting, apart from parents.

Only Children

Conventional wisdom has long held that children with siblings gained an early advantage in acquiring social skills. All those interactions, positive and negative alike, helped train them for school, sports, and later the world of work. Or so this line of thinking went. It has also been a common fear in many cultures that an only child will be self-centered, spoiled, or worse. Wrong again!

In China, where a one-child policy has been state law since 1979 (although 42 percent of Chinese families have two or more children), the results have not reflected this fear. One study of middle school children in the United States found that "onlies" were less anxious and had better social skills than their peers with siblings.

Indicators from several Western countries show that only children do slightly better in school. But the biggest news is that they are not less equipped with social skills.

Children of Divorce

One reason why many parents, particularly fathers, and their children are not spending as much time together as they would like is the continuing high rate of divorce. Between 40 and 50 percent of marriages end in divorce, and the majority of these families include children younger than 18. More than half of children born in the 1990s and 2000s will spend about five years, on average, in a single-parent home, usually headed by a mother.

When a divorce occurs, children usually lose a degree of contact with one of their attachment figures. It is a confusing and stressful time for children, regardless of whether their parents' divorce was amicable or not. There are many factors that may play into how children's attachments are altered after a divorce—gender and age being the two most-documented variables.

Research done during the past three decades consistently shows that divorce increases children's risk for a variety of difficulties by one half—as compared to children living in nondivorced families. Roughly 20 to 25 percent of these children will have academic and behavioral problems. Another way of saying this is that 75 to 80 percent will not experience these difficulties. So while children of divorce are at greater risk, most will not have major problems in adolescence.

Impact on Younger Children

Children from 3 to 5 years of age who go through divorce tend to be fearful and resort to immature or aggressive behavior in the immediate aftermath. They often have difficulty falling asleep at bedtime or sleeping through the night. They might return to security blankets or old toys. Some may have lapses in toilet training. But these types of behavior rarely last for more than a few weeks or months. Most children are confused about what is happening or about why mom or dad has left. Children often try to deny that anything has changed.

Preschoolers also may become less imaginative and cooperative in their play. They may spend more time playing by themselves than with friends. They also may show more anxiety, depression, anger, and apathy in their play and in their interactions with both children and adults. Socially, preschoolers tend to spend more time seeking attention and the nearness of adults. At the same time, they may resist adult suggestions and commands. Some children become much more aggressive.

Children of 6 to 8 years have some understanding of what divorce means. Many young school-age children experience deep grief over the breakup of the family. Some children are fearful and yearn for the absent parent. One 2000 study included a wide sampling and found that the worst initial reactions and behaviors that occur close to the date of the divorce were by the youngest children. In a follow-up study 10 years after the divorce, however, the youngest children were adjusting to their new environments and interactions better than siblings who were older at the time of the divorce.

Older Children and Divorce

Older school-age children, age 9 to 12, try to understand the divorce and keep their behavior and emotions under control. Although they may have feelings of loss, embarrassment, and resentment, these children can actively involve themselves in play and activities to help manage these feelings. They may make up games and act out make-believe dramas concerning their parents' divorce. These activities seem to help the child cope with the situation. Anger is perhaps the most intense emotion felt by this age group of children. Their anger may be aimed at one parent or at both parents. These children may also be more easily drawn into choosing one parent over the other. Children who become drawn into struggles between the parents tend to have more difficulties.

Although adolescents understand the divorce situation better than younger children do, they too experience some difficulties adjusting. Many teens feel that they are being pushed into adulthood with little time for a transition from child-hood. They may feel a loss of support in handling emerging sexual and aggressive feelings. In some cases, adolescents may even feel that they are in competition with their parents when they see them going on dates and becoming romantically involved. Sometimes, teens have grave doubts about their own ability to get married or stay married.

FIELD STUDY

A landmark longitudinal study of children of divorce (Wallerstein, Lewis, and Blakeslee, 2000) surprised many psychologists with the finding that the majority of the 131 participants interviewed after 25 years reported that the major negative impact of their parents' divorce didn't hit them until early adulthood. Then they reported feeling strong apprehensions about marrying for fear of experiencing divorce again as adults. The percentage of the group as yet unmarried was significantly higher than the average for their age group. In general, they reported experiencing high levels of anxiety in their intimate relationships, and identified a common source of lasting dissatisfaction in their lives with the loss of closeness with their parents following the divorce, especially their fathers.

Many adolescents seem to mature more quickly following a divorce. They take on increased responsibilities in the home, show an increased appreciation of money, and they gain insight into their own relationships with others. On the other hand, adolescents may be drawn into the role of taking care of a parent and fail to develop relationships with peers.

Girls, Boys, and Divorce

In the 1990s, divorce was associated with greater conduct problems among boys than girls. But the more general conclusion reached was that most of the disadvantages associated with divorce are similar for boys and girls. The pattern may be somewhat different for boys and girls. Boys are more likely to be aggressive and have problems getting along with their peers and teachers. These problems may lead them to spend less time in school or on their homework.

Girls, on the other hand, are more likely to experience depression, which may interfere with their ability to concentrate on schoolwork or to put effort into their work. School success has long-term implications for children's success in life, so it is important to find ways to support children from divorced families.

By adolescence, both boys and girls post-divorce are more likely to engage in negative conduct and experience bouts of sadness. Adolescent girls are likely to be involved in early sexual behavior, leading to a greater risk of teenage pregnancy and childbirth. This set of events can also have dramatic effects on their completion of school and their ability to enter the workforce and earn a satisfactory living. Adolescent boys are likely to spend more time with deviant peers and engage in delinquent behavior, including substance abuse. Like the young women, adolescent boys are likely to engage in early sexual behavior and become teen fathers.

Children in Nontraditional Families

A review of the psychological literature published in the *Journal of Marriage and Family* in February 2010 compared the impact on children of being reared in single-parent versus two-parent families. Using 33 studies of two-parent families and 48 of single-parent families, they found that, other things being equal, two compatible parents provide advantages for children over single parents. This appears to be true irrespective of parental gender, marital status, or sexual identity. When comparing heterosexual two-parent families to lesbian two-parent families, "scholars have achieved a rare degree of consensus that unmarried lesbian parents are raising children who develop at least as well as their counterparts with married heterosexual parents." In lesbian two-parent families the style of parenting was best described as "a double dose of mothering." (There were not a sufficient number of male-male households represented in the studies to draw any equivalent or divergent conclusions.) They also found that single dads also displayed more "maternal" capacities than married dads.

Ample research has also demonstrated that there is no basis for the speculation that growing up as a child with gay or lesbian parents will produce a homosexual orientation in the adult child. A 2004 study showed that more than 90 percent of adult children of homosexual parents develop a heterosexual orientation. This number is the same with heterosexual parents.

The Least You Need to Know

- The irreducible needs of children from their parents include affection, time, setting boundaries, mutual respect, and positive role models.
- Parents who do too much for their children, called "too-good" parents, deprive them of important growth experiences.
- Counter to conventional wisdom, "only children" do not suffer in emotional-social skills.

- In the immediate aftermath of divorce, grade school and older boys are more prone to misconduct, while girls are more likely to develop depression.
- Other things being equal, two compatible parents provide advantages for children over single parents.

Authority and Discipline

In This Chapter

- The most effective authority style
- The origins of self-control and self-discipline
- Why patient 4-year-olds score higher in high school

One way parents show respect and caring for children is by disciplining them. Discipline is different from punishment. Discipline is a code of conduct. To discipline is to teach children. Punishment is what happens when a child breaks a given code of conduct. Of course, parents have different rules and different styles of setting and enforcing them. In some families, swearing is not tolerated. Under other roofs, the worst thing a child can do is show up late for dinner. This chapter looks to child psychology for insights into how different styles of parental authority and discipline shape a child.

The Study That Changed Everything

In her pioneering 1971 study, child psychologist Diana Baumrind did something that hadn't been done before when she observed how actual parental authority styles correlated with children's real-life behaviors. Earlier research had examined only children's behaviors, not how a parent approached authority. She was also the first researcher to examine whether particular parenting styles affected girls and boys in different ways.

In choosing a population for her study, Baumrind opted for a homogenous group of 130 white, upper-middle class nursery school children in Berkeley, California.

Her priority in choosing this population was its homogeneity; that way she could rule out confounding variables that might lessen the reliability and validity of her results. The boys and girls in this group had an average age of 4 and an average IQ of 125, placing them in an above-average intelligence range.

Measuring Authority

The method used in this study was the naturalistic observation of the children in two different situations: in their nursery school class and while taking a standardized test. The behaviors the observers noted in the children included the following:

- Hostile or friendly

- Resistive or cooperative

- Dominant or submissive

- Purposeful self-starter or aimless and disoriented

- Achievement oriented or not achievement oriented

- Independent or does not question authority

Parents were observed at home beginning just before dinner and until the child's bedtime. Specific measures of parental behaviors in researchers' observations included whether parents required chores and set rules, how flexible or inflexible they were about household rules, how much intellectual stimulation and affection they gave their child, whether punishments for misbehaviors were punitive and harsh or firm and nurturing, or whether there was punishment at all.

Four Authority Styles

In her assessments of the parents, Baumrind used four parenting style categories:

- **Authoritarian**—Parent's word is final; uses punitive discipline methods and demands conformity.

- **Authoritative**—Parent is strict and sets rules but is willing to discuss and change them when warranted. Among this group were some parents who were noncomforming in that they encouraged independent noncomformist thinking but had strict rules.

- **Permissive**—Parent places few demands or rules on child; sees herself as a resource but not an authority figure to child. Parent may be conforming or noncomforming. At their most extreme, permissive parents are overindulgent; they allow their children to misbehave without consequences.

- **Rejecting-Neglecting**—Parent provides little or no structure and is emotionally rejecting of a child's needs. Some of these parents also are neglectful of children's basic physical needs.

In the study, Baumrind found that the label of rejecting fit some but not all authoritarian parents. It also fit some but not all permissive and nonconforming parents.

When determining which parental styles produced the best results in child behaviors, Baumrind first had to define "best" in the context of these children. She chose the criteria of "adaptive," meaning those behaviors that would help a child in this population adapt to society.

COMPLICATION

Critics of Baumrind's study claimed that a behavior that is adaptive in one community could be a recipe for failure in another. For example, critics pointed out that cooperative and friendly behaviors in a high-crime, inner-city neighborhood may not be adaptive. They may put the child in greater danger.

Which Works Best?

Based on Baumrind's observations and calculations, one style of parental authority clearly emerged as producing the best outcomes—authoritative:

- **Independence**—Boys and girls from authoritative parents showed the highest levels of independence, followed by boys of authoritarian and permissive parents. Girls from authoritarian and permissive households showed the least independence.

- **Achievement orientation**—Girls and boys from authoritative households scored highest in this category, with boys in authoritarian and permissive households scoring much lower.

- **Social responsibility**—Authoritative households produced the most socially responsible children. But this was not the case when the authoritative parent is also a nonconforming type.

Research completed after the Baumrind study (using the same authority style categories) has largely reinforced these original results.

A Longer-Term View

Multiple studies done during the past two decades have shown that children raised by authoritative parents fared better in several key areas of performance:

- They perform better in school.
- They are less hostile and aggressive.
- They have greater self-esteem and are more popular.
- They have fewer behavioral problems in adolescence.

When all four parental authority styles are included, the research has shown that children of permissive and rejecting/neglectful parents showed results that were inferior to both authoritative or authoritarian parenting. Permissively raised children were found to be more impulsive and perform worse in school. They were less self-assured, independent, and confident. They were also more prone to alcohol and drug abuse.

INSIGHT

From the Baumrind study and its successors you can see that strictness by itself is not bad; it's how a parent administers household rules that counts. When strictness is accompanied by rules that the child can understand, the outcome is best. The authoritative parent who communicates, responds to questions, and is flexible with rules when warranted has the best style for delivering a positive outcome.

Children raised by rejecting/neglectful parents fared worst of all four categories of parental authority styles. They show higher rates of school delinquency, alcohol and drug use, and early sexual activity. They also show poor cognitive and social development.

Since this study was done, other researchers have added two important over-arching dimensions to Baumrind's parenting style categories. These are ...

- **Responsiveness**—Parent acknowledges, accepts, and tries to meet the child's needs

- **Expectations**—Parent has high expectations about the level of maturity the child is capable of and gives responsibilities to match

Although these criteria are not necessarily correlated, research has found that the combination of high responsiveness and high expectations in authoritative parents produced adolescents who were less likely to use drugs and showed greater competence in school.

The Authoritative Parent

According to child psychiatrist Jack Westman, two basic principles underlie the exercise of legitimate parental authority in the authoritative model of parenthood:

1. Recognition that from the time they are born, children are individuals with valid needs and feelings. Effective parental authority adapts to children with different temperaments.

2. To model effective living for children, who are influenced more by what parents actually do than by what they say.

Westman expands on this by saying that when parents demonstrate a model of controlling their impulses, their children learn how to behave civilly and tolerate the inevitable frustrations of life. When parents model delaying gratification, children learn how to schedule pleasant and unpleasant activities (work comes before play). With these skills, they learn the ingredients of effective living. By developing hopeful visions for their own futures, children learn how to surmount obstacles in their daily lives. They also gain inspiration for making the world a better place in which to live. All of this is nurtured by an atmosphere of respectful parental authority.

Basis of Parental Power

Westman goes on to explain that the foundation of successful parenthood is mutual respect between parent and child. It is not based on a reward-punishment paradigm. Knowledge of child development is helpful in engendering parental respect for the needs of children. A child's respect for a parent depends upon a parent's ability to convey to the child that she means what is said (of course, the parent has the responsibility to mean what is said as well).

Most disciplinary issues arise around testing limits. There inevitably are times when conveying "I mean what I say" to a young child requires a passionate voice and physical intervention. The latter can be done by firmly holding a child with eye contact and speaking in a convincing tone.

Problems with Fear-Based Authority

Westman and others opposed to using harsher physical means of punishment with children believe that ritualistic spanking relies on fear of punishment rather than respect. Although they would concur with authoritarian parents who believe that children should fear their parents' reactions to their behavior, they differ in an important respect. The fear of parental disapproval for misbehavior should be more from letting their parents down and losing their respect than from fear of punishment.

Spanking: The Research

Spanking and yelling at children are "power-assertive" methods of disciplining. Their purpose is usually to teach a child appropriate behaviors and discourage inappropriate ones. In real life, these methods often occur in response to a parent's loss of patience. Researchers observing parent-child interactions report that some parents interrupt their children on average every seven minutes in an attempt to get them to change a behavior. With 2-year-olds, a full 65 percent of parent-child interactions consist of the parent telling the child to stop a behavior. It all adds up to a great deal of conflict and frustration for parents. And in the short run at least, spanking often seems to work. Children do stop what they're doing.

In surveys done in 1989 and 1994, 84 percent of Americans said they believed that "it's sometimes necessary to discipline a child with a good hard spanking." According to data from the National Longitudinal Study of Youth, two thirds of mothers reported hitting or spanking their 6-year-old children. They said they used this form of punishment an average of 150 times a year, almost every other day. One out of every four parents used an object such as a paddle or belt to spank a child. Other studies show differences between economic classes: a greater percentage of parents with middle than higher incomes use spanking, while those lower-income parents who spank do so more frequently than other classes.

According to the psychological research, the problem with spanking and other power-assertive methods of discipline come later. For one thing, spanking is not particularly effective. Yes, children stop their immediate offending behavior, but they eventually return to it. Why else would parents have to spank their children so often?

A meta-review of 88 studies on spanking was done in 2001. This review showed that children who are spanked more often are …

- More physically violent and aggressive with peers.

- More likely to commit assaults and delinquent acts in adolescence.

- More likely to become depressed and suffer from low self-esteem, alcoholism, and addictions.

- Those hit or spanked in adolescence are more likely to hit their spouses and abuse their children; they are also more likely to link pain and sexual activity.

COMPLICATION

Researchers found that with mothers who were generally warm and affectionate, occasional spankings did not increase children's misbehaviors or anti-social tendencies. In the same study, mothers who spanked and were generally less warm, involved, and affectionate with their children produced the same negative behaviors seen in other studies. These results were consistent across African American, non-Hispanic whites, and Hispanic families.

Appropriate Discipline

The American Academy of Pediatrics advises a positive approach to child discipline that excludes spanking. This approach is based on evidence-based research and recommends that adults ...

- Manage situations with their children, preventing conflict wherever possible by adhering to regular schedules and creating a child-proofed environment (e.g., keeping breakables out of reach).

- Set and enforce clear rules of behavior for everyone in the family; some call this a family culture of respect.

- Offer occasional praise for appropriate behavior (not constant, or its positive effect will reverse).

- Use explanation and reasoning.

- As a negative consequence, use removing privileges and time-outs, where a child is removed from the situation in which he's misbehaving.

INSIGHT

So how does a parent reason with a toddler who's repeatedly stealing his baby brother's toy? They don't. Physical redirection and restraint are necessary to demonstrate that a parent's words are to be taken seriously. Using their feet and firmly restraining hands by directly intervening instead of yelling across the room is the most effective way for parents to help a toddler learn the meaning of the most important word at that age: "No."

Nearly every rule in this list should be adapted to the family and child's unique circumstances.

How Children Affect Parents' Behaviors

Is it possible for a child's temperament or behaviors to shape a parent's authority style instead of the other way around? The answer is yes. This issue is known in psychological research as "the direction of effects." Let's say a 4-year-old child in the Baumrind study has an active, impulsive temperament, and the child's parent uses an authoritarian style of parenting. If a correlation is made between these two variables, it is legitimate to question whether this child's parent became more authoritarian and less open to negotiation about rules in response to the child's frequent, out-of-control behavior.

Other researchers point out that two children in the same family can elicit different authority styles. And they say this is often an appropriate adaptation on the part of the parents. In response to the question of which direction of effects is most influential in setting a parent's authority style, the "transactional model" of understanding parent-child relationships settles it with a draw. Using this perspective, parenting is seen as a two-way street. Many variables affect a child's temperament and individual behaviors. Just as many variables shape the authority style used by a parent with that child. By examining these variables, it may be easier to see why one parent's authority style may differ when applied to her two different children:

- Temperament of parent

- Temperament of child

- Birth order

- Gender differences

- Unshared experiences among the siblings

- Differences in children's physical or intellectual abilities

- Changes in parents' work situations

- Daycare experiences

- Age of child in the event of a divorce or death of a parent

FIELD STUDY

Research has shown that there are more temperamental differences within families than there are between different families. What's still not clear is why this is so. What's clear is that family dynamics can be especially complex when it comes to the interactions of children and parents with different temperaments. For example, in certain families shyness may be acceptable in a girl but not in a boy. When looking at psychological data from experiments in this area it's especially important to see whether confounding variables such as those previously listed are controlled.

Where Self-Discipline Comes From

Other terms used for self-discipline are "self-control," or "self-regulation." The same concept is also characterized as the "modulation of desires" or "delayed gratification." Impulsive is what people who lack self-control are called. And although most people concur that self-discipline is a good thing, and many bemoan the fact that too many adults and children don't have enough of it, not as much attention is put on where self-discipline comes from.

It may seem obvious that self-discipline is something a child learns from a parent. And that if a child has self-discipline early in life, he will have greater success in his school performance and career. But common sense is not enough for a statement to qualify as an accepted theory in the science of psychology.

When It Shows Up

To begin to check the accuracy of these assumptions, let's look at when and how self-control first manifests in children:

- Self-control first appears in 1-year-olds when they notice that other people are imposing demands on them. And, if they want to fit in and get their needs met, they comply.

- By 2 years of age, a toddler has internalized these earlier lessons to the point where they're capable of self-control when mother or another primary caregiver is not around.

- At 3, children are capable of "self-regulation." They can adapt to different situations and control their own behaviors.

Studies show that although preschoolers have a modicum of self-control, the ability to delay gratification takes until high school to fully manifest in a youngster. For example, in one 1990 correlation study, children were given a task to complete and a choice of rewards if they succeeded: a small reward immediately or a larger one the next day.

About one third of the 6- to 8-year-olds chose to wait the extra day for the larger reward, while one half of the 9- to 11-year-olds chose to wait. But by 12 to 15 years old, nearly all the participants chose to delay their gratification by waiting the extra day for a better payoff.

Similarly structured longitudinal correlation studies have shown that the choice made as a preschooler about whether to wait or get the goodies right away tends to stick with children as they age. Researchers tracked down nearly 200 adolescents who had been tested as 4-year-olds in a similar self-control experiment and who were now 15- to 18-year-olds. In the original study they had been placed in a room with a bell and told that they would receive a bigger reward if they sat and waited until the experimenter returned. But if they rang the bell sooner they would receive a smaller reward.

Experimenters were able to make significant correlations between the children who waited the longest for their reward at age 4 and a variety of positive coping skills and personality traits, even higher SAT scores in the same children as adolescents. Remember that a correlation between variables is measured as r, in a range between –.01 and +.01.

Measure	r
Yields to temptation	–.50
Distractibility	–.41
Plans and thinks ahead	.36
Handles stress	.34
SAT verbal scale	.42
SAT quantitative scale	.57

Notice that the correlations of the kids who waited the longest at age 4 were now in the positive range for positive coping, personality, and academic characteristics, and in the negative range for characteristics demonstrating less self-control and more impulsivity when the same kids were retested as teenagers.

Why It Sticks

To answer this question, Albert Bandura and Walter Mischel carried out a study to determine if children's self-control could be changed by watching adult models. Specifically, they wondered if children who exhibited little self-control would have more after watching an adult demonstrate self-control. Conversely, they wanted to know whether a child who showed more self-discipline would have less after watching an undisciplined adult. For their methodology, the experimenters gave children a choice between an immediate or delayed reward:

- **Who:** Approximately 250 fourth- and fifth-grade children.

- **Study design:** Experimental. A comparison of the children's choice of immediate or delayed reward was made before and after they watched the adult model make either choice.

- **Independent variable:** Whether or not the child had yet seen the model make choices.

- **Dependent variable:** The number of choices that matched the model's choices.

- **Results:** Of the children exposed to a model who delayed gratification, 50 percent shifted their own preferences from immediate to delayed rewards on a second test. Similarly, most of those who chose to delay gratification shifted to immediate gratification choices after being shown models who did not delay gratification the next time they were tested.

Bandura and Mischel concluded that children often model adult behaviors of self-control. Since this experiment was done, other studies have raised some caveats and added some details to this generalization. Among the most important ...

- When parents are very strict and controlling of their children's behavior, the children have less self-control.

- Even with children as young as 1 year, when a child agrees with a parent's request to change his behavior ("Don't touch that", "Put away your toys before you have a snack"), compliance (and thus self-regulation) is much higher.

- When parents encourage their children to be independent and make their own decisions, they have greater self-control.

These experiments demonstrate that nurture, in the form of an adult's positive modeling, is a significant influence in shaping a child's ability to self-regulate from the earliest years onward.

> **INSIGHT**
>
> The maturation of the frontal cortex of a child's brain, seat of executive functions and reasoning, is key to the development of his self-control. This growth in the frontal lobes, which happens in two spurts at 1 year and between ages 4 and 7, helps children resist temptation and inhibit responses that will get them into mischief.

A child's innate temperament is also considered an important factor in determining his levels of self-discipline and impulsivity. Researchers have linked several aspects of temperament in infancy, including inhibition, effortful control, and fearfulness to later behaviors as older children, such as the ability to follow rules, the tendency to cheat, and the ability to show emotional self-control under stress.

What Works, What Doesn't

So based on the psychological research, how do parents exercise their legitimate parental authority to produce the best possible outcomes for their child? The following principles reflect the consensus of child psychologists and pediatricians:

- A grown child's relationship to authority as evidenced by his relationships with teachers, employers, and eventually toward his own children, is shaped by his original relationship to his parents' authority style.

- A child's unacceptable behavior cannot be ignored. It sends the signal that he's not important and his behavior doesn't matter to his parents.

- Spanking may bring about an end to the objectionable behavior but it produces negative long-term effects including more aggression and depression in children.

- Parents often have strong emotions when they disapprove of their children's behavior. Children learn from feeling those emotions, but parents also need to try to avoid overreactions. When they do overreact, their acknowledgment of doing so and subsequent apology to their children is an important learning experience for both parent and child.

- Parental rules should be consistent, and children should understand the reasons for them.

- Children should be permitted to explain their reason for disagreeing with or violating a rule. In a dispute, the parent's will should prevail.

- Different children may require different authority styles and negative consequences.

- Parents should praise positive behavior as willingly as they voice objections to negative behaviors.

A majority of parents say that exercising parental authority and disciplining their children for misbehaving are the two most challenging parts of being a parent. In the business world, people go to graduate school for two years to learn how to motivate and manage people. When they're finished they receive an MBA and usually a higher-paying job. To manage a family and children, it's all on-the-job training—with no paycheck. An important aim of child psychology is to disseminate established and new findings about the most effective childrearing practices to those who need them most: today's parents.

The Least You Need to Know

- An authoritative parent, who presents firm rules but allows communication and flexibility in rule setting and discipline, produces the best outcomes in children.

- Permissive parenting and parental neglect are the least-effective parental authority styles.

- Spanking works to stop offensive behavior in the short term but not in the long term.

- Greater levels of self-control at age 4 predict better SAT scores and higher performance on other academic measures.

- Until the frontal cortex of a child's brain matures between the ages of 4 and 7, self-control is fleeting and more dependent on parental constraints and modeling.

The Big Picture

A child's growth from birth to young adulthood has three principal themes or dimensions: the development of social-emotional, moral, and cognitive abilities. The next three chapters go in depth about how the field of psychology approaches each of these dimensions, past and present. We look at the sequence of steps for development in that area, how growth is measured, and what happens if sensitive periods are missed.

A Child's Emotional Development

In This Chapter

- Love and the brain
- Why too much praise weakens a child's school performance
- Three-year-olds' emotional and social wisdom
- The ABCs of emotional IQ
- Studying "happiness": positive psychology

Love is all we need. So goes many a song and now a growing body of psychological research supports this view. But loving actions don't always come "naturally." Parents seeking to give a child unconditional love can shower her with too much approval and too many rewards. It turns out that even 7-year-olds know when they deserve a trophy or an A, and when they don't. That's the quandary: emotions are natural and yet they need to be managed for a child to be happy and be successful in every area of her life.

Love as Brain Food

Emotional competence includes self-regulation and being able to read other people's feelings. Both are important personal and social skills. Children who are adept at these skills are more liked by their peers. How do you spot these abilities in a child? These are the children who don't act out when they're upset or angry, but ask for help. They can tell when a friend is sad, and so might try to console the friend by touching them or saying something supportive. This is called empathy, another manifestation of a child's high emotional-social competence, also called *emotional IQ* by child psychologist Daniel Goleman in his 1995 book *Emotional Intelligence*.

DEFINITION

Emotional IQ is the ability to recognize and control one's feelings, as well as to read and respond to the feelings of others.

Lise Eliot, Ph.D., in her book *What's Going on in There? How the Brain and Mind Develop in the First Five Years of Life*, compares a baby's brain to a computer but points to one big difference between the two. A child's brain programs itself. No loading of software is necessary. The programming is in her genes, wired and waiting for the right environmental influences to help it manifest as behavior. This genetic activity happens on a molecular level with a unique pattern of electrical excitation that subtly alters synapses in the child's brain.

What is the best first "food" for this brain growth that is necessary for all other growth? In a word: love. As was made clear in this book's previous discussions of attachment theory, a baby's emotional IQ is shaped by his earliest bonding experiences with a parent. A secure attachment functions like rich soil for a seedling. As the baby matures, the continuing experience of unconditional love from parent to child then serves as the sunshine and water for the seed to grow. From this start, other kinds of learning will blossom.

Emotional Competence: How It Develops

Happiness, anger, and surprise along with fear, disgust, and sadness are considered the basic universal emotions. People have them everywhere in the world in every culture.

In psychology, an emotion is understood to have three parts:

- A physiological change
- A subjective feeling
- An overt behavior or expression

Child psychologists working during the past three decades have paid special attention to how children's emotional competency affects other areas of their development. In a longitudinal study completed in 2003, psychological researcher Susanne Denham looked at the question of which emotional experiences in preschool (ages 3 and 4) are most closely linked with a child's later social abilities in kindergarten (ages 5 and 6). Denham wanted to know what emotional behavior predicted social behavior. The approach used to determine the child's earlier emotional behaviors included naturalistic observation and an interview with each child's mother.

The child's later social competence in kindergarten was measured in two ways:

- Researchers asked the teacher to rate the child's cooperativeness and sensitivity to peers.

- Other children in the class were asked to rate the likeability of each child.

This study's results showed just how predictive early emotional learning is of later social behaviors. The steps taken by Denham and her colleagues in this process show the particulars to support this point:

- **Emotional expressivity**—While observing the younger children for five-minute periods, researchers noted the frequency of their smiles and frowns, as evidence of their positive and negative emotions.

- **Emotional knowledge**—Emotional knowledge was determined by asking the child to name what emotion a puppet would be experiencing in eight common situations. Among these: having a nightmare and receiving an ice-cream cone.

- **Emotional self-regulation**—Mothers were asked how well their children could control their emotions in the course of everyday life.

These three factors were correlated with the child's social competence in nursery school, and then again two years later, in kindergarten.

Among the Denham study's findings …

As expected, children who expressed mostly positive emotions at 3 and 4 were more knowledgeable about emotions and were better at regulating their own emotions than those children who expressed more negative emotions.

But positive emotions were not enough to ensure a child's popularity in nursery school. For 3- and 4-year-olds, social competence was only predicted by the child's ability to regulate her emotions. These children were rated highest by teachers and peers as likeable.

A surprise came in the later results: by the ages of 5 and 6, if a child in kindergarten expressed mostly positive emotions and knew a lot about emotions (their own and others), they were rated more socially competent in class. By this age, emotional self-regulation rated lower in predicting social popularity.

These results raise additional questions but clearly establish the early importance of a child having a modicum of emotional intelligence for social success.

Self-Esteem

Self-esteem is defined as a person's feelings about her worth. Self-esteem and self-respect may appear to be synonyms, but as Jack Westman points out, they are not. He explains self-esteem can be on a low-high continuum based on fantasy, whereas self-respect is based on reality. Self-esteem arises from within. You can have a good feeling about yourself—high self-esteem, which is based on fantasy—and still be a selfish, inconsiderate person. Children who have been "spoiled" can have high self-esteem, which crashes when they are frustrated or don't get the sort of approval they have come to expect. In contrast, self-respect arises from without and refers to how you value yourself in relation to other people. It is having a good evaluation or judgment of yourself validated by realistic accomplishments and experiences with other people. Self-respect gives rise to authentic high self-esteem from internally generated feelings based on reality.

This authentic self-esteem in children is important for a child's emotional, social, and—now the research makes clear—also for her intellectual development. Sources of self-esteem include the following:

- A child's innate temperament helps shape her self-esteem. Easy, friendly temperament children tend to develop more self-esteem than children with difficult, inhibited temperaments.

- When parents are willing to discuss household rules and discipline with them, their children's self-esteem rises. A child then internalizes the message that she is important enough for her opinions to be heard.

- Parents' consistent warmth, affection, and involvement with their children builds self-esteem. A hug sends the simple message: "You are important to me."

- Self-esteem also comes from the peer comparisons a child makes and approval or rejection she experiences from peers.

- Self-esteem comes from a child's emerging "belief system" which can be seen as an accumulation of all of the preceding.

> **INSIGHT**
>
> When measured by researchers, self-esteem is highest in preschool and lowest at the start of junior high school. Why? One view says the transition from elementary to high school is when children fall from a secure social position to a new unfamiliar one, and find themselves at the "bottom of the pecking order."

In one study of 2,000 low- to middle-income children living in the greater Detroit area, 25 percent of 9- to 12-year-olds had negative self-esteem. Their negative views of themselves showed up on all three scales measured: academic competence, social acceptance, and global self-worth. On each scale, 5 to 10 percent more girls than boys displayed negative self-esteem.

What Self-Esteem Is *Not*

Authentic self-esteem in children does not come from adults offering unearned rewards or praise. Kids as young as 7 know when they're hearing an untruth about themselves. For instance, if an adult tells a child how fabulously he just did at bat after he struck out, he'll sense the adult's false praise.

So what is effective praise? What works with children is the same as with adults. Praise works when it is …

- Specific to an accomplishment

- Sincere

- Intermittent

Adults shouldn't give kids praise willy nilly. Simple, right? Apparently not, because in one national survey 85 percent of parents think it's important to tell their kids—early and often—how smart they are.

A Surprising Praise Study

Carol Dweck and her team of investigators at Columbia University carried out a revealing experiment with 400 fifth-grade students in the New York City schools. Dweck's question was whether praise for intelligence would boost or inhibit the students' academic performance on IQ tests. The first test contained a series of simple puzzles. When the students completed the test, they were all given their scores. Randomly divided into two different groups, one group was praised for their intelligence: "You must be really smart." The other received praise for their effort on the test: "You must have worked really hard."

For a second test, both groups were given a choice: they could take a more difficult test or opt for another easy test. Can you guess who chose which test?

- Of those students praised for their effort, 90 percent chose the harder test.

- A majority of the students who'd been praised for being smart chose to take another easy test.

What does it mean? Dweck summarized the implications saying, "Emphasizing effort gives a child a variable they can control." In contrast, when a student is simply told how smart she is, she has no way to emotionally handle failure if she doesn't ace something. Even the risk of failure in the study caused extreme stress for those students who'd been told it was their smartness that had brought success. When Dweck repeated her experiment in schools of different socioeconomic populations, she found the outcome to be the same. It was also the same for boys and girls, with the brightest girls who were praised for intelligence being the most inclined to take the easy test.

Pitfalls of Praise

The dangers of false praise for children are many and far reaching. The psychological research says too much false praise does more harm than good for children by making them …

- More competitive.

- Grade-oriented rather than learning-oriented.

- More prone to lie and cheat in school.

- Less able to handle failure or frustration.

A child can get addicted to false praise. The reward system of the brain will anticipate it and begin sending out dopamine when praise is received. Not receiving praise then becomes a problem for the child.

Meanwhile, the ability to sustain a task and accept a certain amount of frustration and failure is essential to learning and creating in school and in life. When a child is too afraid of failure and too dependent on false praise, she is at greater risk for failure. Praise should be given for sustained effort and rewards should come only with success, not a near miss. From these experiences a child will develop authentic self-esteem and *emotional resiliency.*

> **DEFINITION**
>
> **Emotional resiliency** is the ability to cope with stress and adversity and bounce back. Emotional self-regulation is the "how to" part of emotional resiliency. A child with lower self-esteem has less emotional resiliency.

Conditional vs. Unconditional Love

If getting a parent's love and approval depends on a child's external achievement, the child learns that love is conditional. It depends on him doing something; there's a condition he must meet first. A condition can be sitting quietly at his desk in first grade or getting accepted by an Ivy League college later. If this dynamic is dominant in a parent-child relationship, the child's ability to trust will suffer and his relationships may become superficial. He will lack emotional resiliency. After all, if someone is only as good as his latest accomplishment, he has every reason to feel insecure, and good cause not to trust anyone. One of the ways that parents misunderstand unconditional love is when they use unearned praise for a child as a way to offer it. As we've seen in the research just discussed, false praise has the opposite effect of what is intended.

In her book *The Price of Privilege: How Parental Pressure and Material Advantage Are Creating a Generation of Disconnected and Unhappy Kids,* child psychologist Madeline Levine warned of the negative consequences she attributed to misdirected parental involvement in her young psychotherapy clients' lives. By this she meant too much "enrichment" and too many expectations, and not enough plain old ordinary unconditional love. Levine writes: "The reason that so many of my patients feel empty is because they lack the secure, reliable, welcoming internal structure that's called the 'self.' The boredom, the vagueness, the unhappiness, the reliance on others, all point to kids who have run into difficulty with the very foundation of psychological development."

Levine goes on to explain that by being overcritical and overinvolved in their children's lives, well-meaning parents contribute to their child's lack of self or self-identity. All this frenetic, externally focused activity on the part of parents and children can bring about parental burn out, making Mom and Dad emotionally unavailable when a child most needs support. Parents often have to work many extra hours or take on another job to pay for these privileges, robbing children of the thing they need most from their parents: unstressed, nurturing time together.

Emotional Resiliency: Can It Be Taught?

This question arose largely from the fieldwork done by child psychologist Daniel Goleman. He observed that children who are well-nurtured and whose parents model and help them learn how to calm down when they're upset seem to develop greater strength in the brain's circuits for handling distress. Conversely, Goleman wrote that those children whose parents neglect them or fail to model such behaviors will be more likely to act on aggressive impulses or have trouble calming down when they're upset. He accounts for this by pointing to the brain's prefrontal cortex where circuits for inhibiting disruptive emotional impulses and for applying one's focus to schoolwork are both located. If emotional impulses competing with attention to schoolwork for brain power are not inhibited, less attention will be available to the child for academic learning. As Goleman puts it, distress kills learning.

School-Based Emotional Learning

Goleman advocates that parents and teachers teach children emotional expressivity, along with emotional knowledge and self-regulation. He co-founded a center at the University of Illinois in Chicago to develop a curriculum and train teachers to accomplish this goal. The resulting program is called SEL, for social and emotional learning. After a decade of implementation of SEL programs in American schools, a meta-analysis (a study of all the studies done to date) compared students who had experienced the SEL program to those who had not. The data showed significant differences between the two groups. Not only had the SEL students gained mastery of abilities such as calming down under stress, they also benefited academically. Their scores on academic achievement tests were 14 percentage points higher than their non-SEL-trained peers.

ABCs of Emotional Resiliency

What are the crucial skills to produce a high emotional IQ? In the SEL program there are five competencies which, these researchers say, can be cultivated at school and at home:

- **Self-awareness:** A child learns to identify her thoughts, feelings, and strengths. She makes the connections between these and her habitual actions.

- **Social awareness:** A child identifies and understands the feelings of others, developing empathy and being able to take the perspective of others.

- **Self-management:** A child learns to handle emotions so they help rather than hinder the task at hand. This helps her set short- and long-term goals and deal with obstacles.

- **Responsible decision-making:** A child learns to come up with solutions to problems and implement them, as well as how to consider long-term consequences of decisions.

- **Relationship skills:** A child learns to resist distracting peer pressure, work to resolve conflicts, and keep healthy connections with others.

By learning and using these five competencies, the children in SEL programs exhibited higher scholastic achievement and lower behavioral problems in adolescence.

FIELD STUDY

Psychology researcher and author of *Raising an Emotionally Intelligent Child*, John Gottman, carried out a longitudinal study of 56 families focused on emotions. His purpose was to measure the impacts on children when parents modeled and encouraged emotional competency techniques, compared to families where the parents did not model these behaviors. Controlling for IQ, Gottman found that the children whose parents did what he called "emotion coaching" showed better performance in academics, social competence, emotional well-being, and even physical health. For example, they had lower levels of stress hormones in their urine and were sick less often.

Therapeutic Approaches

In-school programs can help prevent low self-esteem in children by building their emotional and social skills. But what about those children already suffering the negative consequences of not having positive self-esteem and emotional competence? There is sufficient psychological research to positively correlate a child's educational underachievement with social, emotional, and behavioral difficulties. And the problems seem to only get worse over time.

In response, a form of psychotherapy called Rational Emotive Behavioral Therapy (REBT) has been developed and has been shown to effectively address social and academic problems related to low emotional competence in adolescents. Using this therapeutic approach, child psychologists and counselors seek to illuminate the negative beliefs and habits of mind that often accompany poor self-esteem and unhealthy emotions. Their goal is to help the adolescents with these problems and reframe their thoughts with positive beliefs about themselves and their abilities. The most common course of treatment is a series of 12 weekly group counseling sessions. Among the coping strategies participants learn are changing their thinking, getting exercise, and getting emotional support.

A 14-year-old boy who had taken part in REBT sessions described his experience, saying: "Before coming here everything went wrong. I used to blame myself. I used to think only of my bad points but now I'm able to think about my good points. I am able to use rational thoughts."

Although human beings are wired to form close ties with their peers, the research presented in this chapter points to the importance of helping children learn the skills that make strong emotional relationships possible. Children can learn self-regulation and relationship skills—the building blocks of emotional resilience—at home and at school.

The Science of Happiness

Is happiness something that can be scientifically studied? A newer branch of psychology that goes by the name of "positive psychology" answers this question with a resounding "yes." Its proponents also say that this field of study has profound implications for children's social and emotional development.

According to the psychologist credited as its founder, University of Pennsylvania professor and former American Psychological Association President Martin Seligman, positive psychology is "the study of the strengths and virtues that enable individuals and communities to thrive." It includes, he says, "positive emotions, positive individual traits, and positive institutions."

Positive psychology generally places more emphasis on techniques for using positive thoughts and emotions to influence behavior, and less on "happiness" as a goal or as a conceptual construct.

One practitioner of positive psychology, psychologist and author Tal Ben-Shahar, made headlines when his positive psychology course at Harvard had the largest enrollment (at 854 students) of any course in the university's catalog. Commenting on the popularity of his class, Ben-Shahar said:

> In our time, depression is on the rise. More and more students experience stress, anxiety, unhappiness. Until a few years ago, we didn't have e-mail; now students check their e-mail 20 times a day … Students today are looking for ideas that will help them to lead better lives.

Positive psychology provides one such avenue for self-betterment. So how does it work?

Since we know that the physical, emotional, and cultural environment in which we live is as important as our genetic inheritance, positive psychology can be seen as a scientific approach to maximizing the positive potential of the 50 percent of who we are that comes from our environment. It does this by looking for credible evidence of ways people can enhance their personal strengths by using attributes such as optimism, courage, honesty, interpersonal skills, and self-understanding. For psychologists working in this branch of the field, it means focusing less on repairing past traumas or the "broken things" in their patients' psyches, and more on promoting individual and collective strengths.

Among the research findings attributed to psychologists and sociologists working in this field are the following:

- Optimism can protect people from mental and physical illness.
- People who report more positive emotions in young adulthood live longer and healthier lives.

- Wealth is only weakly correlated to happiness within and across nations, particularly when income is above the poverty level.

- Activities that make people happy in small doses, such as shopping, eating good food, and making money, do not lead to long-term fulfillment; they have quickly diminishing returns.

- An activity that produces the experience of "flow" (explained later in this chapter) can be its own reward.

- People who express gratitude on a regular basis have better physical health, optimism, and progress toward goals. They also help others more.

- Trying to maximize happiness can lead to unhappiness.

Even with these practical implications, positive psychology, its adherents say, is more descriptive than prescriptive. They explain that they are conducting research in order to teach people about the consequences of their behavioral choices, such as habitual thought patterns. For example, if someone believes it is better not to have hope for a better outcome so as to avoid disappointment in life, a positive psychologist would point out that, to the contrary, positive goal setting is correlated with positive outcomes.

Positive Psychology and Children

For children, the influence of positive psychology can be seen primarily in the domain of education. Its ideas are not entirely new to the school setting. In fact, positive psychology can be seen as conceptual and practical reinforcement for the concepts of emotional IQ and emotional coaching previously identified by psychologists Daniel Goleman and John Gottman.

Aspects of positive psychology that have been adopted for use in the classroom include the following:

- Help students lessen their negative self-talk and see challenges from more positive perspectives. It's the difference between a student failing his math test and thinking "I can't do math," then giving up, and a student failing her math test and thinking, "Okay, I seem to be missing something in this chapter. I'll ask my teacher for extra help."

- Teach students to identify and embrace their strengths. These are the capacities children have to think, feel, and behave in ways that can help them function better in school and with their peers. When students find and use their unique strengths, they discover their capacities to fulfill personal goals such as teamwork, leadership, creativity, self-control, and honesty.

- Pay attention to the positive or negative moods of students and the class as a whole. This is also referred to as the "broaden and build" theory of using positive emotions to improve the classroom learning environment.

FIELD STUDY

Psychologist Martin Seligman, founder of positive psychology, quotes an experiment in which three groups of children were given a mathematics test. One group simply took the test. The second group was given an unexpected piece of chocolate before taking the test. Before the third group took the test, they were asked to think of a time when they were so happy they jumped up and down with joy. The second and third groups did the best on their math test.

Positive psychology applications in the classroom take into account research that has shown the benefits of using positive emotions to enhance learning for both children and adults. Studies have shown that the experience of positive emotions is correlated with a higher quality of attention, a better working memory, and more verbal fluency.

Positive psychology asks teachers and students to focus not on their weaknesses or failures but on their strengths and potentials. They also suggest paying the most attention to what is working for them and for the other children in the class.

Using this approach, teachers and parents seek opportunities to set goals and support children in their activities. They use every opportunity to express optimism and a sense of meaning. The basic idea is that children internalize what they're feeling as they experience the behavior of adults in their lives (more than what adults say).

Finding the Flow

From his observations of artists at work, psychology professor Mihaly Csikszentmihalyi coined the concept of "flow" as a state of being characterized by high concentration and initiative. Flow occurs when a person is working at a level that meets his skills but doesn't exceed them. For a person of any age who is in a state of flow, hours slip by as if they are minutes. They experience this time as joyous and productive.

Positive psychology takes the concept of flow and looks at ways to make the experience more continuous, especially for adults in the workplace and for teachers and children in learning environments. One school-based application of flow encourages administrators to enhance the well-being of teachers so they can create a more positive emotional and learning environment for their students.

Flow as an aspect of positive psychology has been applied to individuals working successfully in groups to understand and enhance the value of these experiences. When flow occurs in groups, people have high levels of social well-being, and they feel a sense of belonging. They also experience the positive emotion of being valued for their contributions to the community. This experience is the basis of positive social engagement and civic duty. Some educators emphasize this community-building aspect of positive psychology. Professor George Vaillant of Harvard University states, "Negative emotions help us to survive individually; positive emotions help the community to survive." It is not surprising that the last few decades have seen team work become a cornerstone not only of academic methodology but also in the workplace.

Flow in the Classroom

If a challenge outstrips a student's existing skill set and ability, anxiety is the result. Anxiety then impedes learning. However, if a task is too easy, boredom sets in. Boredom also impedes the student's ability to learn.

Positive psychology says that the best way to foster flow for students in a classroom is for teachers to adopt activities that include interactivity and a playful attitude toward learning. Professor Ben-Shahar at Harvard University does this by assigning students exercises connecting positive psychology to their personal experiences.

British educational consultant Jenny Fox Eades of The Centre for Applied Positive Psychology offered several pointers for the successful application of these principles in her article "Celebrating Strengths." Among them are the following:

- Encourage students to go outside of their comfort zones into "stretch zones" where they're challenged but do not fear making mistakes.

- Model and teach aspects of resiliency, such as the ability to notice and control your emotions, a good sense of self-esteem, and a belief in your ability to make a difference and achieve goals.

- Demonstrate satisfaction with your ability to store happy memories and use them as a buffer against hard times.

A teacher's most important role, Fox Eades points out, may be to model the process of encouragement by encouraging others and oneself to keep trying.

Positive Psychology in the Community

Another method used by some teachers and school administrators for enhancing student flow is to increase opportunities for young people's engagement in civic projects. The purpose of these community activities is to give children and teenagers the experience of social belonging and the benefit of internalizing this experience at an early age. This can be seen as an antidote to the overemphasis on individual achievement and testing in schools.

The Least You Need to Know

- Praising the effort a child makes is more effective in building her emotional and intellectual IQ than telling her how smart she is.
- Unconditional love from a parent is necessary for a child to learn self-acceptance and to build emotional resiliency.
- In-school programs and new individual and group psychotherapies can help a child with low emotional competence do better socially and academically.

- The abilities to bounce back from failure and to delay gratification are at the heart of a child's emotional and social growth.

- Research in the field of positive psychology supports the effectiveness of techniques that promote positive emotions in educational and family settings.

A Child's Moral Development

In This Chapter

- Evidence of kindness in newborn babies
- Stages of moral reasoning
- How to tamp down aggression
- Eroding empathy in college students

If cognition of morality—that is, simply knowing right from wrong—were enough to make us moral, there would be far less immoral behavior in the world. Behavior also involves emotions and actions. When you think, feel, and act in a moral way, you experience certain emotional rewards: feelings of personal satisfaction and pride. When you commit an immoral act, you feel guilt. So morality involves cognition or reason, emotion, and behavior. Are children capable of making moral choices? According to new psychological research, babies as young as 6 months are equipped with rudimentary moral abilities previously thought to arrive much later in childhood. This chapter begins with these latest experimental discoveries and works backward to retrace how psychologists have come to understand the moral development of a child.

The Evidence of Morality in Babies

From the Infant Cognition Center at Yale University comes this headline: "Some sense of good and evil seems to be bred in the bone." In their experiments, researchers Paul Bloom, Karen Wynn, and Kiley Hamlin observed what they call "glimmers" of moral thoughts, feelings, and judgments in babies who were younger than a year old.

FIELD STUDY

In one baby morality experiment carried out at a Yale lab, geometric objects with faces were manipulated like puppets to behave in a way that either helped or hindered another puppet as it attempted to climb a hill. For example, a yellow circle helped a red square, while a green triangle blocked its way. After viewing the scene, 6- and 10-month-old babies were presented a choice of the helper (yellow circle) or hinderer (green triangle) objects on a tray. Overwhelmingly, they chose the "good guy" yellow circle object, demonstrating their primitive yet clear preference for good over bad behavior.

To take in the importance of this new perspective on baby morality you need only consider the opposite view that had previously dominated psychology. It began with Jean Jacques Rousseau (1762) who called the newborn human child "a perfect idiot." It rose to prominence with William James' 1890 description of a baby's mental life as "one great blooming, buzzing confusion." As it turns out, these were just guesses.

In fact, the difficulty of assessing the minds of preverbal babies proved insurmountable until researchers came up with the experimental method of measuring a baby's "looking time." In these experiments, researchers used the length of time a baby looked at something or someone as a measure of his interest in it. With this technique researchers learned that babies prefer to engage with objects that move, whether mobiles or faces.

From watching babies' eye movements and behaviors, researchers have also determined that they can detect and mimic other people's moods and expressions starting a few days after birth. If a baby sees a playmate or caregiver crying, he frowns. If another child is joyful, he responds in kind. This sort of mimicking is called an "empathetic response." When Charles Darwin noticed that certain animal species acted empathetically and so did his own 6-month-old son, he concluded that empathy must be innate. Demonstrations of empathy in toddlers are the basis for the belief that *altruism* came about as a human adaptation to assure the survival of the species.

DEFINITION

Altruism is a selfless concern for the welfare of others that is expressed through acts of kindness, sharing, cooperating, and helping.

So if empathy and altruism are in part evolutionary in origin, it makes sense that they are present to some degree at birth. The Yale researchers' findings showed that a baby comes into the world with a moral foundation that includes …

- The capacity and willingness to judge the actions of others.

- Some sense of justice.

- Gut responses to altruism and nastiness.

How a child's moral reasoning develops from this foundation then depends on his cognitive growth, his family, and cultural environment.

Theories of Moral Development

On the school bus, the most unpopular (overweight and buck-toothed) girl in the sixth grade is being teased mercilessly by a bully who keeps knocking her books onto the floor and calling her "fatso" and "bucky." Two other boys are watching this scene from a nearby row. Both feel sorry for the girl, and wish the bullying would stop. But what does each actually do about it?

Boy #1 laughs nervously, in effect endorsing and egging on the bully's immoral behavior.

Boy #2 leaves his seat, retrieves the girl's books from the floor, and hands them back to her. On his way back to his seat, he knocks the bully's books onto the floor, saying "See how it feels? Leave her alone."

What is the cognitive and emotional process that leads Boy #1 to take the cowardly way out and Boy #2 to play the hero in this situation? Let's look at past psychological theories on the development of morality for some insights.

"The Rules Is the Rules"

In Jean Piaget's view, preschoolers have no real sense of morality, while children between the ages of 5 and 10 are moral realists who believe that rules are absolute. In this age group, a fight can break out among a pair of card players if one should sneak a peek at the other's hand. They also tend to administer quick punishment for perceived misdeeds, something Piaget called "immanent justice." He pointed to the tendency of a typical child of this age to employ magical thinking to tie unrelated consequences to an act that he considers to be against the rules. In the child's mind, if someone cheats at cards and then falls down and scrapes his knee, justice will have been served.

Based on his observations of different-age children at play and in conflict, Piaget came up with one of the first theories of how morality develops incrementally in concert with cognitive development. At about age 8, Piaget said children move into the stage of "moral relativism." With their maturing ability to connect rules with reasons, at this age children understand that rules can change to fit different circumstances.

Moral Dilemmas

Morality is rarely as black and white as cheating at cards. Culture influences an individual's view of right and wrong. Some moral dilemmas are complex and subjective. When the stakes are very high and personal it can be difficult to assign greater morality to one course of action over another. That was the challenge taken on in the late 1960s and 1970s by psychology researcher Lawrence Kohlberg who refined Piaget's theory. Kohlberg focused on the grey areas between wrong and right to see how both children and adults handled them. In one famous experiment, Kohlberg posed this situation:

> A man's wife is dying. The life-saving medicine that would treat her illness cost $2,000, 10 times what it cost to make. After asking everyone he knew for help, the man had amassed only $1,000 to pay for the medicine. So he asked the pharmacist to sell the medicine to him cheaper and allow him to pay the rest later. The pharmacist refused. The man then broke into the pharmacy and got the medicine by force to save his wife.

After hearing this story, Kohlberg asked children, adolescents, and adults who in the story displayed moral or immoral behavior: the man who robbed and/or the druggist who denied a dying person a needed medicine.

In fact, there was no "right" or "wrong" answer to Kohlberg's moral dilemma experiment. He was more interested in the process of moral reasoning participants used to arrive at their own answers than who they chose as moral or immoral. After studying all the participants' responses and comparing them, he came up with three levels of moral reasoning. Like Piaget, Kohlberg tied morality to cognitive development, most critically to the ability to see a situation from some-one else's perspective.

How Moral Reasoning Grows

Kohlberg's three stages of moral reasoning include:

1. **Preconventional morality: Punishment and Reward**—On this first "me-first, second, and third" level, morality begins with strict obedience to authority and evolves to an exchange: nice behavior for rewards. A child first follows rules because he sees adults as having absolute power, and then because it serves his own interests.

2. **Conventional morality: Social Norms**—As a child progresses to this middle level of moral reasoning, he first wants to live up to others' expectations. Then, he follows rules to maintain social order, a "contract" with which he agrees and wishes to uphold.

3. **Post-conventional or principled morality: Moral Codes**—At the highest level of moral reasoning, the individual first adheres to a social contract only when he considers it valid. Then, usually in the twenties, his personal morality is based more on abstract principles of justice that fit his personal worldview. It may not always conform to the dominant convention of his society.

A person's progression through levels one to three always moves in the same lower to higher direction, Kohlberg said, even though most people will never reach the final stage of level three. Most children operate at a preconventional level of morality. But so do many adolescents and some adults.

Like Piaget, Kohlberg stressed cognitive development that enabled children to take the point of view of others; in effect, to role play. Along with this cognitive ability, Kohlberg also pointed to the child's social experience as a factor. If a grade school child had no awareness of poverty, for example, he may not be able to fully appreciate the moral dilemma in the experiment. According to Kohlberg, at each stage in this progression the basis for moral decision-making changes. A child starts in level one paying heed to external forces, such as social approval or punishment. By level two the child's basis of decision-making has shifted to what everyone else thinks. Finally, if she reaches level three, the adolescent or young adult is making moral decisions based on her own concepts of justice and rights.

To Lend a Helping Hand

But what if helping someone would cause you to sacrifice something? Working in the 1980s and 1990s, psychological researcher Nancy Eisenberg designed morality experiments which would be more realistic and suited to a child's perspective of the world. Eisenberg and her associates brought children of different ages, from preschool through high school, into a laboratory where they were asked to imagine themselves in this situation:

> A child is on his way to a birthday party when he encounters another child who has fallen and hurt herself. Would he stop to help out the child who fell at the risk of missing out on fun and goodies awaiting him at the party? Or would he go on his way without stopping?

Like Kohlberg, Eisenberg was more interested in finding out the motivations behind each child's choice. She found that, for the most part, only the upper elementary school–age children and adolescents helped the injured girl out of a feeling of empathy. Those that did displayed a *prosocial* level of moral reasoning when they considered the injured girl's perspective and how their helping actions would make her feel in spite of the inconvenience it caused them.

 DEFINITION

Prosocial moral reasoning is the type of thinking people do when they're deciding whether to help, share with, or comfort others when these actions could prove costly to themselves.

Eisenberg found that although other children and adolescents said they would help the girl they did so primarily for personal gain, not out of prosocial moral reasoning. Such gains might include social approval from authority figures or favors from the girl in exchange for their help. As such, these helpers were more guided by self-interest than empathy.

Teaching Prosocial Behavior

Age was a critical factor in how participants responded to this hypothetical dilemma. But Eisenberg concluded that age was not the only thing that determines who operates out of a genuine empathy for someone in need. She pointed to environmental factors, especially cultural values and the quality of parental models as also having a role in predicting which children would be led by empathy to employ prosocial reasoning.

> **INSIGHT**
>
> Eisenberg and later researchers studying child morality found that parents who have a warm emotional tone, parents who communicate expectations of mature behavior, and parents who provide explanations for rules raise children who exhibit the highest levels of prosocial reasoning and behaviors.

How Long Does It Last?

Does a child with a high moral compass at a young age hold onto it as she ages? To find out, Eisenberg and her research associates completed a 17-year longitudinal study of some of the 4- and 5-year-olds who had participated in the birthday party moral reasoning test. The purpose of this follow-up study was to see if those children who showed prosocial attitudes at 4 and 5 were still showing them at age 17. The results were affirmative.

The prosocial younger children became altruistic teenagers. They were more helpful toward others and could reason in complex ways about moral dilemmas. Their more self-interested peers at 4 and 5 grew into teenagers who were less morally mature. For example, if faced with someone needing help, these adolescents said they would help someone they personally liked, but they would bypass another person whom they did not know or like. In contrast, the morally mature teenagers said they would help someone regardless of their personal feelings about that person.

The Role of Emotions

Although many researchers studying moral development in children focused on the mind or reason as the primary driver of behavior, others place greater emphasis on how moral affect plays a part. Moral affect refers to feelings, and includes both negative emotions such as guilt and more positive emotions such as emotional attachment to parents and empathy.

The first psychological researcher to weigh in on this issue was none other than Sigmund Freud. Freud's psychoanalytic theory posited that children act in moral ways to avoid the guilty feelings that their superego imposes when they behave badly. Freud saw the Oedipal or Electra stage (described in Chapter 13), between the ages of 3 and 6, as the period when this conflict played out for most children. This was the time when he believed children *internalize* the moral standards of their same-sex parent as they resolve their Oedipus or Electra conflicts.

 DEFINITION

Internalization is the process of adopting the attributes or standards of another person and taking these standards as one's own.

From the thinking of Watsonian behaviorists (Chapter 1) came the view that the best discipline for misbehaving children was to forcefully squash their negative impulses. When children misbehaved, the advice for parents was to threaten the withdrawal of their love and affection. More recent research has shown that this form of parenting, using physical controls, threats, and withdrawal of affection, is counterproductive. It actually produces lower levels of moral behavior in children.

In contrast, parental behavior that teaches children the positive effects of their prosocial actions on others fosters more positive behavior and moral character. This style of parent-child interaction, called "inductive parenting," tells and demonstrates to children acceptable and adaptive ways to behave. It encourages them to take the perspectives of others. Inductive parenting also emphasizes parents talking with children about their expectations of them.

The parenting implications of Freud's theory have been augmented and modified by later research. But Freud is credited with being the first to point out that emotions such as pride, shame, and guilt are important in the development of moral or ethical behaviors and to raise questions about the origins of empathy.

The Origins of Empathy

As demonstrated by the Yale experiments, babies come into this world wired to care about others. A large body of research also shows that parental models and cultural norms play a decisive role in shaping this human instinct into higher levels of moral and prosocial reasoning.

A child's concern for others' feelings and needs appears to develop in four stages. The core feeling is sympathy or empathy, but this emotion changes and deepens to reflect a child's more advanced cognitive understanding:

1. From birth to 1 year, a baby cannot separate herself from her adult caregiver, so whatever Mom or Dad feels, she feels. This is called "global empathy."

2. Knowing she's separate at 1 to 3 years, a child will try to comfort others by offering or doing something that she feels might make them feel better because it works for her. She might share a toy or stroke the other person. This is called egocentric empathy.

3. In preschool and elementary school, a child understands more about the differences between herself and others. When she wants to comfort another, she helps by offering something the other person might like.

4. In late childhood and adolescence, a young person has a deeper understanding of the sometimes complex reasons for the sadness or troubles of another person. She begins to feel empathy for groups of people who may be at a disadvantage.

Learning Altruism

Parents and other adults can teach altruistic behavior to children by using positive verbal reinforcement. On the other hand, bribing children to get them to be nicer or more caring toward others doesn't work, the research shows. Why not? Apparently, children who receive tangible rewards for altruistic behavior become tied to those rewards. When the goodies stop, so does their altruism. Out the window go their positive, helping behaviors.

The foundation for children to learn prosocial actions is a warm and caring relationship with an adult who models caring and helpful behaviors toward others. When a parent models the desired behaviors, children internalize the actions desired of them. Contrarily, children are less likely to internalize the actions of adults with whom they have a cold and mistrustful relationship.

Studies have been done of unusually charitable adults, for example those Christians who risked their lives to help Jews escape the Nazis during World War II. Such studies have shown that these altruistic individuals had been raised by moralistic adults who practiced what they preached.

Moral Thoughts = Moral Behaviors?

Based on research done early in the twentieth century, some behavioral psychologists hang on to the belief that morality depends on the situation a child or teenager finds himself in. They call this the doctrine of specificity. Those holding this view say moral reasoning, moral affect, and moral behavior do not spring from an internalized set of moral principles. Instead, morality is specific to the situation, and is not a fixed character trait.

More recent research presents evidence that those young people who are capable of higher levels of moral reasoning appear to have greater consistency between their thoughts and actions. In a controlled experiment, only 15 percent of college students who reasoned at the "post-conventional," principled level cheated on a test when given the opportunity. This compared with 55 percent of the "conventional" students and 70 percent of those operating at the "preconventional" level of moral reasoning.

Back on the Bus

With this framework in mind, let's return to the school bus incident that began this section. Which level of moral development do you think Boy #2 had reached when he intervened to stop a bully's harmful actions? What about Boy #1 who laughed at the bully's actions?

A case can be made that Boy #2 operated at level two in Kohlberg's schema of moral reasoning. He understood the bully's behavior to not be in line with the social contract governing behavior on the bus. But he also may have been operating at level three when he concluded that justice needed to be carried out in the form of an intervention. In Eisenberg's framework, Boy #2 felt genuine empathy for the girl and was motivated to risk his own safety by getting out of his seat to help her. His actions were empathetic and prosocial.

Meanwhile, Boy #1 can be seen as operating from Kohlberg's lowest level, the preconventional stage of moral reasoning. This is when rules apply only when it suits one's personal interests. In Eisenberg's framework, Boy #1 felt the bullied girl's need for help but made a "safer" choice by staying put. His moral reasoning and actions were not empathetic or prosocial.

Group Morality

Does a lack of action make someone less moral than the person who takes a personal risk to stop a wrong? The answer to this question for most people is an easy "yes." But what about a large group of people faced with evidence of immoral actions, even atrocities being perpetrated by a representative government? This is one of the great unresolved philosophical questions of the twentieth century—for example, when it is applied to the citizenry of Germany during World War II who did little to defy Hitler and stop the extermination of German Jews.

But the question of moral responsibility also arises in small communities. It has been applied in more recent years to particularly heinous acts of violence perpetrated by groups of adolescents on weaker victims.

By assessing the quality of empathy involved in taking prosocial action, Eisenberg extended the usefulness of Kohlberg's levels of moral development. Taken together, their research provides a framework for understanding moral choices made by children on school buses as well as by adults in their workplaces and as citizens. The cultural aspects of prosocial reasoning have also been extensively studied. When a culture traditionally emphasizes group concerns over those of individuals, prosocial reasoning is more valued and thus, more widely practiced.

Aggression in Children

At the other end of a child's moral spectrum are self-serving attitudes and behaviors that are aggressive and harmful to others. Sometimes the words assertive and aggressive are incorrectly believed to have the same meaning. But in psychological terms, they're not interchangeable. Assertive behaviors are goal-oriented actions that help someone obtain legitimate ends. Aggressive behaviors, whether verbal or physical, are carried out without heeding the needs of others. They are intended to cause harm, damage, or injury to another person. In children and teenagers, aggressive actions encompass hitting, name calling, spreading malicious gossip, pushing, shoving, bullying, initiating fights, and stealing. Studies have found that highly aggressive children have a strong likelihood of becoming anti-social, criminal young adults. Because of this outcome, much attention has been devoted to what causes aggression in children.

Why Are Some Kids Mean?

At one time, psychologists attributed children's aggression to their high levels of frustration. Although feeling blocked from having or doing what one wants can lead to aggressive behavior, further research has shown frustration to be below two other causes.

Early family experiences. The use of harsh physical punishment by parents is positively correlated with aggressive behavior in children. In one 1990 study, physically punished children were rated twice as aggressive (by their peers and teachers) compared to other children. At the same time, not all spanked children are overly aggressive.

FIELD STUDY

University of Tulane researchers studied the effect of spanking using a mixed population of 2,500 children between the ages of 3 and 5. The group included 45 percent who, according to their mothers, had not been spanked, 28 percent who were spanked "once or twice," and 26 percent who were spanked more than twice. The odds of a child being more aggressive at age 5 rose by 50 percent if he had been spanked twice in the month before being observed by researchers. This 2010 study stood out from others done previously in that investigators accounted for variables that included the mother's acts of neglect, parents' use of alcohol or drugs, and violence or aggression between the parents.

And some aggressive children did not receive physical punishment. Parents who simply model aggressive behavior in front of their children can also produce more aggressive children. These parents tend to use more forceful rather than coopera-tive means to settle conflicts. They yell rather than speak calmly or discuss an issue. They grab the TV remote out of someone's hands, rather than ask or negotiate a peaceful solution to competing needs or desires.

Violent television. A typical children's cartoon shows on average one violent act every three minutes. What's the impact of all this mayhem on growing children?

There are many correlational and some experimental studies linking children's viewing of violent TV programs with spikes in aggressive behavior.

In the laboratory of social learning theorist Albert Bandura, children were given specially created TV programs to watch. In these shows, an adult acted violently, kicking and hitting a plastic doll named Bobo. Two groups of children were given the same doll to play with; one group watched the violent program, the other didn't. Those who watched were more likely to imitate the on-screen character and act violently toward Bobo than the others.

A longitudinal study looked at how children's violent TV watching at age 8 affected their criminal records at age 30. Those boys who watched the most violent TV committed the most and more serious crimes as young men. The same correlation was true for girls albeit with lower rates of violence for girls in trouble with the law.

Problems with Processing Emotions

In the 1990s, researchers started to investigate whether any cognitive deficiencies might contribute to a child's level of aggressive behavior. This work revealed that aggressive boys often respond aggressively because they are not as skilled as their peers in sensing other people's intentions. They fail to accurately interpret other peoples' intentions. When they're unsure of why someone does something or looks at them a certain way, they tend to respond aggressively.

Another study investigated whether anything could be done to help young people like this overcome their deficiency and be less aggressive as a result. In one correctional facility, incarcerated adolescents were taught how to pay attention to nonhostile cues in a social setting. When they accurately perceived hostility coming their way, they were shown how to use alternative responses. Supervisors at the juvenile correction facility who were questioned after this training program reported less aggression and less impulsivity in those adolescents who had taken the training.

In summary, parents increase a child's aggression when they use physically forceful punishments. If there are a lot of unresolved conflicts in the home, parents model aggressive behaviors which are then internalized by their child. Aggressive adolescents are more inclined to choose aggressive friends, thus reinforcing the behavior in peer groups. Beyond a child's immediate home and school environment, studies show that poverty and high levels of neighborhood crime create a culture of violence with many negative impacts on children.

Kindness on the College Campus

A recent meta-study of 14,000 students done by University of Michigan researchers looked at whether college students' empathy—meaning their concern for the needs of others—had changed compared to earlier generations. The study's results showed that students who entered college after the year 2000 were 40 percent less empathetic than college students of earlier decades. Researchers also noticed that while it would have been easy for the students who took the survey to make themselves look and sound kinder and nicer if they wished to, they didn't bother to try. Another finding was that the students themselves felt that their peers at school are less compassionate.

You can try some of the actual test questions yourself and think about how you might respond:

- I often have tender, concerned feelings for people less fortunate than me.

- Other people's misfortunes *do not* usually disturb me a great deal.

- When I see someone being taken advantage of, I feel kind of protective toward them.

- I sometimes try to understand my friends better by imagining how things look from their perspective.

- If I'm sure I'm right about something, I don't waste much time listening to other people's arguments.

When conjecturing on the causes behind these disturbing results, the University of Michigan researchers focused on four likely factors causing the decrease in empathy on campus:

- Free play—the amount of time children spend playing outdoors and in unstructured activities with other children—declined by a third between 1981 and 2003. As a result, they don't learn to connect emotionally with other children or interact informally in positive ways.

- The resulting increase in time kids spend indoors, alone and in front of screens—TV, videogames, and computers—where they are likely to increase their level of aggression and decrease their positive social skills.

- The misuse of self-esteem by today's parents who reward and praise their children when not merited, increasing a child's narcissistic tendencies.

- Lastly, the study authors cited dominant individualism and a glorification of competition in the culture at large at the cost of cooperation and altruism.

Studies such as this one and others cited throughout this chapter demonstrate some of the new directions being taken in today's psychological research on the origins and impediments to morality. Much of it is geared toward lending insight into current social issues by examining the possible roots of those problems in childhood. Childrearing practices, how and where children play, and how young people who break the rules are punished or rehabilitated all play key roles in shaping the long-term picture of child morality.

The Least You Need to Know

- Babies before 1 year of age demonstrate a rudimentary sense of fairness and morality.
- Moral thoughts don't always produce moral behaviors.
- Aggressive behavior in children has been correlated with harsh discipline methods, watching more violent television, and an inability to read other peoples' emotions.
- In a recent study, college students showed 40 percent less empathy than previous generations.

A Child's Cognitive Development

In This Chapter

- Figuring out your place in the world
- Are children's minds and computers the same?
- The uses for different types of attention and memory
- Sensitive periods for learning one or two languages

Every baby has innate intelligence, with new abilities to learn and information to process arriving in stages until the mid-twenties. Although it initially comes as a surprise, every young child eventually realizes that what she understands to be true is not necessarily the same as what other people think. How she knows what she knows is the story of a child's cognitive development. Along with emotional-social and moral reasoning abilities, we now begin presenting the big picture of how a child develops from birth through adolescence.

Major Cognitive Stages

In a time when children were viewed as passive recipients of knowledge, Piaget saw that children always and everywhere are constructing their own ideas of how the world works. He explained a child's cognitive development using new concepts such as accommodation, assimilation, and equilibrium. With this three-fold process he demonstrated how children come up with mental schemes to organize their reality. They then take in new data and change their schemes to fit. The practical implications of these ideas have led schools to incorporate processes of discovery and self-interpretation into how they teach everything from math to history.

The Foundation

With some modifications and revisions, Piaget's four stages of cognitive development are still regarded as the foundations of how children think and learn. To review, the stages are as follows:

Stage	Age	Characteristics
Sensorimotor	Birth to 2 yrs	Knowledge comes from senses and motor skills
Preoperational Thought	2 to 6 yrs	Symbols and words used with an egocentric worldview
Concrete Operations	6 to 12 yrs	Logic in the here and now
Formal Operational Thought	Adolescence	Abstract ideas and hypothetical situations; Reasons deductively

Falling Back, Jumping Ahead

One area of Piaget's theory that researchers have re-examined and revised is the consistency of children's performance in these four stages. Some studies show that children gain certain cognitive abilities at the appropriate age but they may often revert back to a previous stage for a particular task. For example, a child of 7 years (in the concrete operations stage) "should" be able to watch water being poured from one container into another and understand that it is the same amount of water even though the new container is a different size or shape. In the Piagetian view, on this so-called "conservation" task the child should not fall back into preoperational thinking and assume that merely by changing containers the water is any more or less.

When the same child looked at another task using the same logical structure as the conservation task, in this case the idea that two people looking at three mountains in the distance should both see the same scene, the child should perform similarly as he did with the water containers. If he misses the first task, he should also miss the "three mountain" task. However, researchers have found that children may use preoperational thinking in one task and operational thought in another even when similar thought structures are involved. Children also may jump ahead on a particular task to the next cognitive stage and display abilities that are "ahead of schedule."

> **INSIGHT**
>
> According to Piaget, children younger than 6 or 7 cannot solve conservation problems because they don't yet understand reversibility. This is the cognitive operation that allows them to discover physical attributes such as mass or volume. Neither did he believe that they possess the needed logic to enable such tasks until they reach the concrete operations stage after age 6.

Current thinking differs from Piaget's view of rigidly differentiated stages of children's thought processing. It is now understood that just attaining a particular level of reasoning does not mean a child will always reason at that level. Researchers have shown that children can be trained to use the concept of conservation as young as 4-years-old. Recent research has focused on the ability of some children to hold more schemes in their memory at a time. This, researchers say, accounts for the ability of some to jump ahead to higher levels of reasoning and others to fall behind.

A wealth of additional new research conducted during the past three decades has added to and refined many aspects of Piaget's cognitive learning theory.

What Children Think About Thinking

The term "theory of mind" refers to the intriguing question of what concepts children hold about their and other people's thoughts. For example, when do children begin to understand that each person thinks different thoughts? Or the realization that they don't know what the other person is thinking? This is the terrain of beliefs, desires, and consciousness; pretty heady stuff for a discussion of preschoolers and kindergarteners. Before getting lost in a Rubik's Cube of possibilities, let's use what is known about the stages of cognitive development to help narrow down the answers.

Here's a classic question used by researchers to test a child's theory of mind:

> Jorge puts some chocolate in a blue cupboard and goes out to play. In his absence, his mother moves the chocolate to a green cupboard. When Jorge returns he wants his chocolate. Where does Jorge look for it?

Which cupboard does a 3-year-old say Jorge will open?

Egocentric 3-year-olds say the green cupboard. Why? Because they know that's where the chocolate is, never mind Jorge.

What about a 4- or 5-year-old? The slightly older child who displays what is called a "belief-desire" theory of mind will say the blue cupboard. This reflects their understanding that beliefs determine behavior so Jorge will look in the blue cupboard because, not having seen Jorge's mother move it, that's where Jorge believes his chocolate is still located.

In the last two chapters you saw that as children mature, this ability to put themselves in another's perspective is of critical importance in their social-emotional and moral development.

Social-Cultural Perspective

One persistent criticism of Piaget's four stages of cognitive development concerns its lack of attention to cultural factors in a child's life. Those that hold this view believe that culture not only affects the rate of cognitive maturation but also how and what children think. Rather than viewing cognitive growth as a self-directed process where children function almost as if they were isolated scientists, learning is seen as an outgrowth of children's social interactions.

The original proponent of the social-cultural view of cognitive development was the Russian child psychologist Lev Vygotsky (1896–1934) who was a contemporary of Piaget. He held the view that cognitive development was not universal; instead, that children develop those cognitive skills that are demanded by the values and needs of their unique culture. The aspect of Vygotsky's theory that holds the most interest for psychologists today is his emphasis on socio-historical development. This is the study of how changes in culture, values, norms, and technologies shape how children think and learn. For example, they ask how the seismic shift in the communications systems of industrialized countries (radio, TV, computers) in the last 50 years has changed children's thinking.

Related research focuses on such questions as …

- Does access to keyboards, joysticks, and digital screens at the preconcrete operational ages of 3 and 4 change when and how a child understands such concepts as conservation?

• What about theory of mind? With this technology at her fingertips does the child come any sooner to an understanding that each person holds separate thoughts? Or might it delay such a cognitive epiphany?

As time goes on with an increasing number of gadgets and processing speeds at a child's early disposal, the opportunities for research will grow exponentially.

Social Collaboration and Learning

The focus of the social-cultural approach to cognitive development is on the relationship between the child and a more skilled partner who guides and encourages her to learn. Vygotsky's term for this, though dense and technical sounding, gets right to the point. With the phrase "zone of proximal development" he marked out the range of tasks that are too complex for the child to master alone. But with the help of a more knowledgeable partner, they can be learned. How does this work? In part the child learns by internalizing the problem-solving techniques of her partner. After this process of internalization, she will have those skills to draw on independently.

It also has been found that younger children, who engage with older children and adults in symbolic, pretend play advance in those cognitive skills faster than children who don't. Were you the younger sibling who played and learned from an older brother or sister? What are the skills you might have learned through that play? Children learn about people, objects, and actions through symbolic play. A direct relationship has been found between the amount of cooperative social play a child engages in and her later understanding of people's feelings and beliefs.

Culture as Teacher

Taking this idea a step farther, consider the fact that in some cultures today, particularly agrarian and craft-oriented societies, children don't go to school with other children. Their learning takes place at home, in the fields, in service work, or in small factories. In these cultures, the model of the apprentice-mentor is still very much in place. In such places children's learned thinking occurs in an apprenticeship relationship to elders and more skilled peers. This is called "guided participation" learning.

The major difference between this type of learning and that used in Western countries is that guided participation takes place "in context." Thinking processes and skills are immediately put to use in the place where the learning takes place. In contrast, most learning in the United States takes place "out of context"— usually in a classroom. In Western culture, a student learns skills to be put in effect at a future workplace or a higher level of education.

To study how children learn in both settings, in the 1990s, an observational study was done of children in two out-of-context settings in Salt Lake City and Turkey and two in-context village settings in India and Guatemala. Researchers noted these differences:

- In-context learning is less verbal, and adults use more explicit hands-on teaching methods.

- Out-of-context teachers use more classroom structure and verbal praise to keep students' attention on the tasks at hand.

In measuring and comparing student strengths, these researchers noted that the traditionally in-context taught students had better observational skills and were better at emulating behavior than the out-of-context learners. When these skills are valued in their particular culture, these students are better prepared for success.

But even in industrialized, Western societies collaborative learning has been found to be an effective educational strategy, when compared to having students work on tasks alone. It has particular relevance in preparing students for the modern workplace where team performance is increasingly emphasized.

Child's Mind as a Computer

The psychological school of thought that has received the most research attention in the area of cognitive development since Piaget is the "information processing perspective." Instead of looking at broad stages of learning, this approach focuses on the child's mental manipulation of symbols. Information processing psychologists often use the computer as a model for human thought. They examine and compare the way a computer stores and uses information with human memory and learning.

Storage and Processing Speed

One of the key differences between computers and human brains is the computer's greater capacity for processing information. This refers to how much information a person or a computer can remember and access at one time. Children gain processing capacity as they mature, but they have different capacities within each age group. For example, let's return to Piaget's conservation problem. An information processing perspective would account for a 5-year-old child's inability to understand that the amount of liquid stays the same in different size containers because the child cannot process container height and width at the same time. As children mature, they can work with multiple dimensions and different sources of information.

Some information processing psychologists believe that children don't add quantity to their processing capacity as they grow older. Rather, children learn to process information more efficiently. These psychologists use the example of reading and point to how hard children must work at first to sound out letters and words. But, as they master the basics, their brains are freed up to make room for other learning. Thus reading becomes an automatic skill, and the child's learning process gains efficiency.

Domains of Learning

After a child learns to read, he has to continually read more books or other material to get more proficient. A child with a voracious appetite for reading can speed way ahead of his same age peers in language skills. This is an example of domain-specific learning. The same thing can happen in math, or a specific physical ability or sport. Practice makes perfect.

FIELD STUDY

"This brain is under construction." The process of myelination—the growth of protective fatty material covering the brain's neurons—is thought to be the decisive factor determining when a child gains certain abilities. The neurons for complex cognitive skills are among the last to be myelinated, after sensory and motor neurons. The executive functions coordinated in the frontal cortex of a child's brain and utilizing these neuronal pathways for learning are maturing throughout childhood and adolescence.

When a skill set or ability is called "domain general," it is one that tends to arrive in most children around the same age. Harkening back to Piaget's stages of cognitive development, these abilities don't depend on how much practice a child has had with a particular activity. They come naturally as she ages. Examples of domain general abilities are the capability to remember names and add "in your head."

Paying Attention

Try learning Spanish while thinking about soccer. Hard, isn't it? The ability to focus on one stimulus without becoming distracted is the thing that makes all kinds of learning possible. Newborn babies pay attention to their mother's faces and most moving objects. But certain types of attention skills are acquired with age:

Sustaining Attention. A child is reading aloud at his desk. He can hear another child reading a different page just two desks away. Will he be able to continue reading without being distracted? Children develop the ability to pay attention for longer periods of time when they can inhibit their responses to irrelevant stimuli in their environment.

Sometimes the distracting stimuli are internal. The child wonders how soon class will break for recess. He panics at his inability to recall a particular word and loses his place. Perhaps he jumps to a conclusion before thinking through the problem he's attempting to solve. When a child succumbs to this type of internal distraction, his problem is referred to as an inability to "inhibit responses." The frontal cortex of the brain is responsible for this type of executive function. Between the ages of 3 and 6 this part of a child's brain makes a major jump.

Attending Selectively. When there are many things going on in a child's environment, he must pick out one thing at a time to focus on. This is selective attention. Children learn different strategies to avoid distractions. They might move away from certain stimuli, or, if it's an electronic gadget, turn it off. Although it sounds simple, many children experience difficulty in focusing and staying focused on the task at hand. In Chapter 16, a brain disorder called attention-deficit hyperactivity disorder, or ADHD, is described. This is a diagnosis given to children who have an extreme problem in this area.

What We Know About Memory

It doesn't matter how well you pay attention if you don't remember what you learn. Two-month-old babies can remember something for a few days. Researchers discovered this when they "taught" babies to pull a string to make a crib mobile move. If placed in the crib a few days or a few weeks later, a baby would typically remember how to make the mobile move again. However, if several weeks went by before getting a chance to try again, the babies would not remember.

Younger children before age 6 or 7 have a more literal way of remembering things. They like to remember and repeat the exact words spoken to them. Older children, like adults, tend to retain general impressions. They might remember the gist of what was said to them, but not recall the conversation verbatim.

This distinction between how and what younger and older children remember has been useful for understanding how children make cognitive progress. Some tasks, for example mental arithmetic, require highly detailed "verbatim" representations in a child's memory. Other problem-solving tasks require only gist memories.

Stored Memory

To illustrate how memories are stored and accessed, psychologists use the model of a network of linked "nodes," which you can think of as gathering spots for similar information. Several nodes might be devoted to a single topic or area. For example, an 8-year-old boy whose skateboarding might have a dozen connected nodes, one devoted to the condition of the board's wheels; while others are about street skating, stairs, flips, etc. These nodes are only activated when needed to complete a memory. Networks that are used more often are activated faster than those with only occasional use. Networks can be activated externally by an image or comment or internally by a thought. The phrase "use it or lose it" is an apt description of what happens if too much time goes by since the last time skateboarding or any other network of nodes in a child's memory were activated.

Your long-term memory has unlimited capacity. The more long-term memory you store at any given time, the more your capacity will expand to hold an even greater quantity. The other surprising fact about long-term memories is that they are never truly forgotten. It's all in there somewhere, waiting to be accessed and then retrieved and reactivated.

There are different categories of long-term memory:

- **Semantic**—Knowledge of words and concepts

- **Episodic**—Memory of events or day-to-day life experiences

- **Scripts**—Episodic memories organized into patterns or habits connected to a certain type of event

As a child matures, he acquires more details about the person, place, or thing that occupies his memory nodes. These details are added in the form of additional links to the child's existing nodes. A 2-year-old, for example, might have a node for bird, with a single-linked node for sky. In comparison, a 7-year-old child's node for bird could have dozens of links to nodes denoting blue, red, large, small, water, marsh, trees, etc.

Why We Forget

Very few adults can recall an event or episodic memory that occurred before the age of 3. Psychologists have a name for this: infantile amnesia. Not remembering early life events is entirely normal. But why? Scientists are not sure but have come up with several possible explanations:

- The immaturity of the baby and toddler's frontal lobes may facilitate the memory of events associated with motor activities but not sensory and verbal cues.

- Children under 3 don't have a sufficiently developed sense of self to relate to and remember what happened to them.

- Children's memories are easily reconstructed to respond to later revisions and descriptions of events that may have taken place. The original memory cues may have been replaced with these later representations.

Although these explanations for forgetting early memories are plausible, there are exceptions. Adolescents and adults appear to vividly recall certain key events from their childhoods. These are called autobiographical memories. It may be the visit to Santa Claus that made a huge impression, the fall that brought you to the emergency room for stitches, or the time your fourth grade teacher caught you passing a love note, humiliating you in front of the class. These are the things that give us our "life stories." They can be viewed as building blocks of childhood, and they can contribute to an adult's sense of self.

Working Memory

The other type of memory important to a child's cognitive development is what she needs immediately in the present to learn the mental task she's working on right now. The length of time that items in working memory can remain activated is short, estimated at 30 seconds on average. Unless something is done to keep the memory alive, it will fade. For example, repeating the spelling of a word, re-reading a passage of text, or practicing an addition or subtraction problem can keep a working memory fresh. That's because your working, short-term memory has a limited capacity. If individual short-term representations are combined into larger "chunks" of memory—for example, if the letters C-A-T are combined into the word "cat"—storage space will be freed up. And then there will be more room available for new short-term representations to enter short-term memory and remain in the "top of your mind."

The Language We Speak

Language is many things at once. It's a tool for making emotional and social connections. It's also an engine for brain development and cognitive learning. There are five components to language and each develops in a timeline corresponding to a child's biological and cognitive maturation:

- **Phonology**—The sound system of a language. Different languages sound radically different from each other. A child learns the sounds of his culture.

- **Morphology**—The rules that govern how words are formed from sounds. It begins with babbling and becomes a lifetime process of learning correct pronunciations.

- **Semantics**—Involves understanding the meanings of words and sentences. Beginning with gestures, vocabulary grows in leaps and bounds.

- **Syntax**—The rules of how words are combined to produce sentences. The relations between words become grammatical knowledge.

- **Pragmatics**—The principles governing how language is to be used in social situations. These include nuances of meaning and tone.

Each of these components must be learned and integrated with the others, a process that typically takes a child through adolescence.

How Language Is Learned

Different psychological perspectives emphasize nature or nurture as the key driver in language development. Learning theorists view a child's verbal interactions with others as all important. This consists of adults using child-directed speech in the first two to three years, and babies imitating what they hear. Those that favor a biological or nature perspective on child development believe that a baby is born with special wiring for language acquisition. This "device" then triggers the young child's speech comprehension when he hears adults and older children speaking.

Most psychologists view a child learning to speak a language as a complex interaction between nature and nurture. Rather than a special linguistic processor for language acquisition, they view normal nervous system maturation as the key for children to develop increasingly higher language abilities. The fact that they do so at about the same developmental times is a biological fact of life.

Substantial evidence also points to there being "sensitive periods" during normal maturation when a child finds it easiest to learn different components of language.

Sensitive Periods for Language Development

One sensitive period for learning a first or second language is thought to occur before puberty. There's also evidence that different parts of the brain are used for second language learning when it occurs in childhood rather than later in adolescence or adulthood.

In every period of a child's development, he takes on and usually masters a different language task. From unusual cases where individuals were unable to hear and speak during infancy and early childhood, psychologists have observed that many aspects of language can be learned later. The exception to this appears to be syntax (how words are combined), which is much harder to learn later. Here are some sensitive periods that have been identified for language development:

- **Prelinguistic**—Before they're 1 year old, babies learn that people take turns talking. Their babbling becomes more purposeful as they receive meanings through repetition. They can understand more than they can speak.

- **One word at a time**—One word says it all. That's the view of most toddlers. In most cultures a baby's first words begin with a consonant and end with a vowel: "ma," "da," and so on. If he's attempting a two- or three-syllable word, such as kang-a-roo, he tends to stick to the syllable that's emphasized in the normal speech he hears—in this case, the "roo."

- **Simple sentences**—In this stage, usually at 18 months to 2 years of age, a child takes single words and combines them into simple sentences. "Da da bye bye," is an example.

- **Preschool**—Between the ages of 2½ and 5, children learn to produce complex sentences. They expand their vocabularies exponentially and learn basic syntax and pragmatics. For example, they master the different uses of grammar that turn a declarative sentence into a question. They don't yet have referential communications skills, which allow them to differentiate when another speaker is being clear or unclear.

- **Middle childhood and adolescence**—In grade school and beyond, children learn exceptions and refinements to the basic rules of language they've acquired. They master referential communications and will ask for clarifications of ambiguous speech.

When learning to speak, young children use several primitive cognitive strategies. For example, they make inferences about new word meanings by contrasting new words with words they already know. Some of these strategies produce the right use of a word while others don't. When "cognitive constraints" produce challenges for a typical 2- and 3-year-old's speech and language comprehension, they often reflect insufficient brain maturation and cognitive development. Chapter 12 covers more about cognitive constraints and compensating strategies used by young children when learning a language.

Bilingualism

The most recent research shows that a child who is exposed by the age of 3 to two languages has little or no difficulty becoming proficient at both. Previous research that claimed the opposite was shown to be flawed. Even when a child learns a second language sequentially and after the age of 3, it takes no more than a year for a typical 4- or 5-year-old to achieve the same proficiency.

Are children who speak two languages smarter than those who know only one? The research suggests yes; there are cognitive advantages for bilingual children. They score as high or higher on IQ tests. They score higher than their single language peers on grammar and written prose. They also perform better on nonlinguistic tasks such as the ability to maintain selective attention and resist distractions.

> **INSIGHT**
>
> Linguists have observed that babies learning English emphasize nouns and verbs first. This was once believed to be a universal processing constraint. But further study has shown that a baby's first word choice and order has more to do with the syntax and pragmatics of his language. Russian and Turkish children, for example, use more grammatical parts of speech with their nouns and verbs and show more variety in word order.

Why might these linguistic and cognitive advantages exist? Linguists speculate that bilingual children's ability to inhibit distractions comes from their advanced training in adapting to a variety of situations to use the appropriate language.

Another hypothesis is that by learning two languages at a young age, a child better understands the arbitrary nature of words and how sentences are constructed. This may predispose them to remember parts and rules of languages because they know they have to tell them apart.

The Least You Need to Know

- The order of myelination—or strengthening of a child's brain neurons—determines what she learns first, second, or third, with cognitive development the last area to occur after motor and sensory.

- Attention and memory are prerequisites to all cognitive development.
- Learning a language is a complex interaction between nature and nurture, with special periods of sensitivity allowing leaps in learning.
- Learning two languages at an early age can increase a child's IQ and school performance.

Ages and Stages

Child psychology has traditionally been studied as a sequence of ages and stages of development. During the next six chapters, we build on our introduction of the foundational ideas in the field and the big picture on developmental themes. We highlight the key area of growth in each period between pre-birth and late adolescence. For example, we take a close look at the formation of trust during the first year of life and the struggle to obtain an independent identity in adolescence.

Prenatal Influences on the Developing Brain

In This Chapter

- Vital brain growth in the first weeks of pregnancy
- Fathers' exposures and habits and baby's health
- The dangers of nicotine, alcohol, and stress
- What's known about other environmental factors

This chapter starts "in-utero"—Latin for "in the womb"—and offers insights into sensitive periods for brain growth during pregnancy. Ninety-five percent of newborn babies make their journey into this world intact, suffering no birth defects or mishaps en route. In this context, the positive and negative forces that shape the fetal brain are examined. Many new mothers and fathers are unaware that nearly everything they eat, drink, and feel before and during a pregnancy can impact the future development of their baby.

Nine Months—Turning Points

The maturation of the future baby's brain and major body systems during the nine months of pregnancy occurs in steady increments and in two major growth spurts. The new brain has its largest spike in growth occurring in the embryo stage. The second major advance in brain growth occurs during the second trimester.

First Trimester

Within two weeks of fertilization, the embryo is implanted in the mother's uterus, held within a sack made of fluid and tissues. This sack is the placenta, the dark, warm, watery home that will support and feed the fetus throughout the pregnancy. Through the highly permeable placental wall and the umbilical cord come blood, oxygen, and nutrients from the mother. The umbilical cord transports carbon dioxide and metabolic wastes from the placenta for expulsion from the mother's body along with her own metabolic wastes.

Hail the brain! Soon after implantation, in the third week of pregnancy, a neural tube appears in the embryo. This tube becomes the fetal brain and spinal cord. Between 22 and 28 days, the neural tube is closing, or fusing, along its entire length. It starts at the top end of the neural tube in the area that will become the brain. It proceeds over these six days to the bottom of the tube, which will become the base or tail of the spinal cord.

This is probably the most delicate time for the baby's developing brain. Neural tube defects are more common when mothers suffer from particular diseases during their pregnancies. Insulin-dependent diabetes is one such illness that raises fetal risk. Others include epilepsy, particularly if the mother is taking certain anticonvulsant medicines. Other medications that are problematic include certain anticancer agents. These risks underscore the issue of neural tube vulnerabilities during the first weeks of the first trimester when a woman may not yet know she is pregnant. A pregnant woman's elevated body temperature as a result of a fever or her use of a hot tub or sauna can also threaten the neural tube at this initial stage of growth.

Neurons, those "thinking cells" on which all human intelligence depends, are being produced in massive numbers starting in this earliest stage of the pregnancy. The potential negative effects on the incipient fetal brain of problems encountered in this stage are often quite subtle and don't manifest until early or middle childhood. Since very few drugs and chemicals have been tested for these potential subtle negative effects, the usual approach recommended for pregnant women is to avoid anything suspected to raise fetal risk. Some influences may be more harmful in the aggregate; for example, cigarette smoking is known to increase fetal vulnerability to other potentially harmful substances, such as alcohol or paint products, while a pregnant woman's exposure to one thing alone may not be as problematic.

INSIGHT

Some research points to a possible biological purpose behind the common pregnant woman's experience of "morning sickness," which generally lasts from morning until night. The fatigue and nausea it brings just may be an evolutionary trick to keep her diet bland and her activity level low. The symptoms of morning sickness peak during the fetus's most vulnerable period—the first trimester—and fade soon afterward.

Between the second and third months of pregnancy, fetal sex selection occurs. In a male fetus, his testes secrete testosterone which is described as "flooding the fetal brain." This male hormone is responsible for the fetal development of a penis and scrotum, as well as the other brain and body characteristics that will make this baby a boy. In the absence of testosterone, female genitalia form and female characteristics shape the fetal brain and body to produce a baby girl.

Middle Trimester

With its new distinctly human appearance intact by 16 weeks, the fetus spends the middle trimester developing its organs, body systems, and five senses in another major growth spurt. Imaging technology has documented the beginning of fetal hearing and visual abilities in this trimester. With these two rudimentary senses, researchers think there may also be the beginning of short-term fetal memory.

During this period of rapid growth, maternal nutrition is of vital importance to the developing fetus, particularly the brain. Babies of malnourished mothers are smaller at birth than babies who received proper nourishment in the womb. Their head sizes are also smaller. The earlier in pregnancy it begins and the longer it lasts, the more the negative effects of malnutrition on the newborn child worsen and become harder to reverse through proper nutrition after birth. Unlike many traits, birth weight is influenced much more by a mother's nutrition than by heredity. Research shows that the brains of malnourished children are both slower and more poorly organized than they should be for the child's proper development. On the other hand, if a newborn child receives proper nutrition coupled with emotional support and intellectual stimulation, especially before the age of 2, much of their cognitive ability can be recovered.

Third Trimester

Certain environmental influences can have stronger negative impact on the fetus during the third trimester of pregnancy. Nicotine is one such agent because of its potential harm to fetal growth at this time of peak maturation. Nicotine causes blood vessel constriction and inhibits the circulation of oxygen between the mother and fetus. The mother's quitting smoking even one month before the delivery is advantageous in that it decreases the chance that the baby will suffer from a lack of oxygen during birth—a major cause of brain damage.

In months 7 through 9, if there are no major problems or deficiencies, the fetus will have reached the point of viability. At 28 weeks, its nervous system has developed to the point where the fetus has distinct wake and sleep cycles. If born prematurely, the baby has a reasonable chance of survival, with the weakest organ system likely to be the lungs.

Environmental Risks

The fact is that most birth defects—an estimated 65 percent—occur without an identified cause. Another 20 to 25 percent are linked to known chromosomal or genetic anomalies, some inherited, others occurring spontaneously. Known diseases or other environmental agents are thought to be responsible for no more than 10 percent of birth defects. Still, the more that's known about these *teratogens*, the better parents can avoid them or cope with any present or future negative effects on their baby.

DEFINITION

A **teratogen** is an external agent such as a virus, drug, chemical, or radiation that can harm the developing embryo or fetus. If exposure to such an agent occurs during a sensitive period, more damage is possible than it would be at another less sensitive time in the pregnancy.

Although the vast majority of babies follow a normal pattern of brain and body development, there are a number of environmental factors that can put the developing fetus at risk. There also are certain periods during pregnancy when the fetal brain is particularly sensitive to the possible damaging effects of these teratogens.

The invisible (or visible later) negative effects of teratogens on the brain include ...

- Slower development of sensory, motor, or language abilities.
- Disorders of behavior, attention, or sleep.
- Poor academic achievement.

Other negative effects are discussed in Chapter 16 on mental disorders and Chapter 17, which covers children's learning disorders.

Sensitive Periods

As discussed previously, because the embryo stage of pregnancy (weeks three through eight) is the period of the fastest growth, it represents the most sensitive period for potential damage to the embryo. The second most sensitive period for exposure to teratogens is during the growth spurt in the second trimester. After a system or organ is fully formed, it is less sensitive to harmful influences. But research has shown that a number of teratogens can be harmful throughout a woman's pregnancy.

Negative Effects of Teratogens

Beginning in the womb, a child's innate traits—both strengths and vulnerabilities—interact with environmental influences and can be changed by them. There are several principles which govern the potential negative effects of teratogens during pregnancy. Here are some of the most important:

- The same defect can be caused by multiple teratogens.
- Not all embryos or fetuses are equally affected by a teratogen; susceptibility is dependent on the mother's genetic makeup and other factors in the prenatal environment.
- Embryos and fetuses can be affected by a father's exposure to some teratogens before conception.
- The long-term effects of a teratogen can depend on the quality of the post-natal environment.
- Sometimes teratogens cause "sleeper effects" that may not be apparent until later in a child's life.

Teratogens that are not apparent at birth can be especially harmful to a child's psychological or cognitive development. A child whose mother consumed as little as an ounce of alcohol a day while pregnant usually displays no obvious physical deformities or neural problems at birth. However, in some research these children processed information slower and scored lower on IQ tests, compared to children whose mothers did not drink at all during pregnancy.

Mother's Health, Baby's Risks

Risks for a child can be caused by maternal age (a mother who is older or an adolescent), obesity or malnutrition, high blood pressure, or any number of infectious diseases. Low birth weight, which puts a newborn at a higher risk for complications due to underdeveloped organs and body systems, has been linked to the mother's use of nicotine, alcohol, and both illegal and certain prescription drugs during pregnancy.

COMPLICATION

A father's health can bring risks to a baby, too. Studies of men in a variety of occupations reveal that prolonged exposure to radiation, anesthetic gases, and other toxic chemicals can alter a father's chromosomes, increasing the risk of miscarriage or genetic defects. And even if the mother doesn't drink alcohol or use drugs, a father who is a heavy drinker or drug user is linked to lower weight newborns. Apparently substances such as cocaine can bind directly to live sperm and cause mutations in them.

Maternal Diseases and Infections

Some disease agents are capable of crossing the placental barrier and doing more damage to the developing fetus than to the pregnant woman. This is because the fetus's immune system and body organs are immature and therefore less able to battle infections. Diseases contracted by the mother during pregnancy and linked to mental impairment in children include the following:

- Rubella
- Genital herpes
- Syphilis

- Chickenpox
- Diabetes
- Toxemia
- Tuberculosis

Mental disorders that have been linked to these infections include schizophrenia and mental retardation.

Malnutrition

Pregnant women need to increase their food consumption by 20 percent and pay special attention to eating from all the food groups to have a healthy baby. Malnutrition, especially if it occurs during the first trimester, can disrupt the growth of the fetal nervous system and induce miscarriages. If it occurs during the third trimester, babies are more likely to be born with smaller heads, have low birth weight, and may be at risk of not surviving the first year of life. Autopsies of such infants showed fewer brain cells and lower brain weights.

Studies across different large populations have shown higher incidences of cognitive defects and mental disorders in places that experienced famines, such as Ireland in the nineteenth century. The Irish famine has been associated with a higher rate of schizophrenia in later generations. The same pattern of famine and elevated level of schizophrenia in subsequent generations is becoming evident in certain African immigrant populations in Western Europe.

Quantity of food is not enough to prevent malnutrition or insufficient nutrition for a fetus's healthy brain development. A mother must be sure to consume a diet rich in protein, certain B vitamins, folic acid, and other vitamins and minerals.

Maternal Hormones, Emotions, and Stress

A mother's hormones have potential negative and positive effects on the developing fetus. Like ingested foods and medicines, they cross the placenta and enter the baby's circulation. Some maternal hormones directly affect fetal cell division and growth; for example, the thyroid hormones are responsible for the production of neurons, synapse formation, and myelination. A mother's thyroid hormone transfer begins in the second month of pregnancy and is essential for the developing fetus which will not produce its own thyroid until much later in the pregnancy. The lack of this hormone during gestation can cause cognitive problems in the fetal brain.

A fetus can also be negatively affected by higher than normal maternal hormone secretions. If a mother undergoes extreme stress during pregnancy—for example, from the loss of a spouse—the fetus also experiences these same elevated stress hormones. Pregnant mothers who experience high-stress events or who are very anxious personality types may "overdose" their fetuses with chronically high amounts of corticosteroids (cortisol) and catecholamines (epinephrine and norepinephrine). These are the hormones that contribute to a person's "fight or flight" impulse. The effects on the fetus can be both short term and long term.

Temporary stresses are not usually harmful to the fetus. But continued exposure to maternal stress can harm the pregnancy by depleting the mother's immunity to infectious diseases. Extended stress is also associated with low fetal birth weight, premature delivery, and other birth complications. Research has shown that babies whose mothers experience great emotional swings during pregnancy tend to be more active during pregnancy and more irritable after birth. Other long-term effects on the child are thought to include a higher level of vulnerability to stress in adolescence and to earlier-onset depression and anxiety.

INSIGHT

Not all pregnant mothers exposed to stressful circumstances experience harmful effects on the fetus. The key to avoiding harm or fetal complications is how well the mother manages the stress she's experiencing in her life. Stress-related complications are more likely when she has ambivalent feelings about the pregnancy, or is missing a base of social and emotional support during her pregnancy. Research shows that counseling for pregnant mothers under stress increases their babies' birth weights.

Pregnant mothers experiencing high stress may also be more prone to eating poorly, smoking cigarettes, drinking alcohol, or consuming dangerous drugs.

Alcohol and Nicotine Exposure

The cumulative research unequivocally makes the case that mothers should abstain from heavy and moderate drinking of alcohol during pregnancy, or even while trying to conceive a child. Binge drinking is especially harmful. The effects of modest amounts of alcohol—a nightly glass of wine with dinner or drinking any alcohol only a few times a week—are still being debated. Some studies show a higher risk of miscarriage and lessening of IQ scores after a mother has had four or more drinks per week. Others do not.

Prenatal alcohol use is thought to be responsible for at least 4,000 cases of mental retardation in the United States each year. In addition, alcohol is linked to "perhaps 10 times that number for children with mild learning or behavioral problems," according to neuroscientist Lise Eliot, Ph.D., author of *What's Going on in There? How the Brain and Mind Develop in the First Five Years of Life*. Babies whose mothers abuse alcohol or drugs are often born with their own addictions to these substances. They must then go through a painful withdrawal in the days and weeks after birth. They can also suffer from long-term, negative cognitive effects.

When a pregnant mother smokes, nicotine enters the fetus's bloodstream. It alters how the developing baby breathes, and research shows it also compromises brain development. Among the problems linked to maternal smoking during pregnancy in one or more studies are:

- Hyperactivity
- Attention and hearing problems
- Mental retardation
- Problems in language and motor skills

Nicotine does its damage to the developing brain by binding to one class of receptors for the neurotransmitter acetylcholine. It interferes with signals normally transmitted through the brain's synapses. In rats exposed to nicotine before birth, and in human babies who were also known to have been exposed to smoking, their subsequent arousal, attention, and motor functioning were impaired.

Other Known Teratogens

We have varying degrees of knowledge about how some of these agents cause harm to a developing fetus, but each is considered a serious risk that should not be taken.

- Cocaine can cause problems for the growth of the placenta, possibly causing it to detach, and trigger premature labor. Babies of cocaine-addicted mothers tend to be smaller, and face a higher risk of fetal stroke and later mental retardation. Cocaine-exposed babies don't respond as well to caregivers or to their environment, often forming insecure attachments.

- Heroin use by a pregnant woman can produce a heroin-addicted baby who suffers extreme withdrawal symptoms after birth as well as many other mental and physical health problems.

- Marijuana use during pregnancy produces the double whammy effect of introducing a potentially harmful drug, THC, to fetal circulation, and exposing the fetus to the oxygen deprivation caused by maternal smoking. Like tobacco smoking, marijuana increases the level of carbon dioxide in the fetus's circulation, depriving the fetal brain of needed oxygen.

- Ionizing radiation includes X-rays, gamma rays, and particles released from radioactive decay. The developing fetal brain is most vulnerable to ionizing radiation between the 8 to 15 weeks following conception. The maximum recommended dose of X-rays or other medical irradiation during pregnancy is 5 rem. For perspective, the average exposure considered acceptable in occupational settings (for X-ray technicians and atomic energy workers) is 0.5 rem.

- Other harmful chemicals pregnant women should avoid include: organic solvents; oil-based paints; all types of herbicides and pesticides; PCB's; carbon monoxide; hydrocarbons, including gasoline; mercury compounds; and other heavy metals such as cadmium, nickel, and lead.

The greatest danger for the developing fetal brain and the baby's other organ systems occurs if a teratogen is ingested or inhaled, particularly in large doses. Brief occasional exposures, such as when a mother pumps gasoline into a car, are unlikely to harm her developing fetus.

Unlikely, Low, or Unknown Fetal Risks

The influences and substances listed here present either very low, unlikely, or unknown risks to the brain or general health of a developing fetus. As a result, in some cases, limited cautions are suggested until further study is completed:

- Caffeine has caused some concern because it crosses the placenta and may concentrate in fetal circulation. Animal studies have shown caffeine in high doses to cause malformed limbs in rodents. Moderate or low caffeine intake is not thought to be a teratogen in humans, although heavy caffeine intake can cause withdrawal symptoms in newborn babies. Pregnant women are advised to drink no more than 300 milligrams or two mugs of medium-strength coffee per day.

- Artificial sweeteners, including aspartame and saccharine, present in diet drinks were once feared to cause problems in fetal physical and mental functions. Again, although they were found in some animal studies to cause tumors when ingested in high amounts, these substances are not considered harmful to pregnant women. On the other hand, diet drinks offer no nutritional value to pregnant women, which should be the more important concern.

- Microwaves can be problematic to human fetal brain health only in extremely high doses, as animal studies have also demonstrated. These dangerous amounts are considerably higher than the amount of radiation put out by the standard microwave kitchen appliances, which are regulated to ensure lower radiation emissions. However, some experts suggest pregnant women not stand in the direct path of a microwave oven, to avoid any possible excessive exposures.

- Computer screens and video display terminals have been ruled out as harmful to a pregnant woman or her developing fetus. These electric and magnetic fields oscillate at frequencies well below those of radios and microwaves.

Environmental factors either not yet studied or inconclusive in terms of their potential harm to pregnant women include electric power lines, electric blankets, and MRI machines. Future studies should shed more light on their potential harm or lack thereof.

The Drama and Trauma of Childbirth

The onset of a mother's labor pains signals the near completion of a baby's biological task of becoming a separate person, a process begun in the third trimester of pregnancy. Under the best circumstances, birth represents an upheaval for the newborn. A first child takes an average of eight hours to make it through the birth canal. Though worn out, a bit bruised, and disoriented, most newborns make the journey without injury or permanent damage.

> **INSIGHT**
>
> Does the baby signal the start of labor? Neuroscientists believe that a part of the fetal brain charged with monitoring the maturation of body organs sends a message to the mother's uterus to say when the time has arrived.

Normal Labor and Delivery

There are three phases of labor and delivery:

- Stage one, the time it takes for the cervix to dilate from 0 to 10 centimeters, lasts from 12 to 24 hours for the birth of a first child and about 3 to 8 hours for subsequent children. When the cervix is fully dilated, stage two begins.

- Stage two often is marked by the mother's first urge to push, using her abdominal muscles. This pushing, along with the involuntary uterine contractions that got everything going, propels the baby down the birth canal. After about an hour, the top of the baby's head appears, an event called crowning. The birth of the baby and cutting of the umbilical cord marks the end of stage two.

- Stage three is called the afterbirth, when the placenta which had been the baby's home these past nine months is expelled from the uterus and exits through the birth canal.

Birth Complications

Despite state-of-the-art technology and medical expertise, childbirth is still risky for a mother but even more so for her child. The source of most risks and complications in childbirth actually hearken back to the mother's health during pregnancy. But if a fetus has been weakened by low birth weight or another factor during pregnancy a difficult birth may exacerbate the problem.

A healthy baby's brain appears to be quite resilient to the rigors of a normal birth experience. The most common problems occurring during childbirth include the following:

- Facial, skull, or spinal cord damage from a difficult delivery or use of forceps or other mechanical means.

- Birth asphyxia, an inability to exchange carbon dioxide for oxygen for a period lasting longer than seven minutes. Asphyxia can harm neurons in the baby's brain and thus cause permanent birth defects, including cerebral palsy. This usually is caused by umbilical cord problems during birth.

- Negative effects of obstetrical drugs, including analgesics and anesthetics used for pain control include irritability and lethargy, but are generally short term.

Infant mortality, defined as the number of babies out of every 1,000 who die before their first birthday, is high in the United States compared to other industrialized countries. The primary reason for this high rate is poor prenatal care, which often results in low birth weight babies. Virtually all the 21 countries that rank ahead of the United States in infant mortality provide complete prenatal care to mothers at no cost, whereas in the United States many mothers receive little or no prenatal care. Many of these countries also provide for paid leaves of absence for pregnant women and new parents. One conclusion we can draw from these facts and discrepancies is that to have the benefits of a healthy brain and a good start in life, a baby needs a physically and psychologically healthy mother.

Certainly one of the most amazing things you'll encounter in our study of how a child grows is the speed and complexity of early brain development. Thanks to the enormous prenatal blossoming of neurons and brain circuits, a child arrives in this world ready to hit the ground running. His brain is prewired, making him more than ready for what comes next.

The Least You Need to Know

- The placenta acts as a protective barrier, but it's also highly permeable, allowing teratogens to reach the fetus's newly developing nervous system.

- Whatever the mother drinks or smokes or feels, the experience is mirrored by her developing baby with potential long-term, negative consequences for the child's cognitive growth and reactivity to stress.

- The evidence is conclusive that moderate and heavy drinking of alcohol during pregnancy harms a baby's brain with later cognitive and behavioral problems well-documented.

- The health of a newborn baby is inextricably linked to the mother's health and well-being.

Birth to 18 Months— Making Sense of Their World

In This Chapter

- The first tests a newborn must pass
- The nature of temperament
- The senses as the gateway to the world
- The way babies develop emotions

Newborn babies are busy people. They grow a central nervous system, figure out which one is Mom, find the balance to walk on two feet, and all the while, bond like crazy. No other period compares with the amount of growth that goes on during the first year and a half of life. It's where nature meets nurture. In this chapter, a baby's inborn abilities are examined as well as the developmental milestones that occur during this critical time for brain development. The first thing explored is what comes to a baby innately: her prewired reflexes and basic temperament. Then how each of the newborn's developing senses expands her interactions with important people and things in her world is outlined. Finally shown is how she puts it all together to lay the foundation for a lifetime of cognitive and emotional learning.

Baby's First Appearance

The evolutionary drive on the part of both mother and child to begin forming a secure bond is in full display in the moments immediately after childbirth. When his cheek and lips are gently stroked, a newborn involuntarily turns his head and looks around. He finds his mother's nipple and instinctively begins sucking.

When researchers present different visual images and objects to newborns in the delivery room, they show a clear preference for a human face.

Mothers, too, follow bonding instincts in the delivery room. When she sees her newborn baby for the first time, a mother usually holds him to allow direct eye contact between them—the better to "fall in love" immediately. It's what nature dictates so that mothers will take care of babies and the human species will continue.

Assessing the Newborn

While the mother is completing the third stage of childbirth—the delivery of the placenta—a newborn gets his first head to toe check-up. The purpose is to quickly assess how well the baby has weathered childbirth by determining his Apgar score.

The Apgar Score

Imagine you are the one responsible for conducting a newborn's first checkup. You'd probably first look to see if he is breathing comfortably. Then take note of whether his skin is peachy or bluish. The Apgar score provides just such a snapshot that records the newborn's immediate response to labor and delivery. It gives the baby's attending physician an immediate and approximate reading on the ability of his body systems to sustain life outside his mother's womb.

The five vital signs measured in an Apgar score are the following:

- Breathing
- Skin tone
- Heart rate
- Muscle tone
- Presence of reflexes, such as coughing

Any red flags that come up in the course of this quick exam are more often the result of a difficult delivery than a long-term health issue for the baby. Still, a poor Apgar result, meaning scoring low on a majority of the five vital signs, could mean the child will have neurological problems that manifest later.

Each of the five vital signs in this exam receives a score of zero, one, or two with two being the highest. When these five scores are added together, a total of seven or more means the newborn is in good physical condition. A score of four to six means he requires special attention. A score of three or less signals a life-threatening situation requiring emergency neonatal care.

It's a Reflex

When a tester pin pricks a newborn's heel, he will withdraw his foot and may cry out. Withdrawal from pain is one of the unlearned, prewired responses that can only be triggered by certain stimuli, in this case the point of a pin on his tender heel. By judging the condition of this and other newborn reflexes, a doctor discovers how well a baby's central nervous system is working.

Here are some of the major reflexes present in a newborn.

Name	Reflex	Function
Moro	Startle, throw up arms	Helps cling to mother
Blink	Close eyes	Protects the eyes
Rooting	Turn head, open mouth	Finds the nipple
Withdraw	Take foot away when heel is pricked	Protection

In a very short time, newborns learn to put together a chain reaction of these reflexes and connect them to a specific stimulus. Consider hunger. After just a few repetitions of rooting, sucking, and swallowing leading the newborn to a full tummy, she probably has made a solid association. The next time hunger pangs strike, her mouth will be ready and she will expect "food" to arrive to meet her need.

The NBAS

To get a more comprehensive evaluation of a newborn's physiological and psychological condition, a physician or nurse uses a longer assessment tool called the

Neonatal Behavioral Assessment Scale, or NBAS, as a guide. Usually done before the newborn and her mother leave the hospital, this test uses a total of 28 criteria. It goes far beyond the baby's response to childbirth to discover how she's responding to her new environment. Among the abilities and behaviors testers look at are the child's ...

- Vigor

- Excitability

- Muscle tone

- Motor activity

- Color changes in skin tone

- Duration of alert periods

- Cuddliness after contact

- Irritability as a result of the NBAS evaluation

Different stimuli are used to elicit the appropriate behaviors, for example:

- Rocking

- Voice

- Facial behavior

- A bright light shone in the infant's eyes

- A pinprick on the heel

- A soft rattle

- A red ball

By the end of the NBAS test, the newborn's responses should shed light on the following five main areas:

1. How he organizes different states of consciousness

2. How he adapts to disturbing events

3. How he attends to and processes events in his environment

4. His ability to control motor tone

5. His ability to perform integrated motor acts

After the Apgar and the NBAS tests are done, hospital personnel will look for the "soft signs" of well-being or distress in a newborn. These are simple observations made of the baby alone and in relationship with the mother that, along with formal tests, can assess whether mother and child are ready to go home.

Asleep, Awake, and In Between

Although it may seem that if a baby is not sleeping, he's either eating or crying, a baby's day is much more complicated than that. A newborn occupies a total of six different *states* in the course of every 24-hour period. Sometimes referred to as six "states of consciousness," this is not to infer that a baby has suddenly taken up Transcendental Meditation. A baby's state tells a parent if he's on his way to sleep or about to awaken, whether this is a good time for play, or to soothe him for a nap.

 DEFINITION

State describes the infant's availability for interacting with others.

The newborn baby's six states:

- Deep sleep, the baby is in restorative rest, still and quiet.

- Light sleep, the baby is more active, yet asleep.

- Semi-conscious, drowsy, the baby is between sleep and awake; in this state stimulation usually makes the infant more alert.

- Alert, the baby is awake and very available for observation and interaction.

- Fussy, the baby is in transition between alert and crying states; can still be soothed.

- Uncontrollable crying, the baby is generally miserable and unavailable.

Early indications of how long a child spends in each state can serve as a preview of what's to come as that child matures. The alert baby is more likely to grow into an extrovert than the quieter, less engaged newborn.

Newborn babies can only stay alert for an average of one out of every four hours, and even within those 60 minutes of wakefulness, they have, on average, four 15-minute cycles where they go from inactive wakefulness, to waking activity, to fussing and crying before returning to sleep.

For half of their sleep time, newborns are in a REM or rapid-eye-movement state. In REM, their brain waves are moving faster, their hearts beat faster, and their breathing becomes more rapid. Eyelids and limbs twitch. Researchers think REM sleep stimulates the brain and fosters growth of the child's central nervous system. In other words, he's working.

What Is Temperament?

A baby's mood and style of behavior is her temperament. A primary criterion used to determine temperament is the newborn's activity level. This refers to the amount and vigor of motor or physical activity in daily situations. Many mothers say they can identify their future child's temperament by the middle trimester of pregnancy based on the number and duration of fetal activity periods in a typical day and night. Today, babies are usually described as fitting one of the following three temperaments:

- Active

- Quiet

- Average

Of course not all active babies are happy. Nor are all quiet babies sad. The most immediate and practical use of this type of labeling of newborns is to help parents and other caregivers gain insights into difficulties they may be experiencing dealing with a child. For example, when a quiet introverted mother gives birth to an active baby who thrives on long periods of stimulation, the mother may find her child's behavior exhausting or off-putting. A deeper understanding of differences in temperament can help the mother manage them.

The Origins of Temperament

The pioneers of temperament theory, Alexander Thomas and Stella Chess launched the New York Longitudinal Study in 1956. Their immediate focus for this first-of-its-kind study was to document which moods and behaviors were most and least common among newborns. Later they would see if a newborn's temperament changed over time. In addition to activity level and mood, Thomas and Chess used the following six factors to evaluate temperament:

- Rhythmicity—Regularity in eating, sleeping

- Approach/withdrawal—Response to a novel object

- Distractability—Ease of disrupting from ongoing activity

- Adaptability—Ease of transition to a new activity

- Threshold—Level of stimulation needed to respond

- Attention span—Time spent on one activity

From the original 141 babies in their study, Thomas and Chess found that about 40 percent fit the general category of "easy" while 10 percent were deemed "difficult." Another 35 percent fit the category of "average," and 15 percent were "slow to warm up."

- The 40 percent of "easy" babies were found to be happy and cheerful most of the time. Easy babies were easily approached and adapted well to regular routines.

- The 10 percent of babies deemed "difficult" tended to be unhappy; they were slow to warm up and had irregular rhythms of eating, sleeping, and wakefulness.

- The 35 percent of newborns who were the so-called "average" babies didn't veer toward either the easy or difficult extremes. They fell somewhere in the middle of the six factors used.

- The 15 percent described as "slow to warm up" had a low activity level and tended to withdraw from new situations and people. They were slow to adapt to new experiences but accept them after repeated exposures.

Temperament provides the basic foundation for personality. Its origins are both inherited and environmentally shaped.

A Window to Baby's Brain

Psychological researchers have developed a number of studies using temperament as a window into an infant's brain. The focus of much of this research is to determine neural pathways for different aspects of temperament. The characteristic of "slow to warm up" which early child development theorists associated with a "difficult" baby continues to be a focal point of psychological research today, although the term "inhibition" is now preferred.

Scientists believe that a newborn's level of inhibition is mostly inherited, based in part on how early and clearly the behavior manifests. As noted before, new is not always better for every young baby. Researchers have found that how a baby responds to a novelty at 4 months predicts how they will respond again at 9 months.

Scientists also have located a likely neural path in the brain to account for inhibition. Harvard psychologist Jerome Kagan found that inhibited children have a more reactive *amygdala*.

DEFINITION

The **amygdala** is the almond-shaped part of a brain's limbic system that regulates fear by activating the sympathetic nervous system, which controls the body's fight or flight response. When the amygdala is stimulated, it sends messages to the frontal cortex, the thinking part of the brain, for processing as thoughts and feelings.

Kagan measured inhibited children's levels of two stress hormones, cortisol and norepinephrine, and found these neurochemicals higher when the inhibited children were presented with mild stresses in the lab.

Researchers found that those 4-month-old babies who frowned at a new color toy had more brain activity in the right frontal cortex, the area that regulates emotions linked to avoidance. The infants who smiled at the same toy had increased activity in the left frontal cortex, which regulates emotions linked to approach (the "go-getter" impulse).

Adapting Mary Ainsworth's strange situation test to new brain scanning technology, 10-month-old babies were monitored as their mothers temporarily left the room. The results showed that test babies' levels of stress differed greatly and correlated with their inhibition levels. Like the 4-month-old babies looking at a new color toy, the more inhibited 10-month-olds showed greater activity on the right side of their brain where feelings of fear and anxiety are processed. Outgoing, less inhibited babies faced with the same stress showed more activity in their left frontal cortex where feelings of joy and affection take place.

Does Temperament Change?

The question of how much your basic temperament changes as you grow from infancy to early childhood and then on to adulthood has long intrigued researchers. The New York Longitudinal Study team found that about two thirds of the preschoolers with difficult temperaments went on to develop behavioral problems in elementary school. In comparison, fewer than one fifth of the preschool children with easy temperaments had such problems later.

Sensory Learning Begins

Within three days of birth, babies can distinguish their own mother's face and voice from those of other women. Let's look closely at what's involved in this sensory feat. Within his first 72 hours, the baby makes a visual imprint of his mother's facial features. He hears and remembers the tone and timbre of her voice. Then he connects her with a unique smell, and, if he's nursing, with the taste of her milk. Perhaps he also learns the distinct feeling of her smooth cheek against his (as opposed to the sensation of father's beard). From the sum total of these sensory experiences the baby forms a perception telling him that this person is special: she is Mom.

Researchers have developed a framework to understand how a baby turns sense experiences into perceptions. First, they point out that a baby's perception is larger than a single or even a group of sense experiences. To have a perception babies must interpret their sense experiences. In other words, cognitive processing of sights, smells, sounds, tastes, and tactile experiences must take place. Because cognition refers to thoughts and knowledge, the question for researchers became how the baby processes the sum total of his sensory experiences. How does he know something is new at the end of this sensation and thought process?

"Differentiation theory" says that babies don't put their sense experiences together one-by-one in a linear fashion. The differentiation theorists insist that babies perceive whole ideas directly from the flow of sensory input that they experience. In the view of the first proponent of this view, Eleanor Gibson, babies constantly look and listen, trying to make sense of what they experience. This means that humans, including babies, have a built-in cognitive ability to organize knowledge through what Piaget called schemas to interpret sensory information. The important point offered by differentiation theory is that this ability to interpret sights, sounds, and more begins soon after birth. It is not something that babies must learn to do later.

Researching Infant Perception

But how do scientists know what a baby is seeing and hearing? Unlike an adult taking a hearing or vision test, a baby cannot hold up a right or left hand or say "yes" and "no" in response to a particular sound or picture. To get past this hurdle, investigators collect data on babies' responses to stimuli by recording their physiological reactions, usually changes in heart rate, facial expressions, and head movements. If two different sounds are played for an infant in a laboratory, one high-pitched and another lower pitched, investigators look for consistent responses, meaning a physical change that indicates whether the baby notices the differences between sounds. If his physical body reacts when the sounds change, and he does this repeatedly, they conclude he can tell the difference. If he doesn't react, he cannot.

The Novelty Principle

A key principle employed when testing an infant's sense perceptions is *habituation*. It is based on the fact that babies, like the rest of us, are more interested in something new and different rather than the same old things.

DEFINITION

Habituation is a decrease in response to a stimulus after repeated presentations. A new ring tone may initially draw your attention or even become distracting. After you become accustomed to it, you pay less attention to the noise and your response lessens. This diminished response is habituation.

Using these techniques and principles, researchers measure sense experiences and perceptions in the womb and in newborn babies.

A Super Sense of Smell

Smell takes the lead in an infant's sensory world. In fact, beginning at 28 weeks of gestation when olfactory neurons have sufficiently developed, the fetus smells whatever odors the mother does. Rather than block smells, amniotic fluid is an excellent conduit for odor molecules. When the pregnant mother is exposed to strong odors, a fetus will react beginning at 28 weeks. A similar result happens with preterm babies. When preemies younger than 28 weeks of age were tested for their ability to smell, they did not respond to a peppermint extract held under their noses. But at 29 weeks, preterm babies reacted to the peppermint smell by sucking, grimacing, and moving their heads.

Researchers have established that each person emits a unique smell and both babies and mothers carry a memory of their respective smells. These smells become imprinted during pregnancy. In the case of the mother, the smell she associates with her baby is actually a combination of her own scent and that of the fetus.

Smell and taste are known as the "chemical senses" because both are activated by nerves in response to certain molecules in the environment. But smell has a unique neural pathway among all mammalian senses. It is the only one where the information (molecules carrying an odor) is relayed directly to the cerebral cortex without going through the lower brain. Because their sense of smell has this direct route to the thinking brain immediately after birth, newborn babies rely more on this sense than any other, and more so in infancy than later in life.

And it's not just because they like to eat. A newborn's super sense of smell may be grounded in an instinctual need to find her mother. Researchers found that 2-week-old babies will look in the direction of a pad saturated with their mother's milk. They're also riveted to a pad dunked in her familiar perfume.

FIELD STUDY

In a controlled experiment, when presented with T-shirts worn by a variety of adults and children, young babies showed a clear preference for those T-shirts carrying the scents of members of their own immediate family—a brother, sister, or father.

A baby's sense of smell is better developed at birth than his sight or hearing. From an evolutionary perspective, it plays a vital role in early attachment formations.

How Sweet the Taste

Like smell, the ability to taste begins in utero, arriving with the fetus's growth of taste buds by 12 weeks. Babies in the third trimester have been observed changing their swallowing patterns when a flavored chemical is introduced into the amniotic fluid. If it's sweet they will swallow more; if the taste is sour or bitter, they'll slow way down.

There's no doubt that the fetus and newborn have a sweet tooth. Some researchers go so far as to say that taste is a baby's primary source of pleasure. When babies were nursed by their mothers in a controlled setting, they consumed more after their mothers ate something sweet. For babies, as with adults, a sweet tastes good because it literally feels good to eat. Beyond providing an energy boost, sugar engages the sweet receptors of the mouth which in turn activate the brain's natural opiates. In other words, unlike most foods, sugar skips the stomach and the normal digestive process and goes immediately to the brain. This kicks into gear the brain's pleasure system. For a baby under stress, consuming something sweet, such as mother's milk, can be a mood-altering, soothing experience. In comparison, the baby's tastes for things that are salty and bitter take much longer to develop.

Touch Me, Touch You

Although a baby's sense of touch is not fully developed at birth, it is a vitally important newborn sensibility. The immediate importance of touch for a newborn is to facilitate her physical growth and emotional well-being.

The baby's first experiences of touch lay the sensory groundwork for later motor skills and the future child's understanding of her physical world.

Touch involves more than skin-to-skin tactile experiences. Temperature and pain sensations also are read through the skin. Look no further than the scowl on a baby's face when given a first inoculation to see that she feels pain. The part of a baby's body that is most sensitive to touch is the mouth, and then the rest of the face. Newborn girls appear to be slightly more sensitive to touch than newborn boys.

Many of the breakthroughs in our understanding of the importance of human touch for babies derive from experiments done with other mammals.

FIELD STUDY

Infant monkeys become distressed when their mothers are removed. Their stress hormones rise and, if continued, their immune systems are weakened. This suppression reverses if the mother and infant monkeys are reunited within 10 days. But if the separation lasts any longer, the negative effects appear to be permanent.

Human babies raised in early twentieth-century American foundling homes—and, more recently, in Bulgarian orphanages—deprived of touching and holding, suffered negative effects similar to those of the infant monkeys. Even when provided nourishment and otherwise cared for appropriately, their limited sensory and social stimulation left these babies stunted emotionally, physically, and cognitively. Given their higher rate of sickness, they also developed weak immune systems. These documented human cases, along with the sum total of animal research and infant observations, prove beyond a shadow of a doubt the importance of touch for the newborn baby. Beyond sensory experience, touch is a vital message system between parent and child that affects every other system of a baby's body.

Baby Talk and Other Sounds

When it comes to auditory perception, babies do not hear as well as older children and adults. The sounds they hear best are neither too high nor too low. They prefer those in the range of normal human speech. Babies also show a strong preference for human sounds over nonhuman sounds.

The term "motherese" has been coined to describe the unique style of speech or baby talk that mothers seem to naturally develop to talk to their newborns. Motherese speech is slower, higher pitched, and highly intonated (with an exaggerated emphasis on each or certain syllables). As with many things new mothers naturally do, this behavior appears to suit the newborn's needs well. The slowness of motherese speech helps the baby's underdeveloped nervous system and hearing follow along. Its wide swings in pitch and loudness enhances the contrast between syllables. This makes it easier for babies to distinguish parts of speech, essential for later language development. Motherese is not just for mothers. Fathers, siblings, and caregivers soon join in this baby-centered conversation.

What a Baby Sees

Like hearing, until her first birthday a newborn's sight is less developed—particularly the aspect of acuity, defined as the smallest pattern visible to the one seeing. Babies respond to light and can track moving objects. Experiments also have shown that newborns see at 20 feet similar to what adults can see at a 200- to 400-foot distance. Until the age of 3 or 4 months, babies see only a few colors. A newborn can better detect short to medium wavelength colors including blue and green; they do not do nearly as well with red and yellow. By the time they're crawling at around 6 months, typical babies can determine changes in depth of field, helpful for keeping a crawling baby safe.

Have you ever noticed how babies appear to stare at you? Beginning at the age of 2 months, they can stare for up to 30 minutes at a time. This is called *obligatory looking*, because the baby's gaze literally gets stuck on something or someone.

DEFINITION

Obligatory looking occurs when the baby's visual cortex—that part of the brain concerned with visual stimuli—is just beginning to exert control over the visual processing center in the lower brain. Obligatory looking fades as a baby's vision develops by the end of the first year.

The development of her five senses and the ability to interpret her sense experiences is the focus of a baby's brain development in the first year of life. It also is the basis for all the cognitive and emotional learning that follows.

Emotional Learning Begins

A baby experiences all basic emotions—and the physical changes that go with those feelings—within her first few months of life.

Trust vs. Mistrust

Erik Erikson in his 1950 classic work, *Childhood and Society*, first offered the now unquestioned insight that the first year of life is the critical period for the baby to develop a sense of trust. As in each stage of his "Eight Stages of Man" theory (see Chapter 1), Erikson saw the baby's attempts to complete the necessary "task" of trusting herself, her parent(s), and the world around her as a challenging but necessary struggle.

By the end of her first year, if a child has accomplished this task of learning to trust, she knows she has the power to engage the important adults in her life through her smiles or cries. She believes they will be there for her when she needs them. Lastly, she thinks the world is a good and safe place to be. When babies resolve the conflict between trust and mistrust, Erikson pointed out they will have formed a secure bond. They then will have the ability to form other significant attachments later in life.

> **INSIGHT**
>
> Not a reflex, researchers say that a baby's earliest smiles are universal and genuine. Babies of all cultures begin making social smiles between 4 and 8 weeks of age.

When attention to her needs is lacking, a baby usually will fuss and cry at first. But when mother or another significant adult still doesn't come, her cries become weaker, her smiles fade, and she turns inward. As she matures, this child may lack curiosity and empathy. She may develop a deep mistrust in her environment.

The Path to Self-Regulation

Emotional learning begins immediately after birth in the form of imitation. Investigators found that babies who are only hours old are capable of mimicking an adult's facial and hand gestures, suggesting a primitive form of empathy. A baby's ability to imitate also equips him to meet the challenge of regulating his emotions.

As researchers see it, throughout the first year and a half, a baby forms stable mental images of appropriate behavior. These are the internal working models of actions and behaviors that work best to get his needs met. They come as a direct result of his accumulated interactions with parents and other caregivers, and help him learn to regulate his own emotional states. A baby's developing frontal cortex, which makes a leap at age 1, helps regulate emotions and behaviors to meet these challenges.

Emotions and Learning

During a baby's first 18 months of life, when sensory and emotional development is proceeding, cognitive learning is a constant by-product. Each of the baby's sensory and emotional milestones builds upon the other. Together they nurture his understanding of the world.

The Permanence of Objects

For the fifth time, Dad hides under a blanket, then sticks his head out and says "peak-a-boo," drawing a smile of delight from the enthralled baby sitting in front of him. The same principle explains the popularity of the Jack-in-the-box as a classic baby toy. So what's the principle? It's called object permanence, the ability to understand that an object (Dad, the Jack-in-the-box) exists even when the baby can't see it. The child who laughs when an object disappears and then reappears does not understand that it is still in his vicinity. Out of sight truly means out of mind.

Piaget believed that babies did not understand the permanence of objects until they reached 12 months of age. More recent research suggests there is at least some understanding of this principle in infants as young as 4 months.

Separation Anxiety

After babies acquire a full understanding of object permanence, they begin to experience separation anxiety. Their increased level of distress at being left alone comes as a result of reaching this cognitive milestone. A 4-month-old will certainly miss his mother when she is not visible, but he will not assume she is within hearing or seeing distance. The same baby at 9 months realizes that mother is not gone permanently; in fact she may be right outside the door.

Who Did That?

In the course of her first year, the advances in a baby's understanding of her environment are astonishing to behold. Take, for example, a newborn's reaction to a mobile toy dangling over her in her crib. If her arm or leg should move one of the items in her sight, she will startle, not understanding that she has made it move. But, by 3 to 4 months of age, the same baby will use her hand to purposely move the crib gym for her own amusement. These differences in the reactions of a newborn and a 4-month-old baby to a crib gym illustrate Piaget's belief about when intelligence begins. A baby's intellect is on display, Piaget said, when her actions and reactions become purposeful.

The Least You Need to Know

- In the newborn's first minutes, hours, and days, instinctual reflexes dominate everything she does.
- Smell and taste develop early in the womb and are the newborn's strongest senses.
- Sensory stimulation is essential for a newborn's physical, emotional, and cognitive growth.
- Learning to trust is the major work of a baby's first year of life.

18 Months to 3 Years—Language and Identity

Chapter
12

In This Chapter

- How toddlers are selfish and altruistic
- Self-talk and healthy brain growth
- How a toddler's missing logic shows up in his speech
- Baby's fast-mapping as a language strategy

The psychological backdrop for a preschooler's dramatic acquisition of speech and communication skills is his emotional maturation as an independent person. Another word for it is autonomy. This is the age when a child is torn between venturing away from his primary caregiver to see what the world has to offer, and hanging on to that person for dear life. These mood and attitude changes, as trying as they are for caregivers, are normal and necessary for a child's development. This chapter looks at the emergence of language—as well as early speech problems—in the context of a 2- and 3-year-old's emerging identity and social skills.

I Want to Be Me

Erik Erikson describes this second stage of a child's development in the second and third years as an ongoing conflict between the toddler's desire for autonomy and the shame and doubt he feels when those efforts are thwarted. The source of these difficult feelings, Erikson taught, is the overcontrolling behavior of parents and other caregivers who attempt to stop the child from exploring or achieving independence. It is, of course, the responsibility of a caregiver to protect the child from harm. Erikson acknowledged that finding the balance between freedom and constraints for a child of this age is not easy for an adult. He encouraged the use of firm and clear limits to reduce the amount of conflict in a child's play environment.

COMPLICATION

Although 18-month to 3-year-olds are acquiring language at a rapid clip, they often can't verbalize their own feelings as clearly as they can talk about people and objects in their environment. The inability to express their feelings results in temper tantrums that brand this age the "terrible twos."

It's not that the average toddler always wants to be apart from his significant caregiver. The same child who runs and hides behind a sofa to demonstrate his autonomy will cling and cry the next time his mother leaves him in someone else's care. In the short term, says Erikson, when a child is too often and too rigidly prevented from acting independently, his frustration increases. In the long term, he internalizes the overcontrolling behavior of the authority figure. According to Erikson, this can result in the child becoming an inflexible, unyielding adult. Erikson's theory of child development was the first to make connections between how effectively this period of growth is navigated and later personality traits.

When a child and his parents successfully navigate this stage the child develops a strong sense of self-control without losing his self-esteem. He is secure, proud, and confident. An unsuccessful navigation of the autonomy-independence conflict produces the opposite qualities in a child. He will doubt himself and experience loss of self-control and excessive shame. In summary, Erikson said toddlers need external limits to develop strong inner controls. They also need clear choices and a chance to choose among options and explore and express themselves freely within those external limits.

The Center of the Universe

With his laserlike focus on how children learn (rather than what they feel), Jean Piaget said that after 18 months and until they reach age 7, children are in the "preoperational stage" of thinking. In this period, a child is egocentric. She thinks of everything in terms of how it relates to her. Further, she can only think about one thing or one characteristic of something or someone at a time. And forget metaphors or abstractions, this age child takes things literally. If you say the playroom looks like a garbage dump, she looks for thrown away food and ice cream cartons.

Piaget points out that this age is when a child's way of thinking is most different from that of an adult (at least we hope adults do not still think this way). For a child to learn at this preoperational stage, Piaget said, he must be given opportunities to explore and construct schemas that explain his world to him in terms he can understand. Think back to Erikson's point on the toddler's need for a sense of autonomy, and this makes a lot of sense. At the same time, because of his limited ability to process information and his dependency on direct experience, the preoperational child makes many incorrect generalizations. For example, if falling down and cutting his knee hurts, he reasons that getting a haircut or clipping his toenails will cause physical pain. If a dog barks and a car drives away, he concludes the bark caused the car to leave.

As discussed in Chapters 1 and 9, Piaget saw learning as a three-fold process. The child forms schemas and, as new information arrives to contradict them, he accommodates the new data by changing his schemas. In this way, equilibrium is restored in the child's world. As a direct result of Piaget's definition of this preoperational stage in a child's thinking, preschools and daycare centers instituted long periods of uninterrupted independent play as essential parts of a child's day.

A Bundle of Contradictions

For normally developing 2- and 3-year-olds, life is full of (necessary) contradictions. She wants Mom, but she wants to run away, too. He guards his toys, but he is newly interested in making friends. She can be sweet and show real concern for a sad or crying child, and she can throw a hair-raising tantrum that gets the attention of everyone in the supermarket. These typically fluctuating emotional states also affect how and what 2- and 3-year-olds learn and how they see the world around them.

A child of this age often surprises with behavior that is both selfish *and* altruistic. By 15 months, a toddler can recognize his image in a mirror and find himself in a group photograph. "Me" and "mine" are his favorite words. Try taking a toy from a 2½-year-old, and you'll discover how strongly he takes this newly learned notion of ownership. Fortunately, the vast majority of these willful toddlers do not become 7-year-olds who are incapable of sharing. Children of this age simply need to establish a sense of ownership of things to clarify their own sense of self.

> **FIELD STUDY**
>
> A group of 2-year-olds were observed as they played in pairs. Most began their play with a series of self-assertions, reciting "my doll" or "my truck" for the benefit of their playmates. The investigator in this study interpreted this tendency to "own" toys that (technically) were not theirs as a cognitive necessity, not a sign of selfishness. To see themselves as separate people, a child of this age establishes her territory through "her" possessions.

As if to balance this tendency to see everything as theirs or about them, the period between 18 and 36 months is the prime time to seed the roots of conscience and morality in a child. Two- and 3-year-olds can begin to tell right from wrong and are ready to learn about personal hygiene, self-control, and responsibility. In several studies, researchers have found that parents who consistently react to their children's misbehavior by focusing on the feelings of the person harmed tend to have children who have greater empathy and become more altruistic.

I Am Girl, I Am Boy

After finishing the work of establishing a separate self (usually accomplished by the age of 2½), a toddler moves on to discover his or her gender. It should be noted that gender is by no means a fixed idea in a child's mind. A boy of this age may believe he can turn into a girl by donning a dress. And if he does put on girls' clothing, it doesn't signify anything other than his curiosity about the opposite sex.

Cultural bias prompts parents to give "masculine" toys (trucks and blocks) to boys and "feminine" play things (dolls and clothing) to girls, thus reinforcing gender roles and preferences. At the same time, substantial research indicates that some tendencies toward male and female styles of play appear to be innate. This topic and other aspects of the child's social self are covered in Chapter 13, where the social identity of 3- to 6-year-olds is examined.

A Critical Period for Language

With their newfound identities taking hold, boys and girls of 18 months are on the threshold of becoming social beings. In order to articulate their thoughts and desires, and to fully take part in the more interactive play of which they are now capable, toddlers need advanced language skills.

The critical or sensitive period for a child to learn her first or second language is between 1 and 7 years of age. That's when a child's brain is the most plastic, when it grows neurons and synapses rapidly and then prunes and refines these neural pathways into circuits. The circuits that get the most use become hard-wired while others fall away. A child's level of skill in using words and sentences provides a window into how her brain is developing in the growth-intensive second and third years of life.

Complex Sentences

By the time a toddler reaches 24 months of age she is using, on average, 200 words, albeit one or two at a time. If a child of this age is reporting on an important event in her day she might exclaim, for example, "Home dada." The same child, on or after her third birthday, is capable of adding complexity to this sentence. Describing the same event she might say: "My dada home now." Her ability to represent relations between people and things reflects new thinking on this child's part. It also reveals the toddler's developing sense of identity as identified by Erikson and described later in this chapter.

What enables a child to jump from two words to a six-word sentence? In a word: grammar. Sentences that include adjectives, possessive parts of speech, and pronouns in addition to nouns and verbs require knowledge of grammar, also called syntax. Both refer to how words are put together to create a certain meaning. When a 3-year-old expands her vocabulary by learning new words, she puts together phonemes that are the sounds of *morphemes*, which are the smallest parts of a language such as syllables, articles, verb tenses, and plurals.

DEFINITION

Morphemes are the basic parts of language, such as syllables (syl-la-bles), articles (the, a), verb tenses (went, going, will go), and plurals (s), that modify the meaning of words and sentences.

Fast Mapping

When this process of increasing complexity starts, it happens very quickly. The term "fast mapping" describes how a child determines probable meanings of words she hears based on the context or situation she's in. She doesn't always get her words exactly right, but in a short time the average monosyllabic toddler becomes a relatively sophisticated conversationalist.

A fascinating new area of recent research focuses on precisely how a budding 2-year-old speaker acquires the rules of word usage and syntax. Certainly you've long known that children learn many words from listening to and mimicking the speech of their older siblings and parents. But, the neurologists say, there's more to it than simple imitation. Grammar is too complex a process to acquire by simple rote repetition of what a baby hears. And then there's the fact that deaf children babble many syllables without hearing. This implies they have some sort of wiring for speech that needs no input from their environment.

Language and the Toddler Brain

As hearing children approach their third birthday, they get help from a newly available neural processing system in the brain that reaches maturation just in time to help speed language acquisition. Research involving children and adults with brain injuries has produced much of the knowledge now available about which parts of the brain control different aspects of language.

Circuits for Speech and Listening

Among the research findings about the brain and language development are the following:

- Most speech and language comprehension is processed in the temporal cortex of the left hemisphere.

- A front part of the left temporal cortex called Broca's area (named for the person who discovered it) is where syntax is controlled. Interestingly, people who have suffered damage to their Broca's area speak much like preschoolers who haven't yet acquired a working knowledge of syntax. They can use one or two words at a time but have extreme difficulty with longer sentences.

- A location in the rear of the temporal cortex called Wernicke's area handles semantics or the meanings of words.

- The right hemisphere of the brain is not completely left out of language processing. The more emotional side of the frontal cortex cues the inflection (emphasis) we give words and the overall musical quality of speech. The right hemisphere also is critical in understanding and interpreting speech.

The two hemispheres working together in sync is essential for normal development of speech and hearing, and, later, for learning the skills needed for reading and writing.

How Self-Talk Builds the Brain

Psychologists specializing in neuropsychology believe that self-talk or "inner speech," the silent conversation that most people carry on with themselves, helps create connections in the brain. They say this occurs at any age, but the ability to engage in self-talk begins between ages 2 and 3.

Although dialogue with parents is still the most critical experience for early language learning, self-talk helps a child build language skills and other cognitive processes. In one form of inner speech, a child talks aloud to himself while he goes about his activities; for example, while he separates different-colored blocks into piles, the child says aloud "red goes here" and "green over here." Later, children similarly mouth or speak aloud the steps to a math problem. All of this self-talk is brain building because connections between speech, actions, and objects are being made and reinforced.

Private speech also helps a child delay gratification, get motivated, and regulate his emotions, and these are all important for cognitive and emotional growth. In one study, psychologists tape-recorded the monologues of a girl while she was alone in her crib from the age of 21 months to 3 years. From the analysis of these tapes came the theory that such toddler monologues are not simply practice or play. Rather, they represent attempts by a child to make sense of her daily experiences.

Put another way, researchers concluded the little girl in the crib study was using speech to recreate her world for herself. Her experience, for example, of being left at nursery school (at 2½ years of age) was recounted verbatim as "Her daddy and mommy will the stay the whole time but my daddy and mommy don't. They just tell me what's happening and then go right to work, cause I don't, cause I don't, cause I don't cry." In this comment, the child's developing sense of self can be detected, as she displays a certain pride over her ability to stay at nursery school without crying.

Signs of Complexity

One clear sign that a child has acquired more complex language skills is her use of compound sentences. This is when she combines two thoughts into one statement or question. For example, the child will combine "I sat down" with "I ate my cookie" saying, "I sat down and ate my cookie."

Another step forward is the grammatical feat called "embedded sentences," or putting one thought inside another. "The girl went home to change clothes" expands to "The girl who got wet went home to change clothes." By the age of 5 or 6, children know up to 14,000 words. They are using most of the grammatical rules of their native language without having taken a single grammar lesson!

The Pragmatics of Language

The rules for how we use language in everyday speech are called pragmatics. Children learn these rules from interacting with people, from being read to, and by watching television. A key pragmatics lesson usually learned by 2-year-old children is taking turns in conversation. Many children's games help teach taking turns, beginning with "peek-a-boo," "Simon says," and countless others. Two other essential language pragmatics learned between the second and third birthdays are speaking clearly and listening well.

Not Quite There

When learning to speak, a young child uses several primitive cognitive strategies. For example, they make inferences about new word meanings by contrasting new words with words they already know. Some of these strategies produce the right use of a word while others don't.

When "cognitive constraints" produce challenges for a typical 2- and 3-year-old's speech and language comprehension, they often reflect insufficient brain maturation for that particular skill.

Some examples of cognitive constraints affecting children between 18 months and 3 years of age include the following:

- A *processing constraint* that leads children to assume whatever new word they hear spoken must apply to the newest object they see in their immediate environment.

- An *object scope constraint* where they assume a new word applies to a whole object, rather than any part of the object.

- A *taxonomic constraint* which has them assume that a new word, such as "kitty" for the furry pet they've known since birth must be the same for all other furry animals.

Knowledge of language must be learned. However, there are certain developmental points in a child's life when he (specifically his brain) is ready to learn them, and not before.

Social Rules of Discourse

The conventions or rules used by speakers in conversation may be fairly simple, such as the taking turns rule. Other rules require more cognitive skills in order to master them. An example of a more advanced language convention is called the "toddlers:language pragmatics:answer obviousness rule." This rule says that if the answer to a question is obvious from the context and speaker, then the listener should interpret the question as a request (perhaps a demand) rather than a question.

For example, a mother finds her child banging his truck on the coffee table while playing with it. She might ask the child "Do you really have to bang that truck so hard?" The child of 4 or 5 who has acquired the answer-obviousness rule will know that his mother isn't really interested in his opinion about banging the truck. Neither does she want to hear about his desire to bang his truck. She wants him to stop banging it immediately.

Other more advanced social rules of discourse include the following examples:

- Saying something relevant to the topic being discussed

- Saying something new and not repeating what has just been said

Another aspect of the rules of social discourse concerns the cultural context for speech in any given ethnic group or community. What constitutes an "obvious" answer in one community may be different in another. For example, Hispanic and African American parents have been found in observational studies not to use question-demands (the preceding truck-banging example) as often as white American mothers.

Speech and Sociability

The typical toddler plays six hours every day. If they are with another child or children their own age, 2-year-olds usually engage in "parallel play," meaning each child carries on a separate activity in close proximity to the other. As you watch them, it may not be obvious, but they enjoy each other's company—just not in the same ways that older children do. As they reach their third year, children have more verbal interaction with peers in their play. That's when language becomes all important. Children also learn very early that different people require different styles and complexities of speech.

FIELD STUDY

Preschoolers adapt their speech to their listeners. This was the conclusion of a study in which 3- and 4-year-olds were asked to explain how a toy worked, first to a 2-year-old child and then to an adult. For the younger listeners, they used shorter, simpler sentences with more attention-getting words such as "hey" and "look." For the adults, they used more complex language.

Some children are more socially outgoing and talkative than others. Other perfectly normal children don't speak much until the age of 3, well past the time when most toddlers are using words and forming elementary sentences. When there are developmental delays in speech that veer far from the norm, and after hearing problems are ruled out, psychologists and speech pathologists usually screen children for the possibility of underlying problems.

Gender and Language

Gender affects language skill acquisition and proficiency. Girls start talking a month or two before boys, and they tend to use longer sentences earlier. The female language advantage stays with girls well into grade school and often into adulthood. A biological explanation for this disparity is reflected in brain scans. The Broca and Wernicke areas in female brains are larger than in male brains. In addition, females tend to use both hemispheres in speech whereas males control most language functions solely from their left hemispheres.

Finally, there are environmental factors such as family size and sibling temperaments that affect how much any 2- or 3-year-old child says in the course of a day. Most children who begin speaking late catch up quickly.

Big Talkers from Birth?

Some people put a lot of feeling into their words. They are said to be more "expressive" talkers. Others tend to use language more for counting, labeling, and mastering things in their environments. Some children are more inclined to use one speech style or pattern than another, although most children use each category when appropriate.

In summary, children use language in the following patterns:

- To express feelings

- To describe objects and events

- To please adults

- To express their thoughts and wishes

Children's use of one speech pattern over another may reflect their temperaments. Try thinking back or asking a parent which style of talker you may have been as a child. Has your speech style or pattern changed over the years?

For the child of 3, the impact of having a bigger vocabulary and a grasp of the rules of language opens new worlds. It serves as a gateway to rapid growth in the cognitive and emotional-social spheres. Complex speech connects a child to the use of words as symbols, essential for learning higher language skills and arithmetic. This newfound ability to say what she sees and wants and to respond to the needs of others paves the way for her first friendships.

Language Milestones

As discussed previously, children learn the rules of language beginning before birth and continuing in earnest throughout their toddler and preschool years. Many key skills are in place by the time they enter first grade. Here is a recap of the behaviors and essential milestones related to language during early childhood:

- Before birth: Receives intonation patterns from mother's voice.

- Birth to 9 months: Cries, babbles, laughs, and begins to imitate word sounds.

- Between 9 months and 2 years: Puts sounds of morphemes together to form words of increasing complexity with increasing accuracy.

- Between 2 to 3 years: Uses one- and two-word "sentences"; understands and uses possessives, negatives, and questions; takes turns; uses different tones for specific purposes; changes topics rapidly; if not answered right away repeats the question; and talks to self to help control his behavior and solve problems.

- Between 3 to 4 years: Expands to longer sentences and more complex grammar, can get an entire idea in one sentence, adds pronouns, uses past tense, gives related response to a question, waits for answers, and adjusts speech to audience.

A normal 3-year-old may or may not have mastered the toilet and may not have total control over his moods, but he has certainly made substantial progress in mastering the verbal and nonverbal language he needs to make sense of his immediate world, to form friendships, and to begin simple learning.

Individual Language Differences

Many aspects of learning a language in early childhood are universal. Different skills are acquired sequentially at about the same ages across cultures. But there are still individual differences—sometimes large ones—between children.

Extroverted children definitely learn language more rapidly than their introverted peers.

Other differences also are apparent very early. In one test, sounds were played for babies while their brain waves were measured. Those with the most active brain waves as babies tended to be more verbal at the age of 3. They were also better readers in school, suggesting an inherited linguistic ability.

Some children lag behind the average maturation speeds in speech and other language abilities. Apart from brain injuries, mental disorders, or hearing deficits, scientists don't know exactly why some children simply don't speak until the age of 3 or older. The probable answer lies in a combination of nature and nurture. Twin studies show that verbal ability is roughly 50 percent heritable. That makes speech more dependent on genes than other academic skills such as reading or spelling, which are closer to 20 percent heritable.

When a Child Stutters

Most 2- and 3-year-olds stammer on their way to mastering speech. It happens usually when the child is in a hurry to say something or simply isn't sure of the word she's looking for. It can be compared to stumbling and falling when learning to walk. Adults often find it hard not to correct a child who makes a mistake in speech. However, it is more helpful to let the child find her own way, rather than applying too much pressure at an early age to say things just right.

For a tiny minority of children, stuttering represents a neurological impairment. One such impairment is called "childhood apraxia." It occurs when a child has trouble coordinating the sequence of movements of the lips, tongue, and soft palate to produce intelligible speech. For these children, a speech pathologist should be consulted.

The Role of a Speech-Language Pathologist

A certified speech-language pathologist is consulted when parents, often in consultation with a pediatrician, suspect that a child's delays or difficulties in acquiring language are outside of the normal range. This would be the 15-month-old who does not babble, or the child of 3 who may stop using language in a way that she had previously mastered. Perhaps she avoids eye contact when her parents address her. Another child may be difficult to understand, even beyond the preschool years.

The speech-language pathologist will conduct an evaluation of the child to determine whether a language delay exists and possible causes for the delay, the skills the child has or still needs to learn, and the intervention strategies that might help.

Some speech patterns that may concern parents but are not outside the normal range for a 3-year-old's speech include the repetition of words such as: "I, I, I, I want my blankie," or "I want to come, come, come home."

In contrast, if the same 3-year-old struggles with a sound, making tics or grimaces or repeatedly prolonging a sound such as "ssssit" or "p, p, p, pot" and she does this with 1 out of 10 words, it may indicate a stuttering condition. As discussed previously, many children grow out of this condition. However, if the difficulties continue into the child's preschool years, a speech-language pathologist will often be called in. In order to be licensed or certified as a speech-language pathologist, a Master's degree in speech-language pathology or communications disorders is needed.

When it's warranted, speech therapy should begin before a child starts kindergarten. Children who have language problems in the first 5 years of life are at elevated risk for reading and writing problems later. Parents are urged to monitor and encourage their children's language skills. Learning and language disorders are discussed further in Chapter 17.

The Least You Need to Know

- In his quest for autonomy, a toddler is a bundle of contradictions, wanting freedom and Mommy with equal fervor.
- By talking aloud to herself, a 2- or 3-year-old learns language and sorts out the important relationships in her daily life.
- This is the age when language problems can appear; some, such as stammering, tend to disappear on their own.
- When a child's talking problems persist past the preschool years, a speech-language pathologist often is consulted for an evaluation.

3 to 6 Years—
A Social Being

In This Chapter

- The silent language of child's play
- What a preschooler knows and how he knows it
- When a child's fluid sense of self goes social
- Why even 3-year-olds can be reasonable when asked nicely

Play is a child's work. Never is this axiom more true than for children ages 3 through 6. Preschoolers play together (instead of next to each other) because they at last have the cognitive and emotional skills to handle the more complicated interactions involved: talking, negotiating, pretending, testing, and laughing. At this age, they're also newly sensitive to the opinions of their peers. The 5-year-old who brought a chewed-up teddy bear with her everywhere will leave that bear at home rather than risk being teased by her preschool friends. She talks more, knows more, and has a new awareness of her own charms. At home, in preschool, or on the playground, her personality blossoms further with each new social interaction.

Developing a Self-Identity

Before there can be a social self, a child must develop a self-identity. For a child of this age, individuality is a work in progress. Most psychologists do not believe that a sense of self is present at birth or during the first year of life. The consensus is that a toddler realizes she has an "I-self"; that is, that she is separate from her mother, somewhere between her first and second years. A "me-self or myself," representing the child's recognition of her own unique qualities—called a self-identity—develops incrementally as cognitive abilities emerge to help move the self-representation process along beyond awareness of "I am" and "I want." This evolving self-identity in turn strengthens the underlying I-self, the consciousness that she is a separate person. Along the way, preschool children develop "working models"—self-concepts—of themselves and significant others.

Adding Traits

As they interact with other people, their unique culture, and their environment, children add certain traits to their evolving self-concepts that comprise their self-identities. Among these may be honesty, a desire to please, impulsiveness, directness, frugality, and loyalty. As preschool children speak and think more like adults, these gains intertwine with new social skills making self-identities that are progressively more tangible. Crucial to this new self-awareness is the feedback received from their peers.

In the preschool years, the toddler's egocentrism gives way to a concern about what others think and feel. Before this point, when what is true only revolves around themselves, children have a distorted view of people and objects. Now, at 4 and 5, they're embarrassed when they attract unwanted attention. Now they feel pride for their accomplishments and envy when other children receive praise. And although a 3-year-old can readily believe she has superpowers, a 6-year-old knows her limits and puts more stock in "the rules."

Who Am I?

For the child of 3 to 6, her self-identity is based on concrete things that are visible to the naked eye. Ask a 4-year-old who he is, and he will cite:

- **Physical attributes**—"I've got red hair."
- **Possessions**—"My cat is white with brown stripes."
- **Preferred activities**—"I can run."
- **Comparisons to others**—"I'm bigger than my sister."

After age 6, a child's description of his self-identity becomes increasingly abstract. It includes intangible qualities such as "nice" and "smart." He also is better able to integrate these separate aspects into a more complete self-portrait.

FIELD STUDY

Researchers looking into the social development of 3- to 5-year-olds found that the level of politeness a child used when faced with a conflict depended on whether the child's playmate explained the reasons for his actions. When the other child explained why he denied a request, the first child responded politely. Niceties were promptly dropped when no reason was given for a refusal.

What Can I Do?

Erik Erikson's third stage of growth addresses the preschool child's need to develop a sense of individual purpose through trial and error. He characterized the developmental conflict at this age as one pitting initiative against guilt. Erikson described the typical 4- or 5-year-old as highly energetic and ready to learn. Compared to children of 2 or 3, they are able to focus, follow directions, and behave less defiantly.

That is, *if* they have successfully navigated the conflicts in the first year of life between trust and mistrust, and in the second stage between autonomy versus shame and doubt. Children who have completed these two previous stages, Erikson noted, will reach the age of 5 with a healthy sense of personal autonomy. They will not be overly burdened by shame and doubt. They learn by trial and error because they don't worry about making mistakes. The tell-tale sign of a child who has worked her way positively through this conflict: after "failing" at something, she feels no guilt. She possesses the initiative to try again.

Initiative

According to Erikson, these preschool years are the time in a child's development when her energy and focus can split off in one of two possible directions: the potential for "glory or destruction." If she's encouraged to learn from her mistakes, her confidence will grow along with a desire to contribute. For such experiences to lead to a child's permanent display of competence, the adults in her life must not try to overmanage her. Nor should they hover around a child "at work" or attempt to do tasks for her that she can do on her own.

To encourage a positive resolution of this developmental conflict between initiative and guilt, Erikson advocated that adults do whatever they can to enhance a child's independence. His primary recommendation was to focus on gains the child makes rather than pointing out and demonstrating how the child can correct mistakes. Instead, a child should be permitted to discover and correct her own mistakes by trial and error and continued effort. Patience above all else is required by adults in dealing with children of this age.

Like Piaget, Erikson emphasized a child's need to play with real objects (not only toys) and use real-life tools to gain a sense of mastery. A salient feature of Erikson's theory was his admonition that adults consider individual differences between children in the same age group. He pointed out that children have different cognitive or emotional abilities or may simply be having an "off day." Such differences must be noted and accommodated by parents and teachers.

Guilt

If children are overly criticized or removed from a task they could master if allowed enough practice, their initiative will turn into guilt and defeatism, Erikson warned. Such children will quit an activity rather than risk making another mistake.

Neither should adults subject children of this age to expectations beyond their abilities, Erikson warned. When that happens, children may conclude they are simply not capable and give up on whatever they're doing. Pushed children may also go beyond their capabilities and succeed against the odds. You may wonder, shouldn't these children then be viewed as overachievers with a bright future? Erikson would say not so fast, explaining that harm comes to a child when his value is determined by what he does rather than who he is. His initiative may not be thwarted immediately, Erikson said, but such a child can still carry a heavy load of guilt and inadequacy.

INSIGHT

Research done in the 1960s showed a link between a parent's hostility toward or rejection of a child and his dependent behavior away from the parent. In an experiment with 100 preschool-age children, those whose parents scored high on a questionnaire measuring hostility had offspring who demonstrated their dependency by frequently asking their teachers for help and by seeking approval.

Cognitive Milestones

During this period of cognitive development, which is still part of the stage Piaget called preoperational, a child is beginning to use simple logic. But the form of logic a preschool child employs comes entirely from personal experience, prompting Piaget to call it intuitive. As we discuss throughout this chapter, there are direct links between a child's cognitive abilities and his social and emotional expressions.

The Missing Pieces

There are some big missing pieces in a preschooler's logic. The 3- to 5-year-old child still doesn't quite get the concept of reversibility, the notion that, if something is done, it can also be undone. For example, pouring liquid from one container to another and then back again. This is key to understanding the reversible processes in basic math problems—such as if $2 + 2 = 4$ then $4 - 2 = 2$. Piaget called processes, such as pouring, adding, and subtracting, "operations." And because a preschool child or child up to the age of 6 can't follow the logic behind these processes, he included them all in the category "preoperational." As seen in the next chapter, after a child passes the age of 6, he is capable of concrete operational thought, and this is when such processes become clear to him.

Mistaken Impressions

Other preoperational cognitive limitations include an inability to understand the concepts of conservation (that the quantity of liquid stays the same in different size containers) and animism (giving inanimate objects conscious life and feelings). Of course, these limitations also are what enrich the play of an imaginative 4-year-old for whom the rules of logic can still be bent to suit fancy or fantasy.

A Peek at the Preschool Brain

An important physiological change that occurs in a child's brain around the fourth year is greater neural communication between the right and left hemispheres of the temporal cortex. This better communication allows a child to employ both the perceptual abilities centered in the so-called right brain with the newly blossoming analytical skills of her so-called left brain.

One manifestation of this brain change is the 4- and especially 5-year-old child's ability to separate appearance from reality. She cannot be tricked into thinking a cloud viewed through red cellophane is really red. The 4-year-old is also beginning to understand that someone can look different and still be the same person. So a 4-year-old would know that Clark Kent and Superman are one and the same character, while a 3-year-old would likely refuse to believe such a possibility.

The Work of Play

Play in the preschool years is considered so important a subject by child psychologists that it has generated thousands of research studies and professional articles. In the 3- to 6-year-old stage, symbolic fantasy play and manipulative activities are important to a child's cognitive and emotional development. Children may appear to simply be manipulating blocks or piles of sand but, psychologists say, they're also testing important scientific ideas. Which ones? How about the science of systems and interactions; or the geometric shapes that can support other shapes; or the physics of how tall a tower can be before it topples to the ground? Let's not forget the concepts of gravity, balance, and stability. All of these concepts are embedded in a typical preschooler's play.

Practicing Patterns

The goal of much preschool learning, whether done in a school setting or at home, is to help a child understand the patterns of people, places, and things. Learning activities to aid this process of pattern-making often follow the order of development of faculties in a child's nervous system. This sequence begins with motor skills, followed by emotional and then cognitive learning.

The following are among the patterns being learned during the preschool years:

- Motor patterns, required in physical games, in the use of tools or utensils and in household chores.

- Visual and other sensory patterns, arising in puzzles, sorting and arranging of materials, and often connecting cognitive skills.

- Sequencing patterns, whether tangible, such as smallest to largest objects, or abstract as in "First put on your shoes, then go outside."

- People patterns, relationships, and comparisons found in stories and pretend play.

- Patterns in the relationships of daily life, often prompting "why" questions which represent a child's need for more information to understand a pattern.

Something that frequently confuses adults who play with children of this age is their rather flexible notion of rules. Left to their own preferences, children often make up new rules as they go along. As long as the changes are agreeable to their playmates, this expansion of imaginative play into an existing game is entirely age-appropriate—even if it frustrates older children and adults.

Constructive Play

With their more refined manual dexterity, preschoolers go about constructing their world using whatever materials are available to them, whether blocks, toys, or household pots and pans. A child learns the similarities and differences among and between things when she gathers and groups things by color, shape, or size. Until age 6 or 7, a child at play is developing the groundwork for abstract thought and an understanding of patterns by mastering his physical environment (and by learning to use language).

Preschoolers' attention stays exclusively in the present, without much regard for the past or future. This makes them "stimulus bound," meaning they're drawn to any new thing in the environment. It also makes one thing at a time the general rule for play. Multitasking is far in the future.

Fun and Purpose in Pretending

With their very basic and limited logic, preschoolers are able to connect symbols (words, gestures, pictures) to things, feelings, and actions. This ability, Piaget said, is what enables their learning of language, which has already taken flight by the age of 3. This is also the basis of symbolic or pretend play, the favorite type of play of this older age group.

After the third year, children can hold some abstract ideas and use concepts that are not tangible. This allows them to go beyond simple imitation to a more creative style of play involving role play. In a nursery school, you often find a small wooden structure with a roof, two walls, and a window. As children play "house" in this structure, they use blocks for food and carry a stuffed pillow they call "baby." With such play, children do something that no other species does: express ideas through symbols. From a learning perspective, play of this kind facilitates an understanding of metaphor. It's also the gateway to later scientific insights and inventions.

Dramatic pretend play also offers avenues for learning in the emotional and social realms. It teaches children social skills more effectively than any kind of didactic instruction. Children also use pretend play to deal with things that bother them in their daily lives, whether they're feelings of jealousy over the arrival a new baby in the house or a conflict with a playmate. They may re-enact intense or scary experiences they've witnessed or experienced themselves. They can do this, for example, by pretending to be a doctor or a nurse working in a hospital or a police-man making an arrest in the neighborhood.

One frequently present aspect of a preschool child's pretend play is the "imaginary friend." When she creates a playmate who is not really there, the child has "some-one" who can act out experiences and emotions she wonders about. Imaginary friends can do bad things without being punished. They can perform miracles. When a parent yells, the imaginary friend can fly away while the real child must stay and listen. A child of 3 and 4 will speak to their created friends as if they are real.

Having imaginary friends is considered normal for a child of this age. They serve as a transition from fantasy play to real-world relationships. When the child of 6 has attained more social skills and confidence, these imagined friends will gener-ally fade away.

Preschool Friendships

In order to form friendships, the 3- to 6-year-old child needs opportunities to socialize with peers. If they don't attend preschool, children of this age make their first friends during other social contacts usually arranged and supervised by parents or other caregivers. These include prearranged playgroups, interaction in playground settings, or casual encounters with neighboring children. In choosing their friends, a preschooler's personal preferences are already at work. By and large, the preschool child seeks out playmates that enjoy the same style of play as they do.

One Friend Above Others

"Best friends" is a meaningful category among preschoolers, just as it is with older children and adults. A best friendship is closer and more exclusive to the preschooler than his other relationships. In one study, Canadian and Scottish children were asked what qualities they expected in a same-sex "best friend." Children beginning in preschool and throughout grade school chose "similar interests" as the most important aspect of this special relationship. Rarely mentioned by children as either a positive or negative factor were physical attributes such as attractiveness. The same went for shared personality traits, such as seeking out children who were either shy or outgoing. These attributes were simply not as important as enjoying the same games and activities.

Interestingly, by the time the children in this study reached the eighth grade, they placed "good character traits" such as generosity and loyalty over shared interests as the factor they held of highest importance in their choice of a best friend.

Boys with Boys, Girls with Girls

The same pattern of like attracting like in a preschooler's choice of friends may be operating in their preference to play with their same-sex peers. By the age of 2 or 3, children show a clear preference for playing with children of their own sex. In observational studies, it was noted that when playing with opposite-sex children, preschoolers tended to play in parallel, or they simply watched the opposite-sex child instead of interacting directly with them. By 6 years, gender segregation is so firmly established that if you were to watch a typical school playground at recess, you would likely find an 11-to-1 ratio of same-sex play groups versus opposite-sex children playing together.

As for the reasons for this same-sex social reality, psychological research offers the following possibilities:

- Play compatibility, as discussed previously.
- Cognitive schemas about what boys and girls are typically like. These may include stereotypes and exaggerated notions about gender differences.

- Operant conditioning, based on parents, teachers, peers, or indirect messages they've received about who and what is appropriate for their play.

Regardless of why gender segregation occurs in childhood, the effects of girls' and boys' separate early social spheres are seen to carry over into adolescence and beyond.

Gender Identities Take Hold

Whereas at the age of 3 or 4 a child may pretend and believe that he can switch his gender, by the age of 6, most children accept their sex as a life-long trait. They notice that boys and girls dress and act differently. Although aspects of gender identity are innate, research shows that children acquire most of the information that guides their learning about how a girl or boy behaves by observation and imitation of their parents, teachers, siblings, playmates, and from mass media.

That's because reinforcement plays a large role in how children express gender traits. By the time a child is 2 years of age and older, the child's subtle differences in behavior are treated differently by parents. When a little girl walks and talks seductively like her mother, she receives positive feedback from Daddy and other family members. She's called cute. The same is true for a little boy imitating his father when he strides confidently across the room and holds back his tears. He's called tough.

Peer Pressure

Notwithstanding any of the preceding, when it comes to sex roles, the last and most definitive word may come from a child's friends and playmates. Researchers watched 200 preschoolers, age 3 to 6, at play and found that boys who prefer dolls to trucks are criticized five to six times more often by their classmates than other children who conformed to sex role expectations. Girls who showed a preference for playing the role of a firefighter rather than a nurse were not treated quite as harshly. Instead of receiving overt criticism, they were generally ignored.

Mind Over Imitation

Lawrence Kohlberg, whose theory of cognitive development was introduced in Chapter 9, has a different perspective on how children acquire their gender identities. His theory puts more emphasis on cognitive skills, and in Kohlberg's view these abilities explain why children develop traditional gender identities even when their parents don't want them to.

In Kohlberg's theory, children's gender roles solidify only after they acquire a cognitive understanding about what girl versus boy means in their culture. Then, they socialize themselves, meaning they're not simply imitators or pawns of social influence. The difference might appear subtle, but notice which of the following statements imparts more self-generated thought and action for a child.

In the dominant social learning model, a boy says (to himself) "I'm treated like a boy, therefore I must be one." In Kohlberg's cognitive-development model, a boy says "I am a boy, therefore I will find out how to behave like one." In this active way, the child then begins gender-typing him- or herself as a self-socializing process. Kohlberg outlines three stages in this process:

- Basic gender identity arrives by age 3, when children label themselves either a boy or a girl.

- Gender stability is an interim stage when children perceive gender identity as a stable aspect of themselves over time, in the sense that they will grow up to be a man or a woman.

- Gender consistency arrives by age 7, as children realize that their sex also is stable across different situations; that is, they are what they are ana-tomically despite changes in appearance or when they're doing different male- or female-type activities.

One implication of this approach is that children begin to meaningfully socialize themselves in ways that "stick" as male or female only after they have achieved gender consistency. This begins at age 5 and usually is completed by age 7.

Other researchers, after testing Kohlberg's theory of gender typing in the labora-tory, argue that the process begins much earlier. There may be a solid middle ground between the differing perspectives on how gender identity develops. An integrative approach combining social learning and cognitive developmental and biological perspectives might begin by acknowledging innate tendencies determined by genetics and subtle differences in brain structure between males and females. It would then credit both imitation and self-direction in the process of achieving a stable gender identity. All of these theorists share the belief that gender becomes a central part of a child's self-identity by the age of 7.

Lagging Timetables

Because of the rapid brain growth and leaps forward in cognitive as well as social-emotional maturation for children in the preschool stage, any lack of progress in one of these areas becomes noteworthy. Allowing for individual differences in child development, there are some warning signs for parents, caregivers, and teachers that a child may have an underlying problem requiring attention.

> **INSIGHT**
>
> Children with social delays often are gifted in other areas, according to pediatrician T. Berry Brazelton and child psychiatrist Joshua Sparrow, writing in *Touchpoints 3 to 6*. The authors speculate that two factors may be at work alone or together. High intelligence takes energy, leaving the child less for social pursuits. Or is it that a shy child tends to prefer solo, quiet activities?

Red Flags

Some red flags in the timetable of a child's social development that should concern parents are:

- When a child past the age of 3 has frequent full-blown temper tantrums with kicking and screaming and cannot be calmed down by caretakers.

- When a preschool child cannot separate from a parent, and spends more time clinging than exploring.

- When a preschool child is completely disinterested in or uncomfortable with pretend play.

- When a child of 6 or older is unwilling to give up imaginary friends for real ones.

- When a child of 3 is not talking in three-word sentences with understandable pronunciation.

- When a 5- or 6-year-old child cannot follow simple directions or listen and repeat basic information.

- When a preschool child lacks social skills and is consistently rejected by same-age peers.

Although not all of these behaviors may require immediate attention, any extreme behavior or more than one of the behaviors on this list may represent early signs of a mental disorder or brain impairment, such as depression, autism, or learning disability. A consultation with a medical or mental health professional is often recommended to assess the child's need for ongoing monitoring and/or therapeutic intervention.

Balancing Factors

Sometimes there are obvious causes for a delay of some kind in a child's emotional-social or cognitive development. Among those that a child psychologist takes into account when assessing a child are:

- Birth prematurity, which almost always causes delays in one area or another.

- A family pattern of slow development; late blooming parents often have late blooming offspring.

- Chronic diseases such as serious allergies, asthma, or kidney or ear infections.

- Physical size; children who are much smaller or larger than their peers may have a lack of physical coordination and slowness in other areas.

- Chronological age, compared to classmates.

- Emotional immaturity due to factors such as the death or absence of a parent or grossly incompetent parenting.

These topics are covered in more depth as they relate to children from infancy through adolescence in Chapters 16, 17, and 18.

The Least You Need to Know

- A child who has successfully navigated autonomy and achieves the capacity for initiative tries again after facing failure.
- Acquiring self-concepts that comprise a child's self-identity is the developmental task of the preschool years.

- Learning patterns among people, places, and things is the basis of preschool learning.
- Pretend play is a learning experience in symbolic logic.
- Preschoolers seek similar interests in their choice of friends, and by the age of 2 they show a preference for same-sex playmates.
- A preschooler's gender identity is not yet established, but it becomes firm by the age of 7.

6 to 12 Years—The Dawn of Reason

In This Chapter

- How to break through to "concrete operations"
- Why fantasy play must make way for structured games
- The size of a child's frontal lobes predicts IQ
- What makes a child's IQ average or superior?

By the age of 6, children reach a new level of intellectual ability. This cognitive growth explains why a child's sixth birthday marks the beginning of formal schooling in most cultures around the world. Children at 6 years have significantly greater language comprehension; their memory and attention have increased; and they show greater self-control and awareness. Although none of these are overnight changes, upon reaching 6, children's higher cognitive abilities coalesce to create a newfound readiness to learn. Theorists Erikson and Piaget noted the change that defines this age and offered analyses that still stand. The latest brain science fills out the picture explaining the physiological basis of what has been called the "dawn of reason."

Hail the Concrete!

When a child reaches 6 or 7 years of age, Piaget believed that he enters the age of "concrete operational thought." It's the third stage in his four phase theory of cognitive development. It's when children use logic to solve real-world problems. Several conceptual pieces that were missing during the preschool years are now in place to help make this leap into the concrete. The 4-year-old who thought juice gained volume by pouring it from a wide, short glass into a tall, narrow one no longer believes it. He readily recognizes that both glasses contain the same amount of juice. He gets such concepts as height and width. And he understands reversibility, noting that subtraction is the opposite of addition.

Children in the concrete operations stage also have the benefit of some new concepts in their logic toolbox:

- **Class inclusion**—A child is presented with three bananas and four apples. He's asked: Which is more, apples or fruits? In the preoperational stage he answers "Apples." After 6 years of age, he knows that the category or class called fruits includes both apples and bananas. He lets you know that he thinks the question is silly.

- **Transitive inference**—A child is told that Sandy is taller than Tom. And Tom is taller than Billy. Who's taller, Sandy or Billy? A child who can use logic to draw inferences understands the relationships between these two pairs and will say that, of course, Sandy is taller than Billy.

Now that he has passed the prime period for fantasy play but still lacks the ability to think in abstract terms, the school-age child bases his logical conclusions exclusively on direct experience. When playing, learning, or problem solving, 8-, 9-, and 10-year-olds typically search for literal meanings, not metaphors. This is the time of life where rules really do matter.

Psychologists say that in these years a child is working to solidify his understanding and mastery of the physical world. If he accomplishes that, he will gain the security that comes from operating successfully within prescribed limits. After that, he can move on to more heady, or abstract, concerns.

I Am What I Learn

This is the phrase Erik Erikson coined to describe a child's self-identity in the years between 6 and 12. Erikson pinpointed the challenge of this, his fourth stage, in a child's development of a healthy personality, as a conflict between "industry and inferiority." All school-age children, he said, want to move beyond the pretend play that previously filled their days to become more useful. They do this by making and learning things. By "industry" Erikson meant the wish to be industrious, saying: "Where he once strode to walk well, or throw things well, he now wants to make things well."

Inferiority vs. Industry

The danger of this stage, Erikson warned, is a child developing a sense of inferiority or inadequacy. This can be caused by an insufficient resolution of an earlier stage, such as not forming a trusting bond in the first year. This unfinished first stage of personality development could manifest at age 6 as a child not wanting to leave his mother to start school. Another risk that can bring about a sense of inferiority at age 6 and older is poor schooling. Here, Erikson referred to any form of instruction that turns off a child's natural drive to become industrious.

Lull Before the Storm

Hearkening back to his Freudian roots, Erikson pointed out that Freud called the 6- to 12-year-old stage the time of "latency." This refers to issues laying low in the psyche for later re-emergence. Erikson agreed that with the child's attention focused on school, any intense inner drives present earlier are less evident at this time. But they're not gone, he said. As he put it, latency is "only a lull before the storm of puberty."

COMPLICATION

Is there play after preschool? Although school-age children largely abandon pretend play, they substitute board, video, and computer games and sports as items of fascination. This shift reflects their increasing reasoning ability, impulse control, and capacity to see other people's perspectives.

It is possible to mistake the industry of school-age children as a lack of interest in play. One reapplication of their imaginative ability is found in their newfound tendency to daydream. This is when they mentally rehearse and replay interactions and challenges from their daily lives.

The School-Age Brain

Neurologists have found that the fundamental change in children's brains during the period from 6 to 12 years of age takes place in the frontal lobes, the brain's centers for thought and executive decision-making. For the school-age child, the most important of these changes occur in those frontal lobe locations regulating attention and inhibition. The abilities to pay attention and take one's time to come up with an answer to a problem after all possible answers are considered are vital processes in learning the subject matter in school and beyond.

The brain of a child of this age consists of a forest of synapses awaiting pruning. As mentioned previously, this process of selecting and eliminating synapses depends on which of the child's neural circuits are used more or less. The period from 6 to 12 years is when most synapse pruning takes place as a result of learning.

Electromagnetic scans show that the brains of children between ages 4 and 8 consume the most energy, demonstrating peak circuit running and pruning activities, after which they gradually decline to adult levels. Surprisingly, the 6-year-old brain is much closer in size and activity levels to that of an adult than to the newborn brain. This doesn't mean they have the judgment of an adult. Rather, it shows the tremendous growth that has already occurred in the first six years.

Why Inhibition Matters

The ability to delay gratification, to think before acting or jumping to a conclusion, is critical to even the simplest of cognitive tasks. Different tests have been used to test a child's inhibition level, such as:

- **The Stroop test**—A child is shown a black card with white stars and instructed to say the word "day." When shown a white card with a bright sun shining, they are told to say "night." A younger child would eagerly say the word matching what he saw on the card, regardless of instructions. The 6 and older child gets the "trick" of the test and repeats the word he is instructed to say.

- **The single tapping test**—The child is told to tap twice when the examiner says "once," and tap once after hearing the word "twice."

In case these tests sound like "no brainers" be advised that the skills they measure do not come easily to most children. However they are essential. The same ability to wait and think before responding comes into play with math problems and reading comprehension.

Thinking Fast

The rate at which your brain processes information is used as an indicator of intelligence. Although babies process stimuli slower than older children and adults, research shows that some baby's "inspection time," or ability to figure out a particular stimulus, are faster than others. These babies get bored with the same old toy or game faster than their peers. A recent study demonstrated that this speed advantage persists through childhood. Babies in the study who habituated faster at 7 months performed faster on perceptual tests at age 11.

Brain Size and Shape

Early signs of intelligence are not just limited to how fast a child sees or hears different things in his environment. It also entails how well a child remembers and stores information. Intelligence tests have found that IQ is modestly correlated with head circumference. Newborn babies with a head size larger than 14 inches will, on average, score seven points higher on IQ tests at age 4 when compared to babies whose heads measured smaller than 12¾ inches at birth.

By mid- to late childhood, in the 6- to 12-year-old age range, the correlation is somewhat greater. At this stage, brain size predicts about 20 percent of the variance in children's IQ scores. With all this heady data, it's also important to note that different forms of higher intelligence and high aptitudes show up in different locations in children's brains. Children with better language skills, particularly those who grasp phonics sooner, tend to have brains where the left frontal lobe (an important language area) is larger than the right. Those whose brains show the opposite asymmetry—their right frontal lobe is larger than the left—do better on spatial intelligence. This is manifest when you have to figure your way out of a maze or follow a map or solve a geometry problem.

Defining Intelligence

Here we take on one of the more contested areas of child psychology: the definition of *intelligence*. We find that different cultural values and the specific testing tools used can skew what is being measured and how it is measured.

> **DEFINITION**
>
> **Intelligence** in Western cultures is defined as the ability to learn and think logically about abstract concepts. It also measures an individual's ability to adapt to changing environments whether that means a "curve ball" appearing in a math or logic problem or a literal, unmapped fork in the road.

In the United States and Europe, IQ is equated with logic and mental speed. In contrast, certain African and South Asian cultures see slow and cautious behaviors as better indicators of high intelligence. Some Eastern cultures, particularly those influenced by Confucian philosophy, believe that moral behavior and one's efforts are the qualities that define intelligence. For the purposes of this book, Western values and measurement tools are our focus. Not surprisingly, most of the available research on this topic comes from the United States and Europe.

What Is IQ?

Enter into this topic and you'll discover plenty of differences of opinion about the definition of intelligence and seemingly endless sub-theories about what is actually being measured in various IQ tests. Because someone's relative intelligence is so much a part of the way we assess people, it's important to understand the different premises and perspectives being used by those who do the testing.

General and Specific Intelligence

The first school of thought on IQ testing, formed around the turn of the last century, was called *psychometric*. Its proponents believed intelligence could be measured by taking physical measurements of people's heads, heights, and perceptual speeds. To these basics they then added simple paper and pencil tests. Although the physical measurement part of this approach was abandoned a few decades later, the notion of measuring intelligence using tests in different subject areas stuck. The heart of this approach is viewing intelligence as a hierarchy of general and specific skills.

DEFINITION

Psychometrics is the measurement of psychological characteristics such as intelligence and personality. Psychologists who specialize in this area are called psychometricians.

In a country school in England, psychometrician Charles Spearman studied children's cleverness, common sense, and academic scores and found strong correlations among all three. He proposed a two-factor theory of intelligence to explain his results:

- **General intelligence**—A broad intellectual ability simply described as how well a child sees how things relate to each other.

- **Specific intelligence**—Abilities in particular areas such as reading, verbal, and spatial skills.

However, leading psychometric IQ proponents soon differed about which and how many abilities should be included under either the general or specific intelligence labels. Some limited it to 7, others included up to 150 different skill types. Among these, two broad factors emerged:

- **Fluid ability**—A biologically based ability to think.

- **Crystallized ability**—Knowledge and skills acquired in a particular culture.

Over the decades, psychometric theories of intelligence have been faulted for placing too much emphasis on static and overly specific crystallized indicators. Examples are facts and vocabulary.

INSIGHT

Ever wonder why IQ tests were first developed? At the beginning of the twentieth century, after a massive wave of immigration, American public schools faced a population explosion. With these increased enrollments, teachers needed a quick way to assess a much wider variation in their students' academic abilities. IQ tests were devised as a way to figure out which students could learn quickly and which needed a slower approach.

IQ = Thinking Speed + Context

In the 1980s, Yale psychologist Robert Sternberg developed his "triarchic theory of intelligence." This theory was largely based on the information processing perspective of cognitive development (covered in Chapter 9). It emphasizes intelligence as the speed of a child's mental processes applied in specific environmental contexts. Sternberg's concept of intelligence defined IQ as having three key parts:

- **Components of thought**—Intelligence that depends on mental processes such as planning, reading, or remembering through which a person gathers and works with information. This is "analytical intelligence," an ability to process information, especially applicable to researching and writing papers.

- **Experience**—With greater experience, a child masters more complex mental processes and learns to apply rational and intuitive thinking to both novel and familiar tasks. This type of intelligence shows when people can quickly figure things out and solve problems. It often is referred to as "creative intelligence."

- **Context**—A child's ability to show adaptive behavior in real-life situations. This is often referred to as practical intelligence.

Sternberg's triarchic theory advanced the concept of different types of intelligence that could be measured separately.

Multiple Intelligences

Also in the 1980s, Harvard psychologist Howard Gardner took the idea of more than one type of intelligence and added shadings and subtleties. He drew on studies of both brain damaged and exceptionally talented persons. He saw eight different intelligences each independent of the others (not a single intelligence with subcomponents like Sternberg's theory). He added a bio-psychological aspect to his multiple intelligence theory, meaning there are genetic and environmentally determined biological factors in every type of intelligence.

Gardner cited cultural and economic factors, such as limited opportunities for women and the disadvantaged to obtain quality schooling as having significant impact on individual intelligence. In summary, Gardner said that a person's overall level of functioning is determined by "his complete profile of strengths and weaknesses within a particular cultural setting."

Gardner's eight intelligences are:

- Linguistic

- Logical mathematical

- Spatial

These first three intelligences are included in psychometric theories of intelligence. The next five are not:

- Musical

- Bodily-kinesthetic

- Interpersonal

- Intrapersonal (within oneself)

- Naturalist

In this theory each person possesses all eight of these intelligences to some degree. However, your individual strengths and weakness define how well you perform and in what context you perform best. There also are differences between people in the timing of the arrival of each type of intelligence. Linguistic intelligence develops much earlier than the others. Each type of intelligence is regulated by a different area of the brain. Spatial intelligence, for example, is dominated by regions in the right hemisphere. In an example of extreme differences between one type of intelligence and another in one person, there are special cases where highly gifted people called "savants" have extremely high intelligence in one area, such as music or mathematics, but these same individuals may function at a mentally retarded level in other areas.

Gardner advocated that schools foster all of these intelligences and allow children to pursue their areas of strength. The education and opportunities each child and adult receive to foster these intelligences become particularly important over a lifespan.

Assessing IQ

The term IQ is used in everyday conversation without reference to its original definition as the outcome of a mathematical formula that produces an "intelligence quotient." The formula used was the ratio of mental age (MA) to chronological age (CA), multiplied by 100:

$$IQ = MA \div CA \times 100$$

The shorthand continues with great meaning attached to a high or low score; some say too much meaning. At any age, children who are of average intelligence will have an IQ of 100 because their mental age equals their chronological age. In this scheme, two thirds of children who take an IQ test will have scores between 85 and 115, and 95 percent will have scores between 70 and 130.

Although a variety of IQ tests have been developed over the decades since this type of testing became popular, two factors are considered essential and apply to all intelligence testing:

- **Reliability**—The consistency of scores for the same child if a test is repeated under the same or similar conditions. There should not be large differences between two tests taken by the same child in the same period of time. Correlations between tests of .80 are considered high.

- **Validity**—How well a test measures what it's supposed to measure. The way this is assessed is by seeing if the test scores accurately predict a child's performance later in school or in other areas of life, such as in a job.

IQ tests have been developed for children of various ages and for adults. For the school-age child, the Stanford-Binet and Weschler Scales tests are the most frequently used. They are also the tests that have been the most revised through ongoing research to increase their reliability and validity.

Stanford-Binet Scale

In its fourth edition, this IQ test provides an overall intelligence score along with four subscores:

- Verbal reasoning; for example, define train, dime, taut, cryptography.

- Quantitative reasoning; for example, what is the smallest whole number evenly divisible by 3?

- Abstract/visual reasoning; for example, when shown a folded up sheet of paper, select the picture that is most likely to resemble it when unfolded.

- Short-term memory; for example, recall a series of digits (4, 6, 9, 0, 2).

The Stanford-Binet IQ test is considered very reliable (in the technical sense of reliability previously defined) and shows moderately high correlations with other measures of intelligence; thus it also is considered a valid measure.

The Weschler Scales

There are three separate Weschler IQ tests: one for children from 3 to 7 years (WPPSI), one for children from 6 to 16 (WISC), and a third for ages 16 and older (WAIS). They provide an overall intelligence score and two subscales in verbal and "performance" areas.

The verbal subscale includes:

- Basic information; for example, who discovered North America? What is the capitol of France?

- Vocabulary; for example, define winter, author, perseverance.

- Arithmetic; for example, if a dress sells for half off its usual price, what is the sale price of a $150 dress?

- Comprehension; for example, why is a person accused of a crime tried by a jury of his peers?

- Similarities; for example, in what way are dozen and quarter alike?

The performance subscale includes:

- Picture completion; for example, draw the missing piece of a given picture.

- Block design; for example, reproduce a design using a greater number of pieces.

- Object assembly; for example, rearrange unconnected pieces into a meaningful picture.

The Weschler Scales have been found to have reliability correlations of .90 or higher. They have validity in that they predict later success in school with correlations ranging from .50 to .65.

COMPLICATION

When a child's intelligence is tested makes all the difference. Traditional IQ testing in kindergarten has proved unreliable in identifying gifted children, with only a 20 to 40 percent correlation to test scores at age 11. Why? The brain of a 4- or 5-year-old is still insufficiently mature to predict a child's later performance. IQ testing done in the third grade has proved to be far more reliable in predicting success in high school.

Ever since IQ tests have been given to children of various ages, critics have complained that they do not adequately take into account ethnic biases and socioeconomic differences among children. In response, supporters of IQ testing say that later versions of the Stanford-Binet and Weschler Scales have compensated for earlier cultural biases.

Others say that any biases that exist in a test demonstrate the same biases that a student will find later in the job market and broader culture he will enter. An increasingly accepted middle position suggests that a low score on an intelligence test means that a child currently lacks some skills needed to succeed in school. Not that the child will always fail in school or is just plain stupid. This debate within the field of child psychology can be expected to continue as new research becomes available.

The Gifted Child

Gifted children's thinking seems to develop in the same sequence as nongifted children's thinking, just more rapidly. In this sense gifted children just think more like older nongifted children. Traditionally giftedness was equated only with IQ scores, with any score higher than 130 viewed as exceptional. However, that approach tended to make giftedness solely a product of scholastic abilities. Today's definition is much broader. It includes giftedness in areas such as music, art, creative writing, and dance.

Whatever the domain of giftedness, the gifted child shares several characteristics:

- A love of the subject and an intense desire to master it from an early age.

- Instruction beginning at an early age from instructors who inspire and nurture the child's talent.

- Parents committed to promoting a child's talent.

This brings us to the concept of creativity in the context of intelligence. In psychological terms, creativity and intelligence are not strictly the same. Why not? Intelligence is associated with "convergent thinking." This is a fancy way of saying the child or person who goes for the norm and uses information to arrive at a standard correct answer. Creativity depends more on "divergent thinking." This is the realm of the person who goes outside the norm to find an answer using novel and unusual lines of thought.

A highly creative person presents new ideas and art forms that may upset or shock the sensibility of their place and time. This was the fate met by artists, such as the nineteenth-century impressionist painter Cezanne, whose contemporaries dismissed his paintings as inept attempts at reproducing landscapes. A similar fate greeted the twentieth-century creators of the World Wide Web, whose invention was regarded as never likely to capture public interest when first introduced in the 1980s.

The Least You Need to Know

- During the years 6 to 12 a child's frontal lobes take large steps forward in growth, permitting reasoning and greater self-regulation.
- The traditional definition of intelligence emphasizes thinking speed, the ability to put thoughts in context and apply experience.
- With an average IQ of 100, two thirds of children who take an IQ test will have scores between 85 and 115.
- If you think convergently, like a conformist (rather than divergently like a creative artist), your intelligence will probably be scored higher on most standardized tests.

12 to 18 Years—An Independent Identity

In This Chapter

- The way a teenager is and isn't like a toddler
- The reason most teens deceive their parents
- The causes of teen mood swings
- The building blocks of adolescent self-identity

In a single leap of epic proportions, or so it seems, a child becomes a teenager. Much of the impetus for this near total transformation is chemical. A 12-year-old's newly awakened hormones have a powerful domino effect on every aspect of maturation. In a physically resculpted body, teenagers' maturing brains and changing chemistry go on to alter their emotions, perceptions, and intellect. Given the intensity and speed of these changes, and the longer time it takes to integrate them into a new and coherent personality, adolescence is a notoriously awkward developmental stage. Still, most adolescents weather these years without significant problems.

This chapter begins with the perspectives of Erikson and Piaget explaining how a teenager's new capabilities in thinking and feeling lay the foundation for a new identity. Then it focuses on how a teenager's blossoming gender identity and sexuality adds to a new sense of self. Finally this chapter takes note of the road-blocks that can sidetrack a teenager along the way.

Ask It Again: Who Am I?

Building a unique self-identity describes the psychological coming apart and putting together experience that is the essence of adolescence. Erik Erikson, writing in 1959 in *Identity and the Life Cycle*, described the changes experienced by teenagers in every sphere of their lives as equal in size and scope to those occurring in early childhood with the added complexity of genital maturity. Imagine the "terrible twos" with hormones and you get the picture.

Refighting Old Battles

According to Erikson, the teen years represent the culmination of each of the earlier conflicts that, if resolved, have resulted in a teenager acquiring trust, autonomy, initiative, and industry. Even so, Erikson said the teenager may have to "refight" these earlier battles to integrate the different aspects of self together into a new self-identity. Also vital: this self-identity has to work for the teenager in the context of his social milieu. The central new conflict Erikson defined for this period is "ego identity versus identity diffusion." In contemporary psychological terms "ego" refers to "self."

How does a teenager acquire a coherent self-identity? In Erikson's view, his self-identity gains real strength only from "wholehearted and consistent recognition of real accomplishments." These he described as "achievements that have meaning in their culture." They might include high grades, making the football team, building a home as a volunteer for Habitat for Humanity, or all of the above.

If such avenues for expression and recognition are denied, Erikson warned, a teenager "will resist with the astonishing strength encountered in animals who are suddenly forced to defend their lives." This thwarted drive to belong and succeed, he said, is what creates the cliques and gangs of America's cities and fiercely nationalistic movements in other societies.

Ego Identity vs. Identity Diffusion

Erikson saw negative adolescent behaviors such as intolerance for differences among their peers, even acts of cruelty, as a "defense against a sense of identity diffusion." He explained that in the face of so many body changes and a self-identity in flux, it is difficult for a teenager to be tolerant of others and himself. He said, "Deep down you are not quite sure that you are a man (or a woman), that you will ever grow together again and be attractive, that you will be able to master your drives, that you really know who you are." The fundamental tension is between developing a solid sense of oneself and feeling insecure, vulnerable, and threatened.

Finally, Erikson advocated for better psychological diagnosis and treatment for even those adolescents who appear to have gone furthest off track. He believed that criminal or delinquent behaviors don't have the same grim significance in adolescence as they do in adulthood.

Inside the Teen Brain

Although many signs of approaching puberty are obvious, the largest as yet unseen transformation is occurring inside the adolescent brain. Right before age 12, the brain's gray matter thickens and expands, mostly in the frontal lobes involved in planning, reasoning, and impulse control. The white matter that connects the brain's different regions—such as the more emotion-bound amygdala to the frontal lobes—also is still growing, thus not yet reliable.

Until age 19 or 20, these new nerve cells lack a full coat of myelin. Myelin is a fatty substance that acts like insulation on an electric wire, making the transmission of information efficient. This means any strong emotion, especially when additional stress is added, gets stuck in the amygdala rather than moving to the frontal cortex where it can be processed with logic and reason. This accounts for the impulsive nature of most teens, as well as their tendency to make immature judgments. It also sheds light on an adolescent's emotional volatility and fragile impulse control.

What Was He Thinking?

On top of everything else happening in a teenager's life, there's a lot of thinking going on. According to Piaget, this is when cognitive development, the ability to think and reason, reaches its fullest potential. He called adolescence the stage of "formal operational thought." Piaget said that two abilities define this stage of thought:

- Hypothetico-deductive reasoning
- Abstract thought

Together these abilities form the basis of the scientific method. To test a child's grasp of this level of cognitive skills, Piaget used several tasks, many of which involved physics or chemistry.

The Pendulum Swings

Piaget's most famous test to determine the presence or absence of *hypothetico-deductive reasoning* was his "pendulum problem." Children of different ages were given a set of weights and strings of different lengths. The weights could be hung from the strings and swung like pendulums. Investigators asked the children to determine what caused the pendulums to swing at different rates. Was it the length of the string, the amount of the weight, or how high the weight was held before being released?

DEFINITION

Hypothetico-deductive reasoning is the ability to use deductive reasoning, going from general to specific facts and then systematically manipulate variables and test their effects to reach correct conclusions in complex problems. Hypothetico refers to the ability to formulate a possibility that can be tested.

Younger children still in the concrete operational thinking stage are not good at systematically testing each of these variables. They tend to come to whatever conclusion occurs to them after only a few tries. In contrast, adolescents using formal operations begin by testing all the variables in every possible combination, reasoning that any one factor could be responsible for the speed of the weights. They then systematically test one factor at a time, holding the other variables constant, until they arrive at the correct answer. This is the systematic manipulation of variables to test effects to reach the right solution.

Formal Operations

A 14-year-old, unlike her 8-year-old brother, can easily contemplate the intangible or mere possibilities. This is an advantage when considering a problem like the pendulum test. But it also makes teenagers' lives more complicated when they're deciding what to wear to a dance or what to say to a friend. Piaget believed that formal operational thought arrived incrementally throughout adolescence, not all at once. He felt that the most advanced ability to manipulate variables systematically did not arrive until the age of 17 or 18.

During this stage of formal operations, adolescents are capable of thinking abstract thoughts about such heady concepts as truth, justice, and fairness. They also eventually learn that any of these concepts can hold different meanings for people. They then understand the concept of subjectivity. Again, in contrast, a younger child might insist there is one and only one "right answer" to a social or moral problem.

Egocentric Thoughts

Piaget also saw an adolescent's judgment as a work in progress. This is especially evident, he said, in the area of subjectivity versus objectivity. He defined adolescent egocentricism as the young person's tendency to not fully grasp the differences between his own and another person's abstract reasoning. Piaget pointed to this egocentricism in two main areas:

* Adolescents believe that other people are as concerned with their behavior, thoughts, and feelings as they are themselves. This can translate into the extreme self-consciousness common to the teenage years. Piaget called this a teenager's "imaginary audience."

* Adolescents also tend to believe that their own abstract thoughts are unique—that no one has ever had such a brilliant idea before them. In this same category which Piaget called "personal fable," you can put the teenager's often ill-advised sense of invulnerability. This leads to self-deception when a teenager engages in risky behavior such as drinking and driving or having unprotected sex.

INSIGHT

In studies done in the United States and France involving tests of concrete operations, today's adolescents perform better than their parents' generation. This is similar to the 3 percent increase in worldwide IQ scores during the past 60 years. Both of these measures of higher intelligence are too large and they occurred in too short a time to be explained by evolution. Other possible explanations include improved education, nutrition, and health care.

Piaget's critics say that he overestimated the abilities of most adolescents and adults. Based on studies done in the 1980s, these researchers found that only 50 to 60 percent of 18- to 20-year-olds in industrialized countries used formal operations. Later in his career, Piaget himself speculated that all adults are capable of reasoning at the level of formal operations. But they only use this level of reasoning when they are solving problems that hold their interest or are of vital personal interest. What do you think? Do you use these thinking processes in the way that Piaget described them?

With the foundation provided by Erikson and Piaget, you can now add insights gained through the more recent understanding of the biochemistry of adolescence. With their immature neurons and oversized emotions, teens get the double whammy of dealing with their changing bodies and the volatile chemistry of their first romantic attractions. For this tsunami of changes, you can blame (or credit) the sex hormones.

Hormonal Onslaught

Pre-puberty is the relative lull before the storm. For girls starting at age 8, and boys by 10, pre-pubescent bodies begin subtle changes which lead to major transformations that are in full swing by age 12. Some of these changes are not complete until the mid-twenties.

Blame the Sex Hormones

Testosterone and estrogen are the producers and directors of these blockbuster body and mind shifts. Before puberty, boys and girls have these hormones in basically the same amounts circulating through their bloodstreams. But when testosterone spikes in boys, reaching 20 times as much as the girls, and the estrogen/progesterone cycle begins in girls, the common denominator between the two sexes is their massive hormonal transformation. Although a hormone doesn't make you do something, it raises the likelihood that you will under certain circumstances.

It is in adolescence that you first get to see the amazing power of hormones to alter mind and body. But, this isn't the first time testosterone and estrogen have brought about structural changes in this same boy and girl. While in their mother's womb, every fetus according to her or his DNA is exposed to testosterone or estrogen, which creates the blueprint of the male or female brain. However, estrogen is not nearly as important as the absence of testosterone because girls have the brains that boys would have if the developing male fetus did not produce and get exposed to testosterone. This drenching of males with hormones causes the prenatal growth of sex-typed receptors on their nerve cells in the brain and on other organs.

Gender-Based Brain Changes

During middle childhood, the structural divergence in boys' and girls' brains shows up in physical, cognitive, and behavioral differences. Girls spend more of their time in bonding activities, and take the lead in learning and language skills. Boys are more active and physical; in play, boys may demonstrate perceptual and spatial advantages. One thing boys and girls have in common during the years 6 to 12: they tend to avoid each other in favor of the company of their own sex. That is certain to change, and soon.

Girls First

With girls in the lead by about two years, puberty arrives. The chemical brakes are taken off a girl's hormonal system, which has been held in check since she was a toddler. With puberty, a girl's brain is programmed so that, near age 12, waves of estrogen trigger her breasts to swell and her ovaries to start menstruation. She starts a transformation into womanhood typically beginning with a budding fascination for boys and a fixation on her own developing sex appeal.

A New Female Cycle

At the tender age of about 12 (depending on such factors as ethnicity, urban vs. rural location, present or absent father) the up-and-down mood and energy cycles that accompany a girl's menstrual periods also begin. It is easy enough for most girls to ride the elevated mood and energy levels of the first week and a half leading to ovulation. With this upswing in estrogen, menstruating girls tend to be emotionally buoyant and intellectually sharper. They're keen to bond emotionally with their girl friends and enjoy flirting with boys.

After the midpoint of their periods, called ovulation, these buoyant feelings start to decrease. These young females come up against a sharp drop in estrogen and a rise in progesterone, wreaking havoc with their moods and energy levels. By week four, many encounter cramps and headaches, along with sudden feelings of irritability and a desire to be left alone. This is the peak period in the teen month for fights between girls and their parents.

Girls Mature Earlier

In 1900, when the great-grandmother of today's typical college student was born, a pubescent girl didn't have her first menstrual period until the age of 15. The same student's grandmother probably got her first period at age 14, and the student's mother, coming of age in the 1950s or 1960s, probably reached the age of menstruation at 13. Today's average age has slipped to 12½. What's going on?

It is thought that this trend of girls' earlier maturation has to do with better nutrition and advances in medical care. Within modern societies where girls receive poor nutrition, they mature into menstruation later, just as their great-grandmothers did. Also, girls who are overweight or tall tend to mature faster.

Changing Relationships

As Judith Harris pointed out in her book *The Nurture Assumption*, peers strongly influence teenagers' interests, fashions, and behavior. Their social lives are oriented around people of the same age.

Even though getting a boy to notice her is one of an adolescent girl's highest priorities, she quickly discovers that it's her girlfriends who share her need and facility for intense verbal interaction. This pattern is one that a majority of women keep for life.

However, not all of girls' relationships are positive. As competition for finding a suitable boy to date begins, girls may begin to ostracize each other, spread rumors about a rival's sexual history, and verbally insult each other. Unlike boys, the nature of competition among girls often is indirect, as though they want to disguise the fact that they are competing at all. Measuring how girls compete with each other has been problematic for psychologists because it is difficult to put a number on a well-worded put down or on the causes of ostracism or rejection.

Becoming a Man

Beginning in puberty, a boy's brain is wired to receive testosterone to order activity of his testicles and bulking up of his shoulders, along with a narrowing of his hips. Testosterone in boys builds up their bulk, increasing the capacity of the body to store calcium, phosphorus, and other elements essential for the growth and repair of bones and muscles.

For boys, growth spurts, physical strength, and sexual awareness tend to come sooner and to a greater degree than girls. Boys start to find ways to stand out from the pack and show off for the benefit of girls, and sometimes this involves taking dangerous risks or physical violence. They also crave independence and respect from their male peers. Many of these adolescent male behaviors become lifelong patterns for adult men.

A Boy's Emotional Rollercoaster

Adolescent boys can be as moody as girls, spending time each day in front of the mirror and obsessing about their appearance. Boys this age (and from here on) tend to talk less than girls, even less than they may have talked before puberty set in. Most boys prefer nonverbal activities, such as videogames and driving cars. Fortunately, boys can also work off their excess testosterone through sustained athletic activity.

A typical adolescent boy tends to act out his emotions physically rather than verbally. The aggression pathway in a young male's brain is tied to direct physical action, whereas a girl's appears to be more closely linked to cognitive and verbal functions.

Teen Male Sexuality

Testosterone rivets boys' thoughts and emotions to the subject of sex. Given the chance, teenage boys will ogle girls' bodies in person, in print, or on screen. With a steady stream of testosterone flowing through their brains and bodies, not fluctuating as estrogen does in a girl's monthly cycle, teenage boys are basically primed for sex all the time. And, unlike girls who often have to be emotionally aroused before sex, boys are often most aroused by visual stimulation, such as seeing a naked body.

Boys' sexuality differs from girls' beginning in adolescence. Whereas affection and touching is enough for most girls at this age, the teen boy's skyrocketing testosterone leads him directly to genital sex—if not in reality, at least in his imagination.

INSIGHT

Why does the United States have the highest adolescent birth rate among industrialized countries? In 2009, 145,000 girls 17 and younger gave birth; more than 6,000 were 14 or younger. The Urban Institute found that poverty is less important than the behavior of her own parents in influencing an adolescent girl's chances of becoming pregnant. Almost one third of all sexually experienced adolescent girls have been pregnant.

Sexual Orientation

Puberty arrives with a blast of sex hormones, but well before typical teenagers have sex, they are fantasizing about their future romantic and sexual partners. This holds true for young people of every sexual orientation. Both homosexuals and heterosexuals say that their sexual orientation was present to some extent in childhood in the form of fantasies about a mate of either the same or opposite sex. Later in puberty, but before they were actually having sex other than masturbation, these fantasies evolved into attractions. You might consider when you experienced such fantasies. They were likely present even if you were not aware of their meaning at the time. By adolescence sexual orientation is clearly an important part of one's self-identity.

Few subjects have historically garnered as much debate and controversy as the question of why an estimated 3 to 6 percent of men prefer a male lover and a slightly lower percentage of women prefer a female sex partner. What is known for sure is that there are homosexuals in every culture and many animal species as well. Also known is that genetic differences play a large role (many believe the largest role) in determining sexual orientation. Roughly 50 percent of identical twins share the same sexual orientation. And given that the other 50 percent do not, you must allow for environmental influences as well. It comes down to this: homosexuality is a quality you discover about yourself and not a lifestyle you choose for yourself. A person's sexual preference is determined by genes, life experience, and opportunity.

Homosexuality and the Field of Psychology

Psychology did not provide leadership on this issue until the 1980s when science finally overtook the religious, social, and cultural biases which had previously dominated the field. Until 1973, homosexuality was classified as a mental disorder in the *Diagnostic and Statistical Manual of Mental Disorders* (DSM). After 1975, this designation was removed.

Today, when sexual orientation is associated with a teenager's higher risk for depression or anxiety, the cause is usually a fear of discrimination or rejection from family and friends. There also is the real threat of bullying of gay and lesbian youth by their homophobic peers, now with Internet and social media being used by bullies to further persecute and ostracize gay youth. This form of violence against homosexual youth has been associated with a rise in suicides by gay teenagers.

A Contrary Gender Identity

Although controversial, the field of psychology still classifies one type of gender identity difference as a disorder. The teenager or young adult who would be given the neutral label of "transgender" by the Gay, Lesbian, Bisexual, and Transgender (GLBT) movement may—if gender confusion causes sufficient emotional distress and functional impairment—qualify for a diagnosis of "gender identity disorder" in the DSM.

In many cases, this preference of boys to be girls or girls to be boys arises in early childhood. In order for this behavior to be considered abnormal, it must go well beyond simple curiosity or experimenting with opposite gender behavior. Rigid cross-dressing and extreme discomfort with one's own gender identity are typical early indications of a serious problem.

By late adolescence or adulthood, about three quarters of boys who had a childhood history of gender identity disorder report a homosexual or bisexual orientation and no longer have a gender identity disorder. The corresponding percentages for girls with a gender identity disorder in childhood or adolescence are not known. Some adolescents may develop clear cross-gender identification and request sex-change surgery.

Roadblocks in Adolescence

Because of the number and scope of the biochemical changes and the cognitive maturation that doesn't always keep up with other drives, adolescent boys and girls have a much greater chance than younger persons of getting derailed during these intense growth years. The vulnerabilities are greatest around the teen's self-identity and blossoming sexuality. These first romantic relationships can set their expectations and patterns in love for a long time to come.

The two sources of a teen's most distressing emotions and irrational actions are …

- Not being accepted by their same-sex friends.
- Not being attractive or appealing to the opposite sex.

Much of teenagers' worst behaviors are attempts to compensate for these fears and anxieties. Boys may display a notorious lack of judgment when it comes to their physical safety. Girls are especially susceptible to eating disorders and self-destructive behaviors, such as cutting. A minority of adolescent boys and girls experiment with illegal drugs and alcohol to fit in and to cope with their own unruly emotions.

Secrets and Lies

Psychological researchers Nancy Darling and Linda Caldwell at Pennsylvania State University studied high school students to determine the facts about how much they lie to their parents. Among their findings: a full 96 percent of students surveyed admitted lying to their parents. The average teenager lies or withholds information on 12 of 36 topics ranging from how they spend their allowance and underage drinking to boy-girl relationships. The biggest surprise: most deception takes place between ages 14 and 15, not among older teens. The study's conclusion: teenage deception is not usually a harmful thing. "By withholding information about their lives, adolescents carve out a social domain and an identity that are theirs alone."

Eating Disorders

In the last 100 years, unlike in previous centuries, Western culture has put a premium on thinness, many believe to an extreme. Most adolescent girls are not satisfied with their physical appearance, and many diet to control their weight. One unfortunate result is the increased number of eating disorders primarily affecting teenage girls and women. According to recent research, approximately 1 of 100 adolescent girls is anorexic, two to three times as many are bulimic, and 1 in 5 are overweight. Researchers believe that adolescents inherit emotional tendencies that make them more vulnerable to eating disorders. These can combine with the low self-esteem and high level of stress experienced by many teenagers and affect their eating habits. For many adolescents with an eating disorder, food is one of the only things in their lives they feel they can control.

Anorexia is a serious, potentially life-threatening disorder marked by a distorted body image; it's when someone, most often a female, believes she is grossly fat when she's average or even thin. She has an intense fear of gaining weight and refuses to eat or just eats enough to survive. Anorexia usually appears between the ages of 14 and 18.

Bulimia is an equally serious eating disorder that involves binge eating, followed by purging (forced vomiting), fasting, or excessive exercise. The bulimic teenager has the same irrational fear that she is or may become obese as the anorexic teen. Bulimia tends to arrive later in adolescence than anorexia.

Although eating disorders have primarily affected females, there is growing concern about body dissatisfaction and related behaviors among male adolescents. This manifests as an increase in the use of anabolic steroids and untested supplements used by males to increase their muscle mass.

The most common eating disorder is obesity. The prevalence of obesity between ages 6 to 11 years increased from 6.5 percent in 1980 to 19.6 percent in 2008. The prevalence of obesity between ages 12 to 19 years increased from 5 percent to 18 percent. Obese children and youth are at greater risk for bone and joint problems, sleep apnea, and social and psychological problems such as stigmatization and poor self-esteem. Obese youth are likely to become overweight or obese adults and be at risk for associated adult health problems, including heart disease, type two diabetes, stroke, several types of cancer, and osteoarthritis.

Treatment for Eating Disorders

Psychological therapy and medications have been used to help adolescents recover from anorexia and bulimia. When there is a related depression or anxiety disorder, antidepressants are often prescribed. If the eating disorder is severe—the teenager's weight is 25 percent less than the average for her height and age—hospitalization may be required. Then food can be introduced and intensive therapy given.

A low-carbohydrate diet with exercise is the most effective and lasting treatment for obesity. Unfortunately, high sugar and high carbohydrate drinks and foods are the most available and least costly for most young people.

The Addicted Teenager

The same pressures and insecurities that lead adolescents to develop eating disorders make them vulnerable to *addiction* to drugs or alcohol. The numbers show that the problem of teen substance use is serious and starting earlier.

DEFINITION

Addiction is the compulsive need to use a habit-forming substance or an irresistible urge to engage in a behavior. Two other important defining features of addiction are tolerance, the increasing need for more of the substance to obtain the same effect, and withdrawal, the unpleasant symptoms that arise when an addict is prevented from using the chosen substance. The word "addiction" is used loosely, but it has a specific meaning in a psychological context.

Teens Abusing Substances

Substance abuse continues to afflict American teenagers, with a dangerous trend toward use of marijuana and other illegal drugs at earlier ages. The National

Longitudinal Study of Adolescent Health found that suburban high school students drink, smoke, use illegal drugs, and engage in delinquent behavior as often or more than urban high school students:

- About 37 percent of suburban twelfth graders have smoked at least once a day compared to 30 percent of urban twelfth graders.

- Around 63 percent of suburban and 57 percent of urban twelfth graders drink away from family members.

- About 40 percent of twelfth graders in both urban and suburban schools have used illegal drugs.

- Urban and suburban students are equally likely to engage in fighting and stealing.

- Half of adolescents have attended parties where drugs and alcohol were available. One third have attended a party at which alcohol, marijuana, cocaine, ecstasy, or prescription drugs were available while a parent was present.

Alcohol Dependency and Abuse

More adolescents in the United States drink alcohol than smoke tobacco or marijuana. Underage drinking accounted for at least 16 percent of alcohol sales in 2009.

Every year, over 5,000 people younger than 21 die as a result of drinking, including 2,000 deaths from motor vehicle crashes; 1,600 from homicide; 300 from suicide; and 1,200 from other injuries, such as falls, burns, and drownings.

In 2007, 2 percent of eighth, 16 percent of tenth, and 28 percent of twelfth graders reported having five or more alcoholic beverages in a row in the last two weeks. Binge drinking by girls is increasing more rapidly than for boys. When compared with non-college-age peers, college students have higher binge drinking percentages (41 percent versus 34 percent).

Illegal Drug Abuse

In 2007, 9 percent, 17 percent, and 23 percent of students in grades 8, 10, and 12 used illicit drugs during the previous 30 days. The estimated abuse rates for illegal drugs are cocaine/crack (10 percent), ecstasy (8 percent), methamphetamine (8 percent), and heroin (5 percent).

Adolescents use over-the-counter drugs for recreation and prescription drugs for specific effects: stimulants for studying, sedatives for sleep, and tranquilizers to relieve stress. In 2007, nearly 20 percent of all adolescents reported abusing prescription medications. Nearly one third believed there is nothing wrong with using prescription medicines once in a while and that prescription pain relievers are not addictive.

Cigarette smoking during childhood and adolescence produces significant health problems among young people, including respiratory illnesses, diminished physical fitness, and retarded lung growth. About 90 percent of smokers begin before the age of 21. Most said they would like to quit, but are unable to do so.

Choosing a Career

How young people go about choosing a vocation or career has been extensively studied by psychologists. According to this research, self-identity is a primary force in an adolescent's choice of work. As Erikson underscored, a teenager's self-identity is influenced by what he likes, the success he has experienced, and the recognition he has received from others.

The most influential factors in an adolescent's choice of future work include the following:

- Parents who recognize their teenager's autonomy and encourage open discussion of interests and possible careers.

- Personal experimentation; teenagers who try different entry level jobs and avocations (hobbies).

- Culture; ethnic identity can be an important factor in which career choices are valued or dismissed.

Choosing a career usually happens in three phases that play out through the adolescent years.

Inspiration

This process begins at about age 13 or 14 when adolescents learn about ideas for possible future careers. An extroverted, highly social teenager may decide that working with people is a good career direction for him. Another student who excels at science or math bases her decision on that success. She may enjoy being in a laboratory doing scientific experiments. Others prefer the world of books and poetry. These early decisions are provisional; they may change when the time for choosing a college major or career actually arrives.

Specification

At about age 18, activities begun earlier usually continue or are dropped. This is the time when adolescents limit their career possibilities. They learn about potential jobs that match their strengths, real-world and school experience, and interests. They also may have begun obtaining education and/or on-the-job experience on the career track of their choice. The extroverted teenager who thought he'd like to work with people may choose a career in sales. The student who loved spending time in laboratories might get an internship as a laboratory assistant.

Implementation

Erik Erikson called attention to late adolescents' need for a "psychosocial moratorium" in which they have an opportunity to "take a time out" from a definitive career choice and "discover their purpose in the world." Many young people do this by going to college and engaging in extra-curricular activities. In addition, the Corporation for National and Community Service helps young people match their interests with opportunities in public and private service organizations, such as Vista, the Peace Corps, Teach for America, Americorps, and the military services.

When they are ready to seek full-time employment, young people learn first-hand about the available jobs that match their interests and training. Beyond the particular field and job they choose, these new workers also learn about getting along with fellow workers who may be quite different from them and work as part of a team. This third phase of the career selection process often is unstable. Reality may not match the dream an individual had back in the inspiration phase. At each stage there is a give and take between the young person's identity and his career.

Studies about what makes people happy and satisfied in midlife rate two things most highly: a vocation or job that matches their talents and interests and close relationships with significant others. Both of these life goals and the skills that make them possible are either furthered or derailed by the experiences of adolescence.

The Least You Need to Know

- A teenager's ability to think abstractly is limited by his egocentricism.
- An adolescent's immature brain, especially the lack of full myelin covering of developing neurons, partly explains his higher impulsivity and lack of judgment.
- A person's sexual behavior is determined by genes, life experience, and opportunity.
- Younger adolescents often withhold information from their parents in an effort to build an independent identity.
- A large minority of teenagers abuse alcohol and illegal drugs with a trend toward the use of marijuana at younger ages.
- Adolescent pregnancy and childbirth rates are the highest in the United States compared to other Western nations.

Issues in Child Psychology

As the field of child psychology acquires more tools and amasses expanding volumes of research, the issues it tackles grow in number and complexity. In this part, we cover some of the issues that have arisen in recent decades that reflect the increasing complexity of our world and the challenges faced by today's children. Among the topics we cover in Part 6 are: children's mental and learning disorders, child maltreatment and abuse, and the digital revolution in children's learning and play.

Children's Mental Disorders

In This Chapter

- Nature and nurture in children's mood disorders
- Behavior problems in childhood and later psychological disorders
- Early symptoms of major mental disorders
- Marijuana and psychosis in teenagers

In addition to studying normal development, child psychologists define the boundaries between normal and abnormal behavior in children and adolescents. This chapter assesses the most common mental disorders and reviews their symptoms, causes, and treatment. Then it takes an in-depth look at one anxiety disorder—obsessive-compulsive disorder (OCD)—to illustrate how the latest psychological research is being applied in the clinical treatment of children with this diagnosis. It then moves on to cover the major psychiatric disorders that may appear in later childhood or adolescence: bipolar disorder, schizophrenia, and pervasive developmental disorders, including autism. Finally, it looks at the frontiers of psychiatric research, including genetics, brain imaging, and family studies.

Classifying Mental Illness

More than one in five American children suffers from a diagnosable mental disorder. Drawing upon U.S. Surgeon General estimates, 13 percent of persons younger than 18 have one of nearly a dozen anxiety disorders, 10 percent have conduct disorders, 6 percent have mood disorders, and 3 percent have severe mood and thought disorders, such as bipolar disorder, schizophrenia, and autism.

There obviously are overlaps between these disorders. Another way of saying this is that the *comorbidity* rate for children with different disorders is high.

> **DEFINITION**
>
> **Comorbidity** refers to the existence of two or more disorders in the same person at the same time. For example, someone who has been diagnosed with both social anxiety disorder (SAD) and obsessive-compulsive disorder (OCD) is said to have comorbid SAD and OCD.

When a child suffers from multiple disorders, one disorder usually occurs first and dominates. For example, an anxiety disorder often precedes depression. It's also possible that long periods of anxiety and the accompanying social isolation may cause episodes of depression. In other words, being anxious can make people depressed.

The classification system for diagnosing mood and thought disorders and other psychiatric conditions is encoded in the so-called bible of psychology, the *Diagnostic and Statistical Manual of Mental Disorders* (DSM). The purpose of this manual is to present uniform standards for psychological diagnosis. The DSM lays out the criteria for matching a patient's symptoms with established mental disorders. Communicating through professional associations and journals, mental health professionals then devise standardized procedures to treat individuals with any of these diagnoses.

The Depressed Child

Major depression is a mood disorder, meaning the individual has a neurobiological problem that causes negative changes in behavior and related emotional states. The most salient symptom of depression is an inability to enjoy life due to an overwhelming sense of sadness. There are two types of depression. A mild to moderate level of depression that is more or less constant is called dysthymic disorder or dysthymia.

Depression that is more severe and occurs in episodes of two or more weeks is called clinical or major depression. Children and adolescents can have both types of depression at once. The symptoms of depression are the same in adults and children, but they often show up differently for people of different ages.

Depressed Preschoolers

When young children are clinically depressed they often are highly sensitive or irritable. They lack emotional resiliency and may take slights more personally. They cry often, seemingly without cause. Without sufficient vocabularies or self-awareness to articulate their feelings, younger children may "act out" their emotional suffering with negative behaviors. They may resist interactions with other children and teachers. They may sulk in a corner. Depressed preschoolers may commit self-destructive acts, such as banging their heads against a hard surface. A depressed child of this age often uses negative self-talk, saying such things as "I hate myself" or even "I want to die." All of these indications, particularly in the aggregate, should be taken seriously.

Depressed Teenagers

With the onslaught of the mood altering hormones of puberty, a child already experiencing bouts of depression often manifests more severe symptoms. Although most adolescents experience mood swings, teen depression has specific symptoms that may look like an exaggerated case of "typical" teenage angst, but are much more serious. For example, when a teenager stays in his room resisting contact with family and friends for extended periods of time, this is not normal adolescent behavior. Other signs may include: changes in appearance, trouble sleeping or too much sleep, changes in appetite, and the use of mood-altering substances, such as alcohol or cigarettes. In combination, these symptoms and behaviors indicate teen depression.

Causes of Childhood Depression

Researchers still have not reached consensus on a specific gene for depression. But that doesn't mean there isn't plenty of statistical evidence for a genetic connection. The most likely "cause" of depression is a combination of genetic vulnerabilities and environmental triggers. Twin and adoption studies done since the 1930s show that the chance of a sibling or offspring of someone with major depression developing the disorder is nearly twice that of the general population.

One study found that when one parent has a history of depression, her or his children have as much as a 26 percent greater chance of becoming depressed. When both parents are depressed, the risk goes up to 46 percent. Of course, when a depressed parent raises a child at genetic risk for depression, the blurred line between nature and nurture becomes harder to define. How much does the depressive personality of a mother or father shape the child who takes her emotional cues from that parent? When "normal" in a family translates into a state of depression, how does a child overcome his expectation to be like Mom or Dad?

A Biological Marker for Depression

A visible biological marker, akin to a blood test for diabetes, to confirm the diagnosis of clinical depression has been missing in the mental health field. In 2009, researchers at Columbia University Medical Center changed that when they came up with the first known biological marker for depression: the thinning of certain parts of the brain in persons who, because of their family history, were at risk for major depression.

In this largest-ever brain imaging study of depression, researchers imaged the brains of 131 subjects, ages 6 to 54, with and without a family history of depression. Structural brain differences were observed in the biological offspring of depressed subjects but not in the offspring of those who were not depressed. Investigators found a thinner cerebral cortex that may increase the risk of developing depression by diminishing a person's ability to interpret social cues and to pay attention. The risk of depression for study participants appeared to correlate with the degree and extent of their cortical thinning.

This study's findings suggest that if you have thinning in the right hemisphere of the brain, you may be predisposed to depression and may also have some cognitive and inattention issues. The more thinning you have, the greater the cognitive problems. If you have additional thinning in the same region of the left hemisphere, it seems to tip you over from having a vulnerability to developing symptoms of an overt illness. Thinning of both hemispheres appears to be linked to the manifestations of either depression or an anxiety disorder.

Treating the Depressed Child

The most successful treatments for depression have involved cognitive behavioral therapy (CBT). CBT focuses on changing the faulty thinking that produces or reinforces negative moods and self-defeating behaviors. For example, the thoughts of a depressed child that contain a nearly constant channel of negative self-talk including ideas like "I am worthless," "Nothing will ever get better in my life," or "I don't deserve to be happy" will reinforce a child's feeling of despair and hopelessness. The therapist then gently challenges these thoughts and helps the child change her negative thoughts to positive ones. Substituting a new stream of self-talk containing ideas like "I am okay the way I am" and "I can make friends" can dramatically improve a child's mood.

Track Record for Antidepressants

Severe cases of depression are most effectively treated with an antidepressant medication. For moderate to severely depressed patients, positive outcomes—meaning a significant drop in their symptoms of depression—are achieved for 75 percent of them after taking an antidepressant alone. Improvement from taking an antidepressant is not as consistent with mild depressions.

FIELD STUDY

In one major study, the improvement rate of 30 percent for mildly depressed patients taking an antidepressant was no better than the improvement shown by those who had been given a placebo.

The combination of antidepressant and CBT shows the highest rate of long-term mood stabilization for moderate to severely depressed persons, including adolescents. CBT combined with lifestyle changes can be enough to treat adults and children with milder cases of depression. Lifestyle changes that have been effective in reducing the symptoms of depression include an altered diet containing less-refined sugar and carbohydrates, more exercise, stress reduction, and in the case of a shy younger child, the help of parents and teachers in enhancing social activities.

Roadblocks to Treatment

Sometimes adults can't tell the difference between normal childhood sadness, adolescent mood swings, and the signs of mild or major depression. Another obstacle to getting kids the help they need for depression is a lack of faith in treatment options. Fortunately, the trend seems to be moving in the direction of greater understanding of the signs of depression and the benefits received from treatment.

Only 38 percent of people in 1994 believed that depression is a treatable disease, whereas in 2004 that number had grown to 55 percent. Among women, whose own rate of depression is nearly twice that of men, and who are usually the ones seeking help for a depressed child, the number was higher—64 percent.

Still, current research indicates that around 40 percent of children and adolescents who receive a diagnosis of depression don't get treated for it. One study puts the number of adolescents who need but don't receive an appropriate diagnosis and treatment for depression at 70 to 80 percent. The diagnosis of depression may come about after a drug overdose or a suicide attempt brings a person to an emergency room, or the diagnosis may arise from a pediatric visit. Follow-through from diagnosis to treatment is still a hurdle for many. Reasons for not getting treatment include a lack of access to adequate mental health care and the stigma associated with admitting one has a mental illness.

Common Childhood Anxiety Disorders

Everyone, including teenagers and younger children, experiences passing bouts of anxiety. In contrast, those whose day-to-day routines are disrupted by long periods of anxiety lasting for days and even weeks probably suffer from an anxiety disorder. Examples of fears that can escalate and become disabling include: fear of leaving the house, fear of interacting with other people, fear of contamination, an inability to concentrate on a task, an unreasonable fear of becoming fat, and a generalized feeling of anxiety that makes one's life basically dysfunctional.

INSIGHT

More than three quarters of young adults who have psychiatric disorders were first diagnosed between the ages of 11 and 18 years. The comorbidity of an anxiety disorder with depression and substance abuse during adolescence predicts a greater likelihood of any one or all three of these conditions continuing into adulthood. One half of adults with a mental disorder had symptoms that began before the age of 14.

Social Anxiety

Up to 3 percent of children and adolescents have social anxiety disorder, also called social phobia. This cluster of fears about being negatively judged or scrutinized by others (adults and other children) can cripple a child both academically and socially. For example, if a child is too self-conscious to ask a teacher for clarification of an assignment, his school performance will suffer.

Social anxiety often overlaps with general anxiety disorder (GAD). Generalized anxiety is believed to affect up to 6 percent of children and manifests as chronic or exaggerated worry and unjustified anticipation of disasters. GAD often includes physical symptoms such as nausea and headaches.

INSIGHT

Research shows that although more girls are affected by depression in middle childhood and early adolescence, school-age boys more commonly have an anxiety disorder.

Separation Anxiety Disorder

Many children experience separation anxiety between 18 months and 3 years, when it is normal to feel some anxiety when a parent leaves the room or goes out of sight. It's also common for a child to cry when first being left at daycare or preschool. If a child is older and unable to leave a family member or takes longer to calm down after separation than other children, then the problem could be a separation anxiety disorder. Other symptoms include refusing to go to school, camp, or a sleepover. This disorder is most common in kids ages 7 to 9 and affects about 4 percent of children.

Phobias

A phobia is the intense, irrational fear of a specific object—such as a dog—or a situation—such as flying. Common childhood phobias include fears of animals, storms, heights, water, blood, the dark, and medical procedures. Children try to avoid situations or things they fear or endure them with anxious feelings, such as crying, tantrums, clinging, avoidance, headaches, and stomachaches. Unlike adults, they do not usually recognize that their fear is irrational. Phobias occur in up to 3 percent of children.

Panic Disorder

Panic disorder is diagnosed in children and adolescents who experience seemingly out-of-the-blue, overwhelming attacks of anxiety and are preoccupied with the fear of a recurring attack. Panic attacks occur unexpectedly even during sleep. A panic attack is defined as the abrupt onset of intense fear that reaches a peak within a few minutes and includes symptoms such as heart palpitations, shortness of breath or a smothering feeling, a fear of losing control or "going crazy," and a fear of dying. These attacks usually are related to traumatic events and occur in the context of other anxiety disorders.

Obsessive-Compulsive Disorder

Obsessive-compulsive disorder (OCD) is a neurobiological condition marked by persistent, intrusive thoughts (obsessions) and behaviors (compulsions). The most common symptoms are repetitive thoughts about personal hygiene, an extreme and excessive need for order, persistent counting of things or events, frequent unfounded fearful thoughts about natural phenomena, magical thinking concerning one's power to influence events, and sometimes extreme religiosity. Up to 3 percent of children and adolescents have OCD.

OCD symptoms typically manifest at two developmental stages in young people, with onset often, but not always, linked to gender. For early school-age children, OCD appears most commonly around 7 years of age and more frequently in boys than girls. The second common age for OCD to appear is adolescence, when girls are more likely to develop symptoms. There also are children of both genders who show OCD symptoms as young as 3 or 4 years of age.

OCD as a Family Illness

There's no doubt about OCD running in families. If any of his first-tier relatives (parents, siblings) have OCD, a child's risk of developing the disorder increases more than four times the rate of its occurrence in the general population.

A study of relatives of children with OCD at the National Institute of Mental Health showed that 17 percent of parents and 5 percent of siblings met diagnostic criteria for the disorder. The authors of this study speculated that by loosening criteria to a wider spectrum of symptom severity, a full 30 percent of the children with OCD would have a close family member who also manifests the disorder.

A Tour of the Brain with OCD

Using advanced brain imaging, scientists can try to pinpoint the most likely pathway in the brain which, when malfunctioning, prompts the symptoms of OCD. This OCD pathway involves three key interacting locations in the brain.

First, the frontal cortex, located behind the eyes, regulates behavior, processing stimuli from deep within the brain. It activates thought and behavioral processes in other parts of the brain, for example those regulating thought and emotions, such as the caudate nucleus.

Second, the caudate nucleus is located in the middle of the brain in the basal ganglia, where it monitors danger signals by separating relevant from irrelevant information and by regulating "automatic" behaviors (those not requiring additional brain processing, such as walking or brushing teeth). It then sends those signals requiring action on to the thalamus.

Third, the thalamus, the main switchboard of this neural pathway, screens incoming signals from the caudate nucleus and sends alarm signals back to the frontal cortex, signaling when and to what degree it should react. It is thought that in the brains of people with OCD, the caudate nucleus receives a flood of danger signals disproportionate to the external stimuli from the frontal cortex. Unable to process this overload, the caudate nucleus sends these unfiltered signals on to the thalamus, which in turn sends a deluge of alarm messages back to the frontal cortex. This puts the brain of a child with OCD in a vicious circle of overload.

The Serotonin Connection

Scientists suggest that the link between these three key brain locations lies in the neurotransmitter serotonin, which brain imaging has shown to be at a lower level in people with OCD. In the language of brain science, there is a premature "reuptake" of serotonin in the synapses between brain neurons. This results in less serotonin in the synapses. This shortage of serotonin disrupts processing signals and turns what should be an automatic or normal response into a false alarm or "high alert."

Using a traffic analogy, a low level of serotonin causes the brain to fail in activating a critical stoplight. This malfunction allows too much traffic, in this case danger signals, to enter the intersection, creating the equivalent of a crash or "brain lock." The result is an overreaction to stimuli, which in the case of a child with OCD threaten her and cause her symptoms. Antidepressants containing a serotonin booster are commonly used to treat OCD.

OCD and the Plastic Brain

How this so-called "brain lock" turns into the debilitating disorder called OCD has to do with the repetition and reinforcement of signals along this neural pathway. When a child responds over and over to an obsessive thought by performing a compulsive ritual, it reinforces the brain pathway associated with the OCD symptom. An axiom in neurology says, "neurons that fire together, wire together." This refers to the plasticity of the brain, meaning the brain can be changed by the ways people habitually think and behave.

All of this has important implications for OCD treatment as well as the treatment of other anxiety and mood disorders, especially in children whose brains are more plastic than those of adults. Treatment, both by cognitive behavioral therapy and medication, actually causes improvements in brain functioning. This happens when either or both forms of treatment weaken old patterns of neural pathways and form new ones.

Treatment of Anxiety Disorders

When treating children with anxiety disorders, therapists often use "exposure therapy," also called "exposure response therapy" or ERT. This approach, used individually or in groups of people dealing with anxiety, gradually exposes a person to the thing she fears. This can be, for example, the use of a public bathroom or any social encounter until her fears lessen. Role playing within exposure therapy groups allows participants to act out and conquer the situations they fear. Outcome data from the use of exposure therapy for anxiety disorders is strongly positive. This is encouraging in that this form of therapy can be effective without the use of medication even with young children.

Major Psychiatric Disorders in Children

Bipolar disorder is classified as a mood disorder, whereas schizophrenia is a thought disorder. A child, adolescent, or adult with either of these diagnoses can have psychotic episodes, including auditory (most commonly) or visual hallucinations.

Bipolar Disorder

Some children are troubled by alternating depressed and elevated moods. The child's mood undergoes large swings, shifting from one extreme to the other. Such children are said to be "cycling" between a high mood, also called "mania," and a low state of depression. Bipolar disorder usually shows up in late adolescence or early adulthood, but it also can appear in younger children. It may begin in childhood as depression with or without periods of extreme irritation or as attention-deficit/hyperactivity disorder, covered in Chapter 17 on children's learning disorders.

FIELD STUDY

Researchers at Stanford University's Pediatric Bipolar Clinic suggest that if a grandparent has bipolar disorder a grandchild has a much higher likelihood of having an anxiety disorder or attention-deficit disorder by elementary school age. If that child is not treated with therapy and/or medication, he has a nearly 50 percent chance of developing full-blown bipolar disorder by the age of 15. If he does receive treatment, that likelihood is far lower, and if he does develop it, the severity is less.

During a manic episode, a child with bipolar disorder has a distorted and grandiose view of herself. This can lead to dangerous risk taking; for example, believing she can fly like Superman. She may talk constantly and be unable to concentrate on one activity. Bipolar disorder is increasingly being diagnosed and treated at younger ages. Treatment of children as young as 5 with psychotropic medications for this disorder has become controversial, leading to subdividing childhood bipolar disorder into multiple diagnoses with more clearly defined symptoms and specific treatments.

Schizophrenia

Schizophrenia is a serious form of mental illness characterized by disturbances in logical thinking, emotional expression, and interpersonal behavior. The cardinal symptoms are ...

- **Illogical thinking**—Thoughts that don't make sense.
- **Loose associations**—Unconnected shifts from one thing to another.

- **Hallucinations**—Hearing or seeing someone or something that isn't there.

- **Delusions**—Rigidly held false, illogical beliefs.

Schizophrenia affects 1 percent of the population worldwide and has a large genetic component as revealed by twin studies. Children who have a biological parent who has schizophrenia have a much higher likelihood of developing it even if they are raised by nonbiological parents.

Earliest Signs

The typical age of onset for schizophrenia is in the late teens and early twenties. There also are rare cases of severe early onset schizophrenia occurring in children as young as 5. Recent large-scale studies of youth with a family history of schizophrenia are providing evidence of sub-threshold symptoms of schizophrenia occurring in pubescent children, as young as 12 and even 8 years of age. In response to the recognition of early signs of schizophrenia in younger people, a number of university-affiliated hospitals in the United States, Europe, Denmark, Sweden, and Australia/New Zealand have combined treatment and research projects to further study the first signs of schizophrenia and bipolar disorder. These hospitals also provide early intervention and treatment for these young people.

Pinning Down Risk Factors

Another outcome of the convergence of these high-risk youth studies has been a wealth of new data on the lifestyles of those youth who go on to develop a full-blown version of schizophrenia versus those who do not. Factors that add to risk include the following:

- **Negative life events**—These include any experiences or events in a young person's life that bring high stress or grief; for example, a divorce or death in the family, bullying, extreme poverty, homelessness, child abuse, and a parent's major psychiatric illness.

- **Marijuana**—Attention of researchers has recently centered on marijuana (cannabis) as a factor adding considerable risk to young people already vulnerable to psychosis because of their family history. A New Zealand–based study found that smoking cannabis before the age of 15 increased the risk of schizophrenia from 3 percent to 10 percent by age 26. The study concluded that there is a minority of teenagers who are particularly vulnerable. This is backed up by evidence from Greece in which children with disturbed thought processes at age 11 were at a 25 percent risk of psychosis if they didn't go on to take cannabis and a 50 percent risk if they did.

The most likely reason for the greater vulnerability of teenagers and young adults to the effects of marijuana is that their brains, especially the frontal lobes, are still developing and thus more susceptible to external chemical influences. Given the fact that teenagers are using marijuana at increasingly younger ages, this link between marijuana smoking and early psychosis is being viewed as an increasingly serious public health threat.

Pervasive Developmental Disorders (PDD)

As stressed throughout this book, babies and children need social and inter-personal contact with others. They need interactive opportunities to give and receive spoken language, eye contact, and touch as much as they need food and water. However, children with a pervasive developmental disorder, a category that includes autism, have mild to severe limitations in each of these sense-dependent interpersonal abilities. As a result of their disorders, these children often manifest an inability to respond to touch and other forms of interpersonal contact.

Autism

Autism is a developmental and communication disorder that often is apparent from early infancy when eye contact is avoided. The typical autistic child is aloof and unresponsive to other people. His speech is usually difficult to understand with short bursts of clarity. The prevalence of early infantile autism is probably 1 percent of the population up to 15 years of age. The ratio of boys to girls is about four to one.

Autism may be suspected if a child exhibits any of the following behaviors or characteristics:

- Withdrawn, aloof
- Doesn't like to be held

- Resists touch and cuddling

- Avoids eye contact

- Scarcity of social smiling

- Plays alone by choice

- Exaggerated responses to loud noises

- Engages in odd or ritualistic behaviors; for example, has to touch parts of the room in a certain order

- Has strong taste aversions; eats limited foods

- Less speech than average child or none

- Makes strange body movements; for example, repeated rocking, whirling, teeth grinding, and head banging

As this list of symptoms illustrates, autism can be disabling. Children with autism typically score in the retarded range on IQ tests. However, because their speech and communication skills are often limited, their intelligence is not properly measured by these tests.

Strides forward in the treatment of autism have been made in recent decades with a greater emphasis on early recognition and treatment with various forms of therapy. When a 6-month-old baby avoids eye contact, does not smile or babble, and shows an unusual interest in objects, the diagnosis of early infantile autism can be made and treatment involving parent and child instituted.

Asperger's Syndrome

This disorder shares many characteristics with autism. Children with Asperger's syndrome function at a higher level than autistic children. As with autistic children, they have problems with interpersonal and social relationships. They have little empathy with others and prefer solitary play. Many of these children strongly prefer interacting with objects to playing with or near other children. They tend to count things and focus on patterns.

Unlike autistic children, Asperger's children are usually proficient with language. They often talk by the age of 2. As they grow older, their speech patterns take on a monotone quality. Asperger's syndrome tends to cluster in families, with relatives showing varying degrees of the disorder or its symptoms. Not surprisingly, many adults with Asperger's syndrome gravitate to high technology professions.

Suicide and Teens

Suicide is a leading cause of death in adolescence. Up to 11 percent of all adolescents in the United States have attempted suicide at some point during their teenage years. Although adolescent suicide rates remain relatively high, there has been a decline during the past 10 years. The reasons for this are not well-understood, but a likely factor may be the increase in antidepressant use with adolescents in addition to suicide prevention programs. Still, one quarter of people younger than 18 with schizophrenia or bipolar disorder die by suicide.

Suicide goes beyond young people who are dealing with a severe mental disorder. Only up to 41 percent of people who commit suicide meet diagnostic criteria for major depression. Substance abuse disorders, panic disorders, social phobias, gender identity disorders, and borderline personality disorders also account for many suicides. Mental health practitioners should screen for suicidal thoughts in anyone who expresses pervasive hopelessness regardless of their diagnosis. It is important to note that someone who is contemplating suicide (showing suicidal ideation and perhaps planning it) usually speaks about it to close friends or family members. Any comments made about suicide should be taken seriously. Listening is important. Referrals to a local suicide hotline or outreach program should follow.

Conduct Disorders

This category of disorder has nothing to do with kids occasionally breaking the rules. A small but worrisome number of children and teens—believed to be up to 10 percent—engage in frequent, serious forms of negative acting out. They are considered to have a mental disorder. The specific behaviors in question range from persistent temper tantrums and aggression in young children to acts of cruelty toward animals and other people by older children and teenagers. These destructive, self-destructive, and often dangerous behavior patterns, which have existed for as long as the human species has kept records, meet the following two possible psychological diagnoses.

- Oppositional defiant disorder (ODD) consists of more than six months of rule breaking, temper tantrums, hostility toward authority, and school and home disruptions committed by a child.

- Conduct disorder (CD) applies when a youngster violates the rights or physical person of others. CD includes bullying, harming animals, destroying property, theft, assault, and other serious harmful behaviors.

These diagnoses are usually given to males, but are increasingly being applied to females who engage in similar behavior.

Children's Mental Disorders—Multiple Causes

Brain researchers now believe there are multiple genes and genetic mutations involved in a *predisposition* to the mental illnesses that occur in childhood, including the most common—depression and anxiety disorders—as well as bipolar disorder and schizophrenia.

DEFINITION

Predisposition is an inherited risk of developing a disease or condition. Having a genetic predisposition for a disease does not mean that you will get that disease, but your risk is higher than that of the general population. One can inherit a predisposition to breast or lung cancer as well as to mental illnesses.

Scientists who study mental illness believe that a predisposition is usually not enough to cause the onset of a mental illness. And a mental illness is not always traceable to a genetic inheritance. In many cases, predisposing environmental factors must be present in a child's environment for the brain disorder to manifest in symptoms.

Researching the Causes of Childhood Mental Disorders

Using functional magnetic brain imaging devices—known as fMRI—to directly observe the functioning brain of children and adults with diagnosed mental disorders, researchers measure changes in the size, thickness, connectivity, and activity levels of different locations in the brain both in "real time" and over spans of time. Some studies are even conducted post mortem. Then the brains of those with mental illnesses are compared to healthy brains and differences noted. For example, the hippocampus (memory center) of individuals diagnosed with schizophrenia has been found to be smaller than the hippocampus of normal brains. This finding is thought to correlate with the fact that schizophrenic patients typically show deficient working memory, the type of short-term memory that helps us solve problems.

Family Studies

The bread and butter of psychiatric research are the long-term family studies that are conducted by universities and public mental health agencies around the world. Family studies consist of interviews and sometimes clinical examinations of large numbers of patients who have a particular mental illness, usually along with their first-degree relatives. In some of the most valuable studies, researchers study twins—both identical and nonidentical (fraternal)—who were adopted. The advantage of these twin adoption studies where twins are separated at birth lays in the ability of researchers to minimize environmental factors as the primary cause when both twins manifest a specific mental disorder.

FIELD STUDY

A three-generation family study in New Zealand showed that a family history involving depression, anxiety, alcoholism, and/or substance abuse can predict the course of a disorder in a child showing symptoms of those disorders. With data from his family history screening, researchers could predict the frequency of recurrences, the likely level of impairment, and the child's need for mental health services.

Even an informal analysis of the presence of mental disorders in a family tree can produce important clues that potentially can be of help to family members. Information gathered can contribute to the diagnosis of a child's mental disorder by providing probabilities in one direction or another. In many families, a mental illness, especially anxiety disorders, are found to be present in multiple generations.

Genetic Analysis

More recent family studies—especially those done since the successful mapping of the human genome in 2002—are yielding genome scans (created from blood samples) of large numbers of related and unrelated patients with a mental disorder. These genome scans are then compared to the genome scans of members of healthy control groups. This type of study also is called "DNA linkage analysis." Genome scans are examined in minute detail for genetic similarities and differences in all study participants.

The goal of this research is to find so-called genetic markers (a difference in a particular chromosome or part thereof) that, by their unusual prevalence in the sample population of those with a disorder, can be associated with the presence of that mental disorder. With the advent of genetic linkage analysis, it is possible to discover the genetic factors in mental disorders. It is hoped that these studies will provide guideposts for the more accurate diagnosis and treatment of all children with mental disorders.

Environmental Triggers

Some of the illnesses or events once considered possible causes of brain disorders have been redefined as environmental triggers. Environmental in this usage refers to any nongenetic factor. This means, although not a cause, triggers are capable of catalyzing symptoms of a disorder in genetically susceptible children or adolescents. These can be events that occur inside a child's body, such as an illness or prenatal exposure to toxins in her environment, or negative life events.

Because there are children who develop mental disorders without a known genetic link, many scientists believe they'll eventually discover firm evidence of environmental factors—both social and physical—that alter genes and create the mutations associated with different disorders. These mutations may or may not cause the disorder in the affected individual, but they could potentially pass on a susceptibility to a subsequent generation. The thousands of toxic substances in your physical environment are affecting your most sensitive organ—the brain— especially during fetal development.

The Least You Need to Know

- Mood and anxiety disorders can affect children as young as 5.
- Early identification and treatment can lessen the severity of many mental disorders.
- Studies show that the use of marijuana increases the risk of psychosis in adolescents at genetic risk.
- New research using fMRI technology shows brain changes associated with high risk for depression.
- Clinical research and studies provide statistical evidence of the most likely risk factors for major psychiatric illnesses.

Children's Learning Disorders

In This Chapter

- The neurobiology behind learning disorders
- The signs of learning disorders
- The links between learning disorders and head injuries

This chapter takes a look at conditions and disorders that affect a child's ability to communicate and learn vital skills in school. Although commonly referred to as learning disabilities, the term "learning disorder" is used here to convey the fact that learning problems need not reflect irremediable disabilities. In fact, these disorders usually represent individual differences in a variety of brain functions rather than defects. Still, unless you've had such a disorder, it's hard to imagine the frustration of affected children as they go through a typical school day: the junior high student with poor fine motor control who has difficulty writing or typing, leaving him unable to communicate what he knows on paper; the third grader with an above average IQ but little visual recall who finds copying from the blackboard to be her worst nightmare; and the high school student who's failing because he can't find the words to express his thoughts so he skips class to avoid embarrassment.

Their teachers may think they're careless. Their parents may accuse them of being defiant or lazy, while their fellow classmates may call them stupid. In reality these students are suffering from diagnosable, treatable learning disorders. In this chapter, neurobiological factors that negatively affect a child's reading, mathematics, and writing performance are covered.

Language and Speech Disorders

To speak a language, you must recognize and speak its sounds as they appear in words and sentences. The English language has 44 units of sound, called *phonemes*. Two examples in English are: "kuh" and "ch." These and other phonemes are blended together to form spoken words.

> **DEFINITION**
>
> A **phoneme** is a basic structural unit of speech sounds combined into a syllable or word. Each language has its own phonemes. A phonetic approach to teaching reading emphasizes clearly sounding out syllables.

At birth, babies are sensitive to any phoneme, meaning they'll learn whatever language they're exposed to. By the age of 6 to 9 months, their brains become more specialized. Neuroscientists say that's when they're "neurally committed" to a specific language. This refers to the point when the neural pathways in the brain used for speaking their own language have been initiated; when initiated they develop quickly during the next two to three years. By the time a child reaches the age of 5, any existing difficulties in making speech become apparent.

There are two types of language skills a child must master, each involving different abilities and skills:

- Receptive language is the ability to listen and understand spoken words. Receptive language is used to perceive spoken words and understand what other people are saying.

- Expressive language is used to formulate and speak words that are comprehensible to a listener. With expressive language you communicate with ideas and feelings. To use expressive language a child must call up relevant phonemes and words from his repertoire of learned vocabulary. He then must arrange them in sentences that conform to the rules of grammar. All in an effort to be understood!

Receptive Language Disorders

To understand language, a child must be able to interpret what she hears and assign meaning to specific words and sentences. This requires that she selectively attend to the sounds of speech, singling out phonemes and syllables. She then must make out words and link them to meanings she's previously acquired.

For a child with a receptive language disorder, different vowels may all sound alike. So when they hear the word tin, it sounds the same as ton, ten, or tan. Children with receptive language disorders benefit from intensive drilling and instruction emphasizing the links between letters and sounds.

Expressive Language Disorder

Children with an expressive language disorder, also called a phonological disorder or a type of dysphasia, have problems when they attempt to formulate words and produce certain language sounds (phonemes). The most frequent letters causing a problem for a child with this condition are l, r, s, z, and th sounds. The child might, for example, mispronounce the word "cry" by saying "cwy."

Children with this disorder have difficulty expressing themselves in words even though they may have the ability to understand language. They usually begin speaking later than their peers. When they speak, they also use shorter sentences and have a more limited vocabulary. They appear to have shorter auditory memory spans and may echo words or substitute the wrong words. The inability to form meaningful speech can be frustrating for these children. They tend to be shy in class. To avoid talking, they may use gestures or single words to get their meaning across.

One boy in an expressive language disorder study said: "I have trouble remembering words … Nobody believes me … I know what to say, but I can't find the words."

About 10 percent of preschoolers have mild receptive or expressive language problems. By age 7, that number falls to 3 percent. They also may have a reading disorder, but the problem usually becomes more apparent as writing requirements increase in school.

A child with a combination of receptive and expressive problems has difficulties with both understanding words that are spoken and articulating words.

Causes of Speech and Language Difficulties

The cause of speech and language difficulty actually may be a hearing loss or an abnormality in the structure of the mouth, larynx, or the throat that interferes with the production of proper speech. In many instances, however, there is no structural cause for a language or speech problem. When this is the case, these problems are related to the temporal lobe of the brain's left hemisphere, where speech is produced and modulated.

An estimated 4 to 5 percent of children have one of the speech and language disorders described here. After a hearing test and a physical examination rules out structural problems, speech therapy is indicated.

Learning Disorders

The developmental learning disorders covered in this section involve difficulties with specific skills necessary for learning reading, writing, or mathematics. Children with these learning disorders have average or above average intelligence. They should be capable learners, but their learning disorder slows them down.

Those disorders most likely to negatively impact a child's academic performance affect their ...

- Visual perception
- Language processing
- Fine motor skills
- Ability to focus attention

About 5 percent of U.S. children receive the diagnosis of a learning disorder, although educators estimate that the number of children suffering silently from one or more mild learning disorders may be up to 20 percent. They often go undetected and untreated until the child reaches the first or second grade, when learning problems become more noticeable.

The following three criteria are used to identify a child with a learning disorder:

- The child has difficulty mastering an academic subject.
- The child has normal intelligence.

- The child is not suffering from other conditions that could explain poor performance, such as sensory impairment (a hearing or vision problem) or poor instruction.

All children with learning disorders share an unexpected failure to learn.

Causes of Learning Disorders

There are four categories of possible causes of learning disorders:

- **Brain injuries**—Most children with a learning disorder do not have a brain injury. But there are some links between learning disorders and head injuries in childhood in addition to injuries resulting from birth trauma, oxygen deprivation, high fevers, or seizures.

- **Individual differences in brain development**—Variations in the development of neural pathways at different stages of brain maturation can affect a child's ability to learn. Such a variation usually is located in just one part of the brain. This explains why a child's learning difficulty tends to affect a single ability, such as expressive speech or visual decoding of words.

- **Chemical imbalances**—A variation in the brain's chemical balance, especially its neurotransmitters (too much of one, not enough of another) can cause a learning disorder. Unlike structural variations in brain development, chemical imbalances are functional problems.

- **Heredity**—Recent studies have shown that about 40 percent of children with learning disorders have a parent with similar learning problems. Sometimes, parents don't identify their own mild learning disorder until their child is diagnosed.

Although all learning disorders are caused by one of the previous physiological issues, environmental influences can make the difference between a mild or severe disability for a child. Supportive parents, an orderly home with regular routines, a nutritious diet, adequate sleep each night, and intellectual stimulation are positive environmental factors that can tip the scale toward effective management of a learning disorder.

Reading Disorders

Proficiency in reading is considered the cornerstone of all academic learning. It's hard to learn most other academic subjects without solid reading skills. Reading includes identifying words, pronouncing words, spelling words, using words, and writing words. Children with reading disorders tend to have difficulty predominately with one or a narrow mixture of these skill areas.

The term "dyslexia" has been used traditionally to refer to reversing letters and trouble visually identifying words. But this term has been subsumed under the broader category of "reading disorders," within which the tendency to reverse letters and misread words are symptoms.

To qualify as a reading disorder, a child's reading ability must be substantially below his grade level and what's expected for his age, intelligence, and education. He has trouble recognizing words, and commonly reverses his letters, especially b with d, and p with q. He may transpose letters, making "pot" into "top." He may invert letters, turning w into m. He may make omissions while reading; for example, reading "ton" when the word is "tonnage."

Another type of reading disorder brings a child trouble when decoding words, meaning separating the sounds or syllables in a word. Still other categories of reading disorders involve problems with reading comprehension, spelling, and writing.

Visual-Spatial Reading Disorder

A child may have difficulty in accurately perceiving the visual-spatial arrangement of words. A word recognized yesterday or even a few minutes earlier evades him in a particular moment. He has difficulty reading because he cannot recognize the visual arrangement or sequence of letters or words. He confuses similar letters, alters the sequence of letters in words, or reverses letters.

A child with *visual-spatial* problems can recognize words by sound, if she sounds out letters and syllables and then reconfigures them. As a result, she responds well to phonetic teaching methods, where "sounding out" words is a key strategy. Here's how one girl put it: "I can see words but not understand them unless I concentrate very hard and sound them out either silently or out loud so I can hear their sounds."

DEFINITION

Visual-spatial ability is the capacity to understand and see visual symbols or representations as well as the spatial relationships between things and is used in reading maps, following mazes, and performing mathematical operations. Males may be more adept initially in this ability than females.

Auditory-Linguistic Reading Disorder

A child with auditory-linguistic problems can recognize familiar words but cannot recall their meanings. He cannot sound out or spell words accurately and confuses abstract words. He may have a history of the delayed onset of speech. As one boy said: "I know the word, but I forget what it means."

Visual Coordination Reading Disorder

A child with poorly coordinated eye movements has difficulty reading because of blurring of words, omitting words, and losing her place in a paragraph. Her vision is not impaired, but she may respond to optometric vision therapy.

Writing Disorder

Problems with the physical act of writing, drawing, copying figures, and other fine motor skills involving eye-hand coordination fall under this category of learning disorder. It also manifests as poorly organized writing and errors in spelling, punctuation, and grammar. The large motor skills (running, throwing, jumping) of children with this disorder are not involved. A child with a writing disorder may also have difficulty reading orally.

Mathematics Disorder

Five basic factors are involved with doing math:

- Language
- Visual-spatial ability
- Conceptualization

- Memory

- Writing

Difficulties in learning mathematics are not as well-understood as reading and writing disorders. They can include difficulty counting, memorizing math facts, remembering which operation to use, or remembering which steps to follow when solving math problems. While all children make errors in math sometimes, persistent trouble with basic math tasks can be a sign of a reading disorder in recognizing or misperceiving numbers or of a writing disorder. A child who is failing math may have trouble concentrating and high impulsivity. Both of these traits are common for children with attention-deficit/hyperactivity disorder (ADHD), which is discussed later in this chapter. Having ADHD can make it difficult for a student to organize the details of a mathematical problem.

A child with a mathematics disorder may have trouble memorizing basic math facts and understanding abstract mathematical concepts, such as fractions and values. Another common weakness is an inability to recognize which mathematical operation—such as addition, division, or multiplication—is needed in story problems and how to perform it to arrive at the correct answer. To remedy this weakness, students need intensive remedial instruction that emphasizes the goals of a math problem and how to select the right operation to meet that goal.

Approximately 1 percent of children receive this learning disability diagnosis, which is usually apparent by the second grade. However, based on low scores on standardized math tests, many educators believe that closer to 6 percent are suffering from this disorder.

Many children with learning disorders develop behaviors that compound their difficulties in school. These behaviors may reflect aspects of the learning disorder itself, but they also may result from emotional responses to the learning disorder, such as frustration, depression, or anxiety. Among the typical behaviors seen are social immaturity, inflexibility, clumsiness, absentmindedness, and problems following directions. The most common behavior associated with a learning disorder is hyperactivity. This is an extreme restlessness, often coupled with impulsivity, which affects approximately 25 percent of children with a learning disability.

Attention-Deficit/Hyperactivity Disorder (ADHD)

Children with ADHD have difficulty paying attention. The most common disorder diagnosed in children, ADHD is characterized by the presence of chronic abnormal levels of inattention, hyperactivity, or their combination. Up to 12 percent of children are diagnosed with ADHD. Boys outnumber girls by a 3:1 ratio. Although they are usually of at least average intelligence, children with ADHD perform below average on reading, spelling, and arithmetic tests. For this reason, they are regarded as having a learning disorder.

To meet the diagnostic criteria for ADHD a child's inattention or hyperactivity-impulsivity must persist for at least six months and to such a degree that it impairs his normal development and learning. It also must be accompanied by six of the nine behaviors that fall into the categories of inattention, hyperactivity, or impulsivity. Here are basic definitions of these categories and some examples of symptoms for each category:

1. **Inattention**—Skips from one task to another, does not pay attention in class, and appears unable to concentrate on schoolwork.

    - Has difficulty organizing schoolwork and forgets things.

    - Often avoids tasks or activities that require sustained mental effort.

    - Frequently fails to follow instructions.

2. **Hyperactivity or overactivity**—Unusually energetic, fidgety, and unable to be still, especially in situations where mobility is limited.

    - Fidgets with hands or feet or squirms or leaves seat.

    - Often talks incessantly.

    - Often runs about or climbs on things inappropriately; for an adolescent, this tendency may manifest as a subjective feeling of restlessness.

3. **Impulsivity**—Acts before thinking. May run out onto a street to get a ball without looking for traffic or may interrupt classmates.

- Often blurts out answers before questions have been completed.

- Often has difficulty waiting turns.

- Often interrupts or intrudes on others.

Parents or caregivers usually notice signs of hyperactivity by the time a child is 3 to 5 years old. By age 5 to 7, he also begins showing signs of inattentiveness. Many children, in some studies up to one half, may meet a child or teacher's definition of hyperactive based on classroom observations. But only 4 to 6 percent of children meet the clinical criteria for ADHD as described here. Research shows that many children with the disorder are aggressive and, consequently, are disliked by their peers.

The most common and effective treatment for ADHD is stimulant medication, which has been administered for more than 70 years to children with the symptoms of ADHD. Stimulants, such as Ritalin and Adderall, appear to activate parts of a child's brain that relate to inhibition and self-regulation. Three quarters of children with ADHD who are given this medication show significant improvements. When medication doesn't work or is not an acceptable treatment option in the view of the child's parents and/or physician, behavior management techniques with diet and lifestyle changes have also proved helpful for some children. Soft drinks that contain sugar and caffeine should be avoided.

The least favorable response to a child's learning difficulties is no response at all. Without treatment or assistance, such a child's attitude toward school and his own ability to learn will both plummet into negativity. Children with learning disorders currently receive half of all special education services provided in U.S. schools. If educators and psychologists are right, there probably are more children who need help than are currently receiving it.

The Least You Need to Know

- Nearly half of children with a learning disorder have a parent with the same learning difficulty.
- Most children with a learning disorder have difficulty in one area of learning such as speech, writing, or reading.
- Children with learning disorders have average or above average intelligence, but do not perform well academically without remediation.
- Many kids who don't receive treatment for learning disorders are branded by teachers and other students as lazy or unintelligent.

The Abused or Neglected Child

In This Chapter

- The signs of abuse and neglect (child maltreatment)
- The brain changes caused by sustained abuse
- Symptoms and disorders in abuse victims
- The pathway from victim to survivor

Society is concerned about the numbers that reveal the scope of this problem: 1 to 2 percent of children are maltreated in the United States each year. Then one in four girls and, less known, one in six boys have been sexually violated at some time in their lives, most younger than 10. Child health practitioners and teachers are on the frontlines of those who see and must report signs of physical and sexual abuse in kids. This chapter takes a look at child abuse from the inside out: focusing on how these traumatic experiences change a child's brain and reshape her emotional, cognitive, and social future.

Facts and Fictions of Child Abuse

Child maltreatment, including physical and sexual abuse and the neglect of children, has long been an under-reported fact in the United States. This status quo was challenged in 1993 with the enactment of the National Child Protection Act. This law made it a prosecutable offense for anyone coming into contact with children through work or volunteer activities to fail to report any credible suspicions of child abuse. This now includes teachers, doctors, bus drivers, daycare workers, ministers, scout masters, and many others.

Although reporting and prosecution increased after this act became law, it should still be assumed that any statistics about child abuse under-represent the scope of the problem. The causes of this underestimation are complex. There is often misplaced shame felt by child victims that inhibits them from telling anyone of their abuse. There also is the fear that they won't be believed and the possibility they will be removed from their homes (this occurs in 20 percent of investigated cases) and placed in a fragmented foster care system. Add to that the frequent negative economic consequences resulting from jailing a family's breadwinner. Understandably, there is a continued lack of reporting and investigation of child maltreatment.

The "Stockholm syndrome" stands in the way of detecting child abuse when a victim identifies with the perpetrator and either denies or rationalizes the abuse. The victim may even adulate and express positive feelings toward the perpetrator.

Types of Abuse

From available information, again based only on those cases that have been reported, there are four recognized categories of child maltreatment:

- **Neglect**—This is the largest category of child maltreatment. Neglect entails a failure to provide for a child's basic physical, educational, and psychological needs. It may include abandonment, failing to provide proper nutrition or medical attention, exposing a child to domestic violence, and drug and alcohol abuse in the presence of a child.

- **Physical abuse**—Includes beating, slapping, kicking, burning, shaking, or otherwise causing physical harm to a child. Studies indicate that most of these cases result from physical punishment in which a parent loses control and punishment escalates into battery.

- **Sexual abuse**—Includes fondling a child's genitals or breasts, intercourse or other sexual acts with a child, exposing the child to indecent acts, or involving a child in pornography. When a minor is induced into sexual activity with someone in a position of greater power—whether that power is derived through the perpetrator's age, size, status, or relationship—that minor has been sexually abused. If the perpetrator is an adult, it is statutory rape.

- **Psychological (emotional) abuse**—Includes verbal put-downs and any other behavior that terrorizes, threatens, rejects, insults, or isolates children.

There often is overlap between these categories of abuse. For example, psychological abuse nearly always accompanies other forms of abuse and neglect.

Victims of Child Maltreatment

In abuse statistics, a child is anyone younger than 18 who has been subjected to any of the previously mentioned categories of maltreatment. A recently enacted Florida law eliminated the statute of limitations for prosecuting child sex abusers whose victims were younger than 16 when the crime was committed.

An estimated one in four girls and one in six boys have been sexually abused in the United States. In one study of sex abuse reports subsequently investigated and verified by authorities, more than half of the child victims reported being subjected to more than 50 incidents of sexual abuse. The average age of the first abuse for these children was 7.

There is a great deal of misunderstanding about boys as victims of child sexual abuse. Among the most common fictions are these:

Boys are not as traumatized by sexual abuse as girls.

Not so. Studies show boys, most whom are sexually victimized between the ages of 6 and 10, are just as traumatized by the experience as are girls. By nature of their physiology, older boys might experience erection, ejaculation, and orgasm. It should be understood that these responses are automatic and are not indicative of any reduction in trauma caused by their sexual violation by an adult. The experience of feelings of confusion, guilt, fear, betrayal, shame, and anger are gender neutral in sexual abuse.

Homosexual males perpetrate most sexual abuse of boys.

Wrong. The majority of male sexual abusers of boys identify themselves as heterosexual. Another little-known fact: more than one third of boy sexual abusers are female.

Boys abused by males become homosexuals.

Not true. Abuse doesn't determine sexual orientation. It may, however, cause later sexual dysfunction in an adult male, if the individual doesn't receive support and/ or treatment for residual emotional problems.

According to the U.S. Children's Bureau, an estimated 6 million children are referred each year to child protective services. Of these, nearly 3.7 million children are investigated. Almost 1 million are found to be substantiated victims of abuse or neglect. Of these, the primary maltreatment is neglect in more than 600,000; physical abuse in almost 150,000; sexual abuse in almost 100,000; and emotional abuse in almost 100,000. More than 1,700 children die each year as a result of maltreatment.

The Child Abusers

In more than 70 percent of cases of physical abuse and neglect, the perpetrator is a parent—with mothers constituting the majority, probably because they spend more time with children than fathers do.

In 90 percent of cases of child sex abuse, the perpetrator is someone known to the child: a parent, relative, family friend, or other care provider.

Warning Signs of Child Abuse

Because perpetrators often terrorize their child victims into maintaining silence about their abuse, child protection workers encourage anyone who interacts with children to be aware of potential warning signs that might indicate ongoing abuse. Among these signs:

- Unexplained visible bruises, sprains, or broken bones
- Sudden emotional withdrawal or depression
- Frequent urinary infections
- Sudden aggressive behaviors toward peers
- Trouble sleeping or nightmares

- Irrational fears of places, situations, or people

- Regression to an earlier stage of development, such as bedwetting or thumb sucking

- An onset of acting out in school

- Being socially isolated

- A beginning of frequent school absences

- A deterioration of personal hygiene

- Signs of alcoholism or drug addiction in the home

- Genital bruises seen in medical clinics

Most states require professionals to report any credible evidence of child abuse or neglect to law enforcement authorities within 48 hours. Any previous confidentiality, such as between a minor and her doctor or her psychotherapist, becomes void at such a time. The practitioner is then liable for prosecution if he does not report evidence of such a crime.

Effects on the Developing Brain

When a child is repeatedly sexually violated or physically beaten, particularly by someone he loves and trusts, his brain at first attempts to compensate by activating his body's fight or flight reaction. This bathes the brain with stimulants in the form of neurotransmitters and hormones that are part of the body's *hypothalamic-pituitary-adrenal axis*.

DEFINITION

The **hypothalamic-pituitary-adrenal axis** refers to the glands that release substances, such as cortisol, that are known to be elevated in abused children. These substances are also suspected to cause abnormalities in behaviors or phobias such as sleep disturbances and anxiety disorders.

The immediate effect of these neurotransmitters and hormones on the brain and body is to heighten concentration and boost immune function by decreasing digestion, increasing heart rate, and maximizing energy reserves to meet the threat.

However, as fear persists and a state of stressful anxiety becomes a child's norm, the child's stress hormone reaction goes into overdrive, eventually depleting the brain functions it regulates. As a result, the child's limbic system, the brain's seat of emotions and memory, can be permanently altered in negative ways. Instead of boosting memory and concentration, these excess stress hormones and other chemicals diminish a child's memory functions. Instead of improving immune function, the abused child becomes more vulnerable to illnesses.

Structural Damage

The most serious neurochemical effects stemming from sustained abuse are believed to be long-term changes in the brain's internal structures caused by alterations in the genetic code of brain cells. By negatively impacting gene expression during childhood, the brain's altered DNA causes the hippocampus to shrink—possibly permanently. The job of the hippocampus, the seahorse-shaped structure located in each hemisphere of the brain, is to encode memories through imprinting sense perceptions. This action normally enables memories to be stored in the brain.

Repressed Memories

The disruption of the normal memory process in abuse victims is probably connected to *repressed memories* of abuse, a common phenomena that occurs in early childhood. Because of the amount of brain growth that normally occurs during the first seven years of a child's life, the earlier the abuse takes place, the greater the long-term damage it does to a child's brain and its emotional functions.

 DEFINITION

Repressed memories of abuse may result from structural damage to the hippocampus as a consequence of the severe stress of abuse. It also may occur as a result of a child's need to temporarily deny or disconnect from the emotional and physical horror of abusive experiences. These memories may be forgotten until adulthood when they are triggered, or reactivated, by sense stimuli reminiscent of the abuse, such as during adult sexual activity.

Incest most often begins when a child does not yet have the verbal or cognitive capacities to describe to herself or others what she is experiencing. More confusing, sexual abuse often occurs under the guise of love or other acceptable forms of physical contact. The victim is left doubting her own perceptions, feelings, and memories of the abuse.

False Memory Syndrome

The validity of repressed memories and later recall of incidents of abuse have been questioned because of high-profile cases of false or implanted memories. These imagined and subsequently disproved or recanted experiences of child abuse have been dubbed the "false memory syndrome." The phenomenon has been attributed to brain washing or implanting memories by overzealous psychotherapists or other significant parties.

Although most recovered memories of early childhood abuse are considered credible, it is possible to misremember events that happened long ago. This is true particularly if there is manipulation by a third party, or if the individual doing the remembering has a preexisting emotional agenda with the accused perpetrator. In the "parental alienation syndrome," one parent turns a child against the other parent in the context of false or distorted accusations, often of sexual abuse.

Cognitive Impairments

Although all forms of abuse can cause developmental delays and diminish a child's learning abilities, physical and emotional neglect appears to have the worst overall cognitive impact.

The academic achievement gap for neglected children is greater than for those who have been physically or sexually abused. Language delays and poor school performance are common. Neglected children spend a lot of time unsupervised and receive insufficient mental stimulation at home. They may receive more "parenting" from a television "family" than their own parents. They often receive inadequate nutrition with a negative impact on their ability to learn. They tend to be passive and to show poor impulse control. They also are more socially withdrawn.

COMPLICATION

One common characteristic of physically abused children is called "compulsive compliance." This is a pattern of vigilant, quick, and compulsive behavior intended to please and comply with the wishes of adults. It results from a child's desire to avoid doing anything that might trigger the anger of an abusive parent. This is most common in physically abused 1- to 3-year-olds in contrast to normal children of this age who are appropriately testing limits and developing their sense of autonomy by saying "no."

Studies have shown that physically abused children score an average of 20 points lower than their peers on IQ tests and about two years lower than their classmates on verbal and math skills tests. About one third of these children fail school subjects or are in special education classes. They also cause more disruptions in class because of behavior problems. Victims of sexual abuse generally show fewer cognitive deficits than children who were physically abused or neglected.

Social-Emotional Impairments

Most children eventually heal from the trauma of abuse. But recovery usually occurs after years of struggle with the negative consequences of their abuse. Many mental health professionals who deal with child abuse victims say that the child's emotional development is arrested at the time the abuse begins. For example, if it begins in the first years of a child's life, the essential task of establishing trust with a significant caretaker will be stymied by the violation. The child may then carry an inability to trust well into her adulthood. More specifically, incest survivors say that the damage done by sexual violation actually is secondary to the betrayal of trust they experienced.

Emotional Disorders

Psychological research has documented possible negative effects of maltreatment on every aspect of a child's life. Some behaviors may begin as defense mechanisms adopted by the child to survive the abuse, such as the repression of painful memories that spawns full-blown mental disorders or at least symptoms during the adult years.

Depression

The most common psychological disorder seen in an estimated two thirds of abused children is depression.

Post-Traumatic Stress Disorder (PTSD)

Fifty percent of abused children also show signs of post-traumatic stress disorder (PTSD). This is an anxiety disorder, common to soldiers who've fought in wars and survivors of natural disasters. Anyone who has felt intense fear or been threatened with death or injury can develop PTSD with flashbacks, nightmares, and severe psychological and/or physical symptoms when exposed to stimuli (people, places, or sensory experiences) that trigger memories of the trauma. PTSD sufferers are easily startled and often cannot tolerate crowds of people.

Panic and Other Phobias

Distortions or exaggerations of fear reactions are frequently experienced by child abuse survivors. Agoraphobia, a fear of open spaces, is common. Others are fear of driving and claustrophobia, a fear of entrapment in small spaces that may require an adult survivor to have a door or window open at all times.

Dissociation

The defense of dissociation occurs when a victim detaches his conscious mind from the memory of a traumatic event. This can manifest later as a "zoning out" from the here and now, or a compartmentalization of emotions from other aspects of the self. In its extreme, this can become a "dissociative disorder," when one has multiple personalities (as depicted in the movie *Sybil*) to cope with the after-effects of abuse.

Borderline Personality Disorder

Child sexual abuse can contribute to the development of a borderline personality disorder in later life. This disorder results from projecting a part of oneself on to other persons and a lack of emotional control. As a result of this splitting off of a part of one's own self, persons with this disorder shift between idealizing and demonizing other persons. They may be loving and trustful one moment and raging and distrustful moments later—toward the same person. They tend to be unable to sustain stable personal, social, or professional relationships. They also frequently display self-destructive and impulsive behaviors, for example, driving recklessly and engaging in promiscuous sex.

Addictions

For survivors of child physical or sexual abuse, addiction to alcohol or drugs can serve their need to numb the pain of their memories of abuse. Addiction can be to an activity such as gambling or shopping as much as to a substance or alcohol.

Eating Disorders

Child sexual abuse victims are especially vulnerable to eating disorders including anorexia nervosa and bulimia, as well as obesity from overeating. Some say that starving themselves is an attempt by anorexics to control their own bodies after years of feeling as though their abuser had that control. When a sexual abuse victim experiences compulsive overeating, this behavior often stems from a feeling of shame toward her body and sexuality.

FIELD STUDY

In one experiment, two groups of toddlers, one consisting of children who had been abused and the other of those who had not been abused, were placed near other children who were crying. The abused children reacted with fear, anger, and even hostility to the distressed children near them. In contrast, the nonabused toddlers reacted with empathy and a desire to comfort the crying children. The study concluded that abused children learn negative ways to respond to negative feelings and lack emotional coping strategies.

Other Emotional After-Effects

The following behaviors are common with victims of child physical and sexual abuse or neglect in addition to repressing memories of earlier periods in life:

- Night terrors
- Self-injury, such as cutting
- Sexual activity or promiscuity at an early age
- Inappropriate clothing worn to cover the body, usually too much clothing for the weather
- Gag reflex, overreaction when water hits the face, and difficulty using public bathrooms are specific to incest

The emotional damage is greatest when sexual abuse started before the age of 6 and lasted for several years. Child and teen victims of sexual abuse have a significantly increased chance of suicidal thoughts during adolescence. In the teen years, sex abuse victims show significantly higher rates of prostitution and pregnancy.

When Children Witness Domestic Violence

Teenagers who had witnessed physical abuse and been abused in their homes were observed while living in a domestic violence "safe haven." Researchers noted the following differences between these male and female abuse victims and witnesses:

- Boys displayed "battered" symptoms. They showed higher amounts of anger, aggression, frustration, and hyperactivity.

- Girls displayed "victim" symptoms. They were withdrawn and displayed more worry, grief, and helplessness.

Both male and females witnesses of domestic violence who had been removed from their homes had a sense of loss of their home and personal possessions. They often experienced a lack of appetite and states of high anxiety.

Although the previous cognitive and social emotional effects are common with abused children, the outcomes of child maltreatment vary. Some individuals are more resilient than others due to such factors as temperament and personality as well as the presence or absence of other people who are supportive in their lives.

A Psychosocial Profile of Abusers

Abusers of children come from every ethnic group and economic class. At the same time, research shows that the rates of physical abuse and neglect of children rise sharply during difficult economic times and high unemployment, such as occurred during the 2008–2011 economic recession. Poverty is undeniably linked to child abuse, as is inadequate preparation for parenthood. Communities that have instituted parent support and training programs for low-income families, such as one in the Chicago public school system begun in the 1970s, have found a drop of nearly 50 percent in the rates of child maltreatment.

Who Sexually Abuses Children?

Children can be sexually abused by criminal pedophiles with personality disorders or family members and their companions. Three characteristics that most pedophiles have in common are as follows:

- Because of their own arrested emotional development, pedophiles get emotional gratification from relating to a child in a sexual way.

- Pedophiles find children sexually arousing and are unable to be physically aroused or gratified by peers.

- Pedophiles are not deterred by the taboo against having sex with children.

As a group, pedophiles tend to deny, minimize, and justify their sex crimes against children. They may even idealize pedophilia, as does the North American Man/Boy Love Association. If they do admit to molestation, they usually say it was limited to one incident. They also routinely blame their victim, saying they were seduced or that the sex was consensual, regardless of the age of the victim. More often they claim that the child is lying. Unfortunately, too often they are believed at the expense of a child.

The Case of Incest

Research has shown that parents or other family members and companions (technically not incestuous) who commit incest with children tend to have these qualities in common:

- They tend to sexually abuse children younger than 6.

- They live in isolation and/or in poverty, although it occurs in every economic and social class.

- They often are alcohol or substance abusers.

- They are more likely to be stepparents than biological parents.

The Science of Recovery

From three decades of clinical experience and psychological research, there is ample evidence that people abused as children can recover and live emotionally fulfilling lives.

Steps for Healing

Whether or not an individual enters formal psychological treatment, the steps of healing tend to be the same for an abuse victim. They include …

1. First confronting and acknowledging any disorder that may have resulted from the abuse.

2. Acknowledge and release the painful memories of abuse. To accomplish this, the victim must emotionally return to the experience of abuse and realize that she did not "deserve it" and could have done nothing to stop it or prevent it. Therefore it was not her fault. In keeping with this process the victim must realize that her own feelings of shame and guilt are misplaced; they belong to the abuser. This also is called empowerment, the victim taking power back from the perpetrator.

3. Challenge any core beliefs or ingrained patterns of thoughts and feelings formed as a result of the abuse. Examples are "I am worthless" or "I don't deserve to be loved." In many cases, the victim feels the need to mourn the years of childhood he lost to the abuse.

4. The victim must seek help and support from others, like a psychotherapist or social worker, a minister, and fellow abuse victims in a program for survivors of abuse, such as the Twelve-Step program. Sympathetic relatives or friends can be helpful as well.

Psychotherapy for Victims

A psychotherapist can help unlock unconscious memories to begin the process of healing from child maltreatment for an individual of any age. Before a recovering victim of child abuse is treated by a psychological practitioner, he often takes a diagnostic test called the "Trauma Symptom Inventory." This self-administered exam lists 100 items that are possible symptoms related to child abuse or neglect. The results of this test can help the practitioner and person choose a particular therapeutic course.

Therapy modalities successfully used for adolescent and adult survivors of child abuse and neglect include the following:

Cognitive Behavioral Therapy (CBT)

As mentioned in Chapter 16, CBT focuses on a person's current thoughts, feelings, and conduct. The therapist seeks ways to help the person identify negative or self-destructive reactions and behaviors and replace them with different positive behaviors. For example, a victim of child maltreatment who responds to stress at work by zoning out and cutting off her feelings might be encouraged to take a timeout for deep breathing.

Dialectical Behavioral Therapy (DBT)

Used in treating persons with borderline personalities, this therapy often is administered in groups as well as individually and teaches persons to regulate their emotions. They learn to identify negative behaviors, particularly hostility toward loved ones, and find alternatives.

Eye Movement Desensitization Response (EMDR)

A controversial but often effective method of treating emotional trauma, eye movement desensitization response therapy attempts to address pathological changes in the patient's brain. Just as sensory stimuli can trigger memories of abuse or trauma, this approach uses eye movements as the body's natural way to expose and desensitize a person to a traumatic memory. A therapist uses visual stimuli in the form of hand movements or electronic pictures to trigger memories and emotions and then uses psychotherapy or hypnosis to reframe those experiences while desensitizing persons to their emotional pain.

The "Writing Cure"

For many people recovering from abuse or any other traumatic experiences, keeping a journal can be therapeutic. A controlled study found that the act of writing down one's darkest memories and deepest feelings had psychological and physical health benefits.

In the study, those who were "high disclosers" of trauma in their writings were less likely to develop symptoms. They also had improved immune systems and better overall health. Those who were "low disclosers" had more symptoms and less emotional well-being. Writing also assists in the process of self-discovery and memory retrieval.

Long-Term Recovery and Prevention

Because of children's innate resiliency, contemporary social changes that allow more open discussions of past abuse, and the availability of many avenues to trauma recovery, the long-term prognosis for child maltreatment victims is increasingly positive. Contrary to conventional thinking, the vast majority of child abuse victims do not become abusers themselves.

Many school programs have proven effective in helping children and teens protect themselves from abuse or stopping ongoing maltreatment. These programs focus on teaching children how to "stay safe." For example, by learning the differences between appropriate and unacceptable touching, and how they can create a "safety zone" of at least three trusted people (including one adult outside the immediate family) in their lives, children can be taught their basic rights and how to report incidents of abuse. Organizations offering assistance to victims of child maltreatment are listed in Appendix B.

The Least You Need to Know

- One in four girls and one in six boys have been the victims of child sexual abuse.
- Lack of reporting means that the official numbers for victims of physical and sexual abuse and neglect are lower than the actual scope of the problem.
- Abuse and neglect reshape a child's brain, causing memory and learning problems.
- The passage of laws requiring professionals and volunteers with credible evidence of child abuse or neglect to report it to authorities has increased reporting.

The Digital Child

In This Chapter

- Total screen time and school attention problems
- Correlation between TV and videogame violence and crime
- Positive effects of higher Internet use

It appears that no one worried much about the impact of the new medium of radio on young impressionable minds when it first entered American living rooms in the 1930s. It must have been the excitement of having the whole world wired for the first time. By the time televised images came along in the 1950s, it was a different story. Almost immediately, alarm bells went off for parents and medical professionals alike. In the last 60 years, the number of hours of TV watched by children and teens has skyrocketed with DVDs, videogames, the Internet, cell phones, and other hand-held devices adding exponentially to the total amount of digital content being consumed. With each new decade, unease has risen about the impact of this steady stream of digital media on children's minds and bodies.

These concerns have translated into hundreds of psychological studies investigating links between the act of watching TV (and other media) or the content of programs and children's emotional, cognitive, and moral development. As you'll see in this chapter, those studies, particularly many investigating the impact of media violence, have added weight to ongoing public debate of these issues. But they've also raised persistent questions about the methodology and limitations of correlative psychological research.

Plugged-In Kids

If pictures made TV a more powerful and perhaps dangerous medium than radio, what effect has the interactivity of videogames and the Internet had on children's thoughts and emotions? Does more intensity and engagement change the impact of an image on a child's brain? Is there a tipping point at which school work suffers? Before broaching these questions, let's get an accurate picture of the most important digital sounds and pictures today's kids are plugged in to.

> **COMPLICATION**
>
> Overly eager parents who buy educational DVDs to turn their toddlers into the next Einstein or Shakespeare should know these products don't appear to have any beneficial effect. Babies learn language best from a live human speaker, not a screen. Another tidbit from the research: babies learn a word faster when they hear several people say it, not just one.

More Screens, Same Questions

A 2008 study of 1,000 children done at the University of Maryland found that children from 10 to 12 were messaging each other, playing games, using the Internet for school work, and surfing the web an average of 3.4 hours per week. Those from 16 to 18 spent 6.3 hours weekly on keyboards or joysticks. The reporting methodology of this study combined the following:

- Time-use diaries completed by child and teen study participants
- Parent surveys of the same children and teens
- Academic achievement test scores (Results will be reported later in this chapter.)

The largest increase in media use among younger and older children alike involved computer games. It should be noted that 2008 was before the quantum leap in kids' use of social media, including MySpace, YouTube, and Facebook, which now count billions of people of all ages as regular visitors. If done today, the greater increase may well be in traffic to these social media websites rather than computer games.

Interestingly, although this study found a decrease in TV watching as other media claimed more of children's attention, TV watching still outpaced all other screen time. According to this survey, children of all ages watched about 13 hours of TV per week in 2008. This compared to 6 to 10 hours a week spent on computers and gaming systems combined.

Electronic Media = Attention Problems?

To measure the impact of electronic media on school performance, a research team at Iowa State University looked at one aspect of how children learn: their ability to pay attention and keep a lid on their impulses. Researchers wanted to know whether watching TV and playing videogames could harm a student's ability to pay attention in class.

To answer this question the study compared school and homework performance with the media habits of 1,323 children in grades three to five, and in a separate study of 210 adolescent/young adults. The elementary school children were followed during the course of 13 months with parents helping kids log their TV and gaming time. Teachers were then interviewed to obtain assessments of each child's classroom performance.

Researchers found that classroom attention problems grew worse in proportion to the total time kids spent in front of screens. Further they found that kids who exceeded the two hours per day of total screen time recommended by the American Academy of Pediatrics were one and a half to two times more likely to have attention problems when doing homework. In reaching these conclusions, researchers took into account any attention problems children had before they entered the study.

FIELD STUDY

In the segment of the Iowa State study investigating the link between attention problems and media screen time for 210 senior high school and college students, the finding was similar to that of elementary school students. If the students spent more than two hours a day in front of either a TV or videogame screen, they were twice as likely to have attention problems in school.

So an association between screen time and difficulties concentrating on school tasks has been made. But an association—even a strong one—doesn't prove cause.

The Iowa State study investigators speculated that because the action in most TV and videogames moves very quickly, involving rapid changes in focus, kids who spend more time with these media have difficulty staying focused on slower activities, such as homework. One point raised by critics of the study was that poor concentration also is associated with a lack of sleep and exercise, which may result from too much screen time. An experimental design in which all variables are controlled may ultimately resolve this issue.

The Violence Question

There's no debate about the fact that television programming is loaded with violence. The average hour of television contains four to five acts of violence. Children's programs, such as cartoons, average 20 to 25 acts of violence. One media watchdog group totaled 8,000 murders watched by the average elementary school child.

Two factors fuel the continuing debate about whether watching violent or aggressive acts on visual media directly causes an increase by inspiration or a decrease by sublimation (expressing and discharging a child's violent impulses through watching TV or playing a game) in aggressive acts committed by children and adolescents:

- The soaring popularity among children and adolescents of violent videogames on top of average TV viewing time found in one study to occupy a combined 4.3 hours per day.

- The increased rate of acts of violence committed by youth against the backdrop of a 15 percent drop in the national overall violent crime rate since 1999.

The corollary of this debate is whether or not greater regulation of media content is called for to stem societal violence. Public concern about this issue tends to crystallize around high-profile crimes committed by adolescents. For example, the gruesome 2003 murder committed by Alan Menzies, who stabbed and then drank the blood of his best friend, claiming he was inspired by the vampire film *Queen of the Damned* in which such an act brought the murderer immortality. Then there were eight Long Island teenagers who went on a carjacking and mugging rampage in homage to the videogame *Grand Theft Auto IV*.

So, after hundreds of studies, how strong is the association between onscreen violence and acts of violence committed by youth? There are two principle approaches used in research into the effects of TV and other media violence on youth.

In laboratory-based studies, investigators place participants in front of various videos and record their responses. Participants' responses are correlated with observations of their playground behavior, as well as teacher, parent, and self-reports. These studies tend to be shorter and more focused in their findings. The acts of aggression and violence they measure are limited to wholly or partially controlled settings, such as a classroom and playground.

More recent violence studies have been based on contextual evidence, an accumulation of research linking the TV viewing habits of specific young people with real-life crimes they may or may not commit later anywhere in a community. This longitudinal approach has contributed most of the recent research on the question of media violence and children.

TV Time and Juvenile Crime

A limitation of earlier studies examining the association between TV watching and real-life aggression and violence was their focus on young children. How playground behavior translated into real-world actions later in life was unknown. This was the knowledge gap filled by a 2002 Columbia University and New York State Psychiatric Institute study. It followed children in 707 families who lived in two northern counties of New York for 17 years. Several things about this study were unique:

- Researchers looked at how many hours of total TV programs were watched, not just violent TV.

- The study accounted for other known risk factors for aggressive behavior, including childhood neglect, growing up in a dangerous neighborhood, low family income, low parental education, and psychiatric problems.

- Children were between the ages of 1 and 10 when the study began. In 2000, when their average age was 30, they filled out a questionnaire about any acts of violent or serious aggressive behaviors they had committed. Aggressive acts included assaults, fights that led to injuries, and the use of a weapon to commit a crime.

• Self-reports on aggressive behaviors were then checked against state law enforcement and FBI crime records.

This study found that 45 percent of the men who had watched three hours or more TV a day at the age of 14 went on to commit an aggressive act against another person; this compared to just 9 percent of the young men who had watched less than an hour of TV daily as 14-year-olds. More than 20 percent of the group that watched three hours of TV a day went on (beyond the single act of aggression) to commit robbery, threaten to injure someone, or use a weapon to commit a crime.

There was an interesting difference for young women in the study. For 30-year-old women, the strongest TV predictor of violence was watching three hours of TV or more at the age of 22. Of these women, 17 percent had committed at least one aggressive act (as defined previously) compared to none in the group watching less than an hour a day.

Even with this hefty evidence for an association between TV watching and aggressive behavior, there is a problem: the possibility that the association between watching violence and committing acts of violence is strong but indirect. One critic suggested that families high in TV viewing may be lower in character and moral education. The study's chief investigator rebutted this line of criticism, saying in a *New York Times* interview that his study had accounted for such risk factors and that, if anything, they had underestimated the amount of TV watched by their study participants. Summing up, he said: "By decreasing exposure to media violence we may be able to prevent millions of Americans from being raped, murdered, and robbed at gun point."

One significant implication of this study is that the effect of TV violence is not short term and limited to children's behavior. Rather, it may last well into adulthood.

Tracking the Chain Reaction

So if you accept the evidence that watching screen-based violence might increase the risk of aggressive behavior, the question that emerges for psychologists is how. What is the internal mechanism that turns a youngster's watching an act of violence into violent behavior? One psychological process that may hold the key to this dynamic is called *desensitization*.

DEFINITION

Desensitization is the result of repeated exposure to something that lessens a person's cognitive, affective, and behavioral responses to that stimulus. In the case of violence—either TV-based or violence in the home or community—it is thought that such exposure may undermine a child's development of emotional self-regulation skills; so, after repeated exposures, cues that normally elicit empathy are dulled or missing.

Researchers at the University of Toledo in Ohio did a study to investigate this process using 150 fourth and fifth grade students. They measured such factors in the children as:

- Real-life violence witnessed

- Violence exposure from all media

- Empathy

- Attitudes toward violence

The research team found that ...

- Only movie and videogame violence exposure were associated with strong pro-violence attitudes.

- Only videogame violence exposure was associated with lower empathy.

- Although children who play large amounts of violent videogames may be slightly more aggressive, they are not necessarily more violent than children who do not.

As to why, researchers speculated that the active nature of playing videogames, where players must identify and then choose violent strategies if they are to succeed in the game, provide reinforcement of those pro-violence strategies and attitudes. At the same time, researchers point out that desensitization is difficult to quantify. They called for more research where individual differences and causal relationships can be more specifically identified.

A Child's Online World

According to a Neilson Online report, kids from 2 to 11 years of age were spending 63 percent more time online in 2009 than they did 5 years previously. Their time online rose to an average of 11 hours for the month of May 2009 compared to just 7 hours during May 2004. So usage is increasing, but researchers want to know if it changes students' school performance.

The Internet and Schoolwork

The University of Maryland study mentioned earlier that rated the popularity of various media produced some surprising answers on the measurable impact of students' Internet use on their school performance. Even with the large increase in computer and Internet usage, investigators found little evidence of academic harm done to children from 6 to 12. Moreover the study found academic benefits for two groups: girls and African American boys. Both showed improved reading scores.

Only Caucasian boys showed a decline in their reading test scores as their screen time increased. Investigators associated this finding with boys' greater tendency to randomly surf the web rather than spend time reading individual websites, as girls did. As a whole, this study adds credibility to the perspective that it isn't the medium that matters as much as its message or content. Other studies, however, contradict this conclusion. Some say that it is the passive nature of watching any screen—particularly TV—that produces negative effects on children.

The effects on thinking of "hypermedia"—in particular clicking, skipping, and skimming—on working and deep memory are being studied. There is evidence that digital technology may be diminishing the long-term memory consolidation that is the basis for true intelligence. Hyperlinks and overstimulation mean the brain must give most of its attention to short-term decisions. True, there are compensations: better hand-eye coordination, pattern recognition, and the very multitasking skills the machines themselves require. Skeptics rightly point out that similar concerns have accompanied each new technology. Something is always lost, and something is gained. Some evolutionary biologists claim with tongue in cheek that the scholarly mind is a historical anomaly: that humans, as with other primates, are designed to scan rapidly for danger and opportunity. If so, the Internet delivers this shallow, scattered mindset with a vengeance.

"If It's Online, It Must Be True"

The Kids and Family Reading Survey by Scholastic measured both the quantity and quality of kids' reading habits. One worrisome statistic was the finding that 39 percent of the 9- to 17-year-olds surveyed agreed with the statement "The information I find online is always correct."

As most teachers are well aware, there is a persistent tendency for students (and some adults) to hold to this woefully wrong assumption. The antidote many teachers have found is strict sourcing standards for student research, whether online or off. Accounting for who said what and determining whether the content came from a credible source is a skill like any other learned in school.

The Wrong People in the Wrong Places

One wrong click and a 7-year-old who is looking for an "animal behavior" website can land on a site extolling a wholly different kind of behavior not suitable for his sensibilities. A 2010 survey of more than 2,800 kids and more than 7,000 adults in 14 countries about their online lives found that more than 6 in 10 kids had accidentally landed on web nudity and violence. Many also had a stranger make an online bid to meet them in real life. A parent's worst nightmare is, unfortunately, an existing social reality.

> **INSIGHT**
>
> An Internet security firm found that no fewer than 92 percent of children in the United States have some kind of web presence posted by their parents by the time they are 2. From photos to full profiles on social networking sites, parents say their purpose is to share with friends and family. Only 3.5 percent expressed concern that such personal disclosures might be available online for decades to follow. Should they be concerned?

Although 7 in 10 kids in the Scholastic survey said they would turn to their parents for help if something bad happened to them online, only 45 percent of parents acknowledged that their children may be having such bad experiences online. The facts present a starker picture than most parents apparently realize:

- Around 41 percent of the kids had a stranger try to connect with them on a social network.

- About 10 percent said someone they did not know tried to arrange a real-life meeting with them.

- One fifth of kids said they regretted something they did online.

Parents are encouraged to set rules for their children's online use, including such safety steps as …

- Not "friending" people unknown to them, including "friends of friends." This survey provides some reassurance on this point: most youth using social media are associating with people they already know in their offline lives. Texting, e-mail, chat, and online gaming have simply been integrated into their normal social routines.

- Never agreeing to meet someone in real life without a parent.

- Making agreements about how much private information the child will put on any web page or social media site. Always exclude home addresses, telephone numbers, Social Security numbers, and other data that might make the child or family members vulnerable to identity theft or other crimes.

- For younger children especially, consider installing a content filter on a home computer.

- Setting limits for the child's daily Internet surfing time.

Parents and other adults are advised to pay special attention to any evidence that a child may be a victim of "cyber-bulling." This is an extension of other forms of bullying but brings with it a high level of potential humiliation for its victims. High-profile suicides and legal prosecutions of child and adult bullies have put this issue increasingly in the public eye. The take-home message is to report any such bullying actions to school and law enforcement authorities.

In sharing personal information online, youth are practicing self-expression and reciprocity at the risk of losing control over the audience and permanence of that information. Bullies are emboldened by the disinhibiting effects of online anonymity. Youth with mental disorders may be especially at risk for the negative consequences of digital living.

The Unplugged Child

For those child development experts sounding a warning about the digitalization of childhood, the perceived risks are varied.

Some point out that the overuse of technology by teens may enhance other gaps that tend to arise in adolescence, such as the wedge between parents and their teenage children who are naturally separating from parents as they search for an independent identity. If parents are clueless about the media gadgets that have captured their kids' every waking hour outside the classroom, it's another zone for disengagement between child and parent.

Many psychologists point to a growing trend of addiction by children and adults to their favorite technology choices. Videogames appear to create the most compulsions for constant play at the expense of relationships, work, schoolwork, and even basic self-care.

Others worry about the amount of time that plugged-in children aren't spending in nature, doing sports activities, or even just being in the physical presence of friends. Rather than viewing the curtailment of time in front of screens as a punitive gesture, it's suggested that the emphasis be put on positive replacements for plugged-in hours. The restoration of family dinners with conversation (minus TV and perhaps with an after-dinner board game) would go a long way to righting the imbalance.

The Least You Need to Know

- Spending more than two hours a day in front of any combination of screens increases a child's risk of attention problems.
- Even with the large increase in computer and Internet usage, investigators have found little evidence of academic harm done to children from 6 to 12.
- Videogames have the most addictive potential for children, while violent videogames show the highest association compared to other media with aggressive child and adolescent behaviors.
- The booming science of decision-making suggests that overloading brains with too much information leads to objectively poorer choices.

Therapeutic Approaches in Child Psychology

Part

7

Today's mental health practitioners must use all the resources and methods at our disposal to help children cope and thrive. Here you'll find an overview of the theories and therapeutic practices used in individual psychotherapy for children and adolescents. Family therapy involving children with their parents and siblings under the guidance of a family therapist is then covered in its own chapter. We conclude by using general systems and ecological/transactional and chaos/complexity theories to view the "whole child" in the context of his or her society. We introduce the concept of "juvenile ageism" as a way to get the big picture on what's ailing today's families. Finally, with all these tools, we invite you to join us in making the world a better and less perplexing place for our children.

Psychotherapy with Children and Adolescents

In This Chapter

- How "Little Hans" overcame his fear of horses
- Why a child's play is free association
- What it means when a cat bites a dog

When a child or an adolescent has a psychological problem, there are two basic approaches used to address it. One is to change the child's external world; for example, to switch schools or place him in a special education class. Or if the family is found to be the major source of the problem, a child may be placed in foster care. The other approach is to change the child's internal world through psychotherapy and/or medication. This chapter deals with this latter approach.

Most professionals help people through the services they provide. Psychotherapists help people to help themselves. Child psychologists, child psychiatrists, social workers, and marriage and family therapists practice psychotherapy with children and adolescents. They work with youngsters suffering from a diagnosable mental disorder, such as those covered in Chapter 16. But they also may treat those whose development is not proceeding smoothly. An estimated 10 percent of children and adolescents receive some form of psychological intervention—approximately one half of those who need it.

When the Patient Is a Child

The approaches and techniques originally used in child and adolescent psycho-therapy came from the theory and practice of psychotherapy with adults. But those treating children soon discovered the need to adapt therapy to the ages and developmental levels of their patients.

The biggest difference between treating youngsters and adults is how and why the patient comes to be in the therapist's office. The vast majority of children and adolescents are there because their parents and/or teachers are concerned about their behavior and bring them to a professional to "fix" them. Understandably, a child may then see the therapist as someone who sides with his parents rather than as his ally. This often makes the first stage of psychotherapy—gaining the patient's trust—a longer and more complex process with children and adolescents than with adults. It also makes parents an essential part of the therapeutic process both as sources of information and as participants.

A comfortable office or room makes it easier for a child and therapist to do the work of therapy. Unlike adults who are comfortable with chairs and desks, youngsters of all ages are more comfortable in places where they can "do things" and in which there are furnishings and objects of interest to them. For younger children, a playroom is helpful, although any office can be adapted to their use by providing play materials. And then there is the therapist's attitude about the physical space; if she treats it as a place in which "we can do things" rather than "just a place to talk," a child is more likely to be approachable.

Other key differences between adult and child-adolescent psychotherapy include the following:

- A youngster is viewed in her social context; her home and school life are important factors in therapy.

- A youngster is less verbal; therefore therapy often is an activity-based process.

- The principle of confidentiality between therapist and patient—a given in adult psychotherapy—is handled differently. With younger children, information usually is exchanged freely between therapist and the child's parents. With adolescents, a degree of confidentiality usually is important to encourage trust and openness.

The Qualities of Therapists

These differences all spell out the need for patience and a high tolerance for frustration on the part of therapists who treat children. Patience is important in all aspects of living but is especially important for therapists.

The next important quality is empathy both for a child's perspective and for childhood in general. A therapist's ability to relate to young persons at their age levels is essential for successful psychotherapy. The nurturing aspects of a mature adult and a therapist's ability to find the child within himself are the wellsprings of interest and success in working with children, adolescents, and families.

The growth of childhood spans many years and participating in that process as a therapist gives one an opportunity to become closely acquainted with the complexities of life and the awesome, but inevitably rewarding, odyssey of human maturation.

Why Am I Here?

The goals of child and adolescent psychotherapy also are somewhat different from those of adults in psychotherapy. They can be summarized as …

- Reduction of symptoms, such as aggressive behavior on the playground or school failure.
- Promotion/resumption of normal social, emotional, and cognitive development.
- Fostering autonomy and self-reliance.
- Bringing about change that is reflected in real-life settings (not just in the therapist's office).

The Therapeutic Process

A window into a young person's world and a road to his self-understanding lie in psychotherapy, often referred to as "play therapy." Conversations with children may hide as much as clarify a question. There is a difference between conversing with a child and gaining access to his inner mental and emotional life.

The purpose of psychotherapy is to help a youngster comfortably accept things she already knows about herself and discover parts of herself previously hidden from her awareness.

There are five stages in child and adolescent psychotherapy, with some differences depending on the theoretical approach used:

1. **Establishing a working relationship.** This is required for the therapist to gain access to a youngster's fantasy life. Most psychotherapists find that words describing psychotherapy with a connotation of "working together" rather than "playing together" help young children understand the therapeutic intent of the process.

2. **Analysis of the problem and cause.** This is more of a cognitive process between therapist and patient, particularly with an older child or adolescent. Youngsters who are aware of the discomfort or negative effects of their own problem behavior tend to contribute more to this stage and benefit more from psychotherapy in general.

3. **Explanation of the problem.** The therapist uses direct talk or indirect communication through play to educate and lend insight or self-understanding to a youngster regarding her problem. Sometimes a child in psychotherapy gains an insight into her behavior after (rather than before) making a behavior change and seeing the results in her life.

4. **Implementation of a formula for change.** When a corrective action is discussed or enacted through play, ways to carry it out in daily life are identified.

5. **Termination.** This involves helping the youngster (and his parents) reinforce attitudinal and behavioral changes in real-life situations.

In general, children and teenagers who are inclined toward introspection and are less inhibited tend to respond best to psychotherapy.

A Freudian Legacy

In Chapter 1, Sigmund Freud was introduced as the first prominent medical doctor to treat mental disorders with psychotherapy. So you will not be surprised to learn that he and his psychodynamic heirs were the founding practitioners of the psychological treatment of children. In fact, Freud's daughter Anna Freud, along with psychoanalyst Melanie Klein, pioneered child psychoanalysis and adapted its core tenets to the needs of children beginning in the 1920s.

Although Sigmund Freud did not directly treat children, his consultation with one father and son provided some insights for psychoanalysts and other therapists who would follow.

Little Hans's Phobia

Freud met Little Hans through the child's father, whom he had previously treated in psychoanalysis. The 5-year-old boy's symptom was a fear of being bitten by horses. Recognizing the difficulty of gaining a child's trust, Freud opted to work through his father, in effect giving Hans's father on-the-job training as a psychoanalyst. Under Freud's direction, the father engaged Hans in frequent free-ranging conversations with a purpose: to uncover the unconscious cause of the boy's fear and to bring that cause to his conscious awareness.

Freud credited alleviation of Hans's symptoms to the father helping Hans discover that his conscious fear of horses actually was based on an unconscious fantasized fear. Freud related Little Hans's problem to his understanding of the developmental conflicts of childhood. He believed inner conflicts stem from frightening aggressive and/or sexual urges. He regarded Hans's fear of horses as displaced fear that his father would castrate him because of his wish to get rid of his father and marry his mother (the Oedipal complex).

Therapist-Patient Relationship

Another possible reason for Little Hans's "cure"—put forth by other psychodynamic theorists' writings since Freud's day—was simply the substantial time and tender attention Hans received from his father. They surmised that a fearful relationship between father and son had been at the root of the boy's phobia. The fact that this relationship was in effect healed by trustful interaction with his father sheds light on the first requirement for effective psychological treatment of children: the quality of the child's relationship with his therapist.

Another Freudian concept central to the therapist-patient relationship with special relevance to child psychotherapy is *transference*. This refers to the tendency on the part of patients to transfer attitudes and emotions from family members to a therapist. By creatively using the transference, a psychotherapist gains insights into a patient's troubled relationships and helps the patient change the negative behaviors that resulted. For example, a patient's irritability with, and anger toward, her female therapist can be interpreted as really directed toward her mother.

DEFINITION

Transference in psychotherapy is the transfer or reproduction of repressed painful childhood experiences and emotions—usually relating to a parent—on to a therapist. When the therapist does not respond in the same negative relationship pattern, the patient has the opportunity to see and change his negative behavior.

Establishing a relationship with a child involves demonstrating one's usefulness to the child rather than on becoming his friend or "pal." In fact, most successful psychotherapy does not include friendship or even mutual affection.

The core elements of the therapist-patient relationship that evolved from the Freudian model include the following:

- **Identification with the therapist.** A trusting relationship between psychotherapist and patient is fundamental to the success of any psychotherapeutic process. The patient adopts the therapist's open, problem-solving, rational attitude and behavior.

- **Corrective emotional experiences.** The patient has new, objective experiences while interacting with the therapist. For example, a girl with a harsh judgmental father experiences a gentle, supportive male therapist and gradually loses her fear of men and becomes more open to men in general.

- **Therapist as educator.** The therapist helps the patient alter distorted thinking about himself or the values he has been taught; for example, "All sex is bad," or "If I make a mistake, I'm bad or worthless."

Talk Becomes Play

The "talking cure" at the heart of psychoanalysis with adults involves two essential elements:

- Free association, where the patient talks spontaneously, expressing without inhibition his ideas and memories, in order to discover repressed material in his unconscious.

- The insights that come from this talk, shedding light on the patient's thoughts, feelings, and behaviors.

The talk therapy process seemed to work with Little Hans when the therapist was his father. But how could an unfamiliar therapist engage a young unwilling patient in such a dialogue and receive a child's trust? The answer found by Anna Freud and Melanie Klein was *play therapy.*

> **DEFINITION**
>
> **Play therapy** involves the use of toys, blocks, dolls, puppets, drawings, and games to help a child recognize, identify, and verbalize feelings. Through a combination of play and talk, the psychotherapist observes how the child uses play materials and identifies themes or patterns that help understand that child's problems.

Whereas an adult plumbs the depths of her unconscious by engaging in free associations with her psychoanalyst, a child free associates in fantasy play. Anna Freud and Melanie Klein recognized how play functions like free association at a symbolic level to reveal a child's unconscious fantasies and emotions. This recognition made these two psychoanalysts major contributors to the field of child psychotherapy.

Fantasy play in which a child interacts with props—such as dolls, clay, sand trays, or finger paints—while telling an emotionally laden story to a therapist is a fundamental part of child psychotherapy. It is used by therapists in every school of child psychology, not just those with a psychoanalytic or psychodynamic orientation.

With play and props, a child can use a third person to distance herself from her fears or feelings of shame or guilt. For example, a story about a child trapped behind a wall unable to reach her mother can be plumbed in a nonthreatening manner. Why is the child trapped? Why is the fantasized mother unable to see, hear, or touch the child? In this way, the therapist gathers information about imagined or real problems in the child's relationship with her own mother.

Just as the "royal road to the unconscious" of adults is through dreams, the royal road to the fantasy lives of children is through their play. It is quite possible for a child to be consciously unaware of hostile wishes toward a parent, so he provides no clue of his hostile feelings when speaking to the therapist. If asked directly, he will deny having such feelings. However, the same child may infuse his play and creative productions with violence and hostility.

Here are some examples of how play reveals a child's subconscious inner feelings:

- A child's hostile feelings toward a father become quite clear when male dolls come to tragic ends in the child's play.

- A child's negative feelings and attitudes toward his own body can be inferred from the way that he avoids or approaches nude anatomical dolls.

- A child's attitudes toward herself and the world also are expressed through the manner in which she either hesitates or rushes to approach and use inviting toys and creative tools.

- A child's painting of an idyllic house with trees, sky, and sun says something about the child's fantasy life, especially when it next becomes the scene of a tornado.

 COMPLICATION

Although play is revealing, plain talk also is relevant and important to the therapeutic process. The point is that play is used to facilitate communication with a child, to clarify her actions, to aid her in expressing thoughts and feelings, and ultimately to confirm attitudes and feelings that are expressed through her play or other behavior.

Information conveyed verbally should be evaluated in light of a child's developmental level, her powers of observation, her dominant feelings, and her desire to please the therapist. Youngsters may quickly discover that the simplest way to minimize their own anxieties is to agree with therapists and provide what they believe are desired answers.

Changing Behavior

The question remains: How does a child get from insight about "bad" behavior to trying on and adopting a new behavior? Or does he? Start from the assumption that most youngsters are not particularly receptive to analyzing their own stories. Nor do they wish to "own" their resemblance to a story's main character.

Let's take the example of a child who tells a story about a cat who bites a dog. A therapist might ask the child: how are you like the cat? The child is asked to make the cognitive leap between a symbol (cat) and himself to reach an insight about his own behavior.

Anna Freud and Melanie Klein were impressed by children's insights gained through fantasy play and storytelling. They viewed these insights as key to alleviating children's symptoms. But others who use the same therapeutic process see the reason for its effectiveness differently.

Insight Not Required

Those who downplay insight as an important component in child psychotherapy cite Piaget's stages of cognitive development. They point out that children are not capable of having such insights until they've reached the "formal operations" stage at 11 or 12. Only then can a child separate a symbol (cat, doll) and an object or person (patient, parent, sibling) and move back and forth between the two.

A therapist attempting to use fantasy play and storytelling without relying on a child's insight would take a different approach to the cat bites dog story. This therapist would remain in the frame of the child's story and characters and ask a question such as: why did the cat bite the dog? And then follow up with: is there any other way the cat could get the dog to stop bothering him?

Some call this technique "mutual storytelling," where the therapist's questions encourage the child to give his story a complete plot (action with a beginning, middle, and end) and character motivations. The behavior change, such as being less aggressive with peers or siblings, comes from changing his story. This occurs even if the story remains directed only to the dolls and is not applied to the child himself. Central to reaching this positive behavioral response through play, its proponents believe, is a lifting of the child's guilt about his actions and receiving his therapist's approval. All of this is achieved without ever requiring the child to acknowledge his own actions.

INSIGHT

Most children have a natural resistance to expressing their inner thoughts and feelings directly. They also may sense that the ideas and feelings expressed in fantasy play may reveal things they don't wish to divulge. The techniques and materials used by child therapists are intended to overcome this natural resistance.

Storytelling Aids

There are a number of media or props with therapeutic advantages and limitations to each:

- **Doll play**—Figurines representing family members have long been used in therapy with young children. Therapists note not only the stories a child tells with these figures but also the child's movements and other nonverbal cues.

- **Drawing**—A child's creations have the advantage that unlike doll play a drawing is entirely self-created and has no "contamination" by association with evocative images. A child begins to draw recognizable human figures around the age of 4. Many child therapists use drawings to uncover attitudes and emotions and to discern family dynamics, thus making them a useful information-gathering technique.

- **Clay**—Because of its ease of manipulation, malleability, and three dimensionality, clay is used to help draw feelings out of an inhibited child.

- **Dramatization**—Many children of preschool and school age love putting on costumes or hats, holding props, and acting out roles and scenes in pretend play. By play acting in the presence of a therapist, a child can desensitize herself to an anxiety-provoking situation, such as separation from her mother.

Other media used in therapy with children of different ages are board games, finger painting, water, sand, and blocks.

Current Approaches and Methods

Methods used in child and adolescent psychotherapy fall into three general categories: non-behavioral, behavioral, and group or family therapies. Some have been introduced in previous chapters; here the emphasis is on the therapeutic process employed. Any form of psychotherapy can be short term or long term in duration.

Non-Behavioral Approaches

Psychoanalytic principles and methods have been applied to other non-behavioral approaches including active play therapy, relationship therapy, and release therapy.

- Psychodynamic psychotherapies are based on the assumption that a child's behavior and feelings will improve after unconscious inner struggles are brought to light. They emphasize understanding the issues that motivate and influence a child's behavior, thoughts, and feelings. They can help identify a child's typical behavior patterns, defenses, and responses to inner conflicts and struggles.

- Nondirective or client-centered therapy attempts to help older children and adolescents achieve full expression of their "self-actualizing impulses." In this approach, the therapist takes a passive and nondirective role. The therapist helps the youngster achieve self-expression by reflecting back his feelings and verbalizations to assist building self-awareness. Conceived by Carl Rogers in the 1960s, this approach was subsequently applied to children and adolescents by Virginia Axeline.

- Interpersonal therapy is a brief treatment specifically developed for depression, but also used to treat a variety of other clinical conditions. Interpersonal therapy focuses on how relationships affect an individual's emotional state. Individual difficulties are framed in interpersonal terms, and then problematic relationships are addressed and improved.

Behavioral Approaches

Behavioral therapies involve a more structured, educational approach to changing behavior than do the non-behavioral therapies. They encourage specific behavioral changes through directed assignments and tools for self-monitoring and self-regulation.

- Cognitive behavioral therapy (CBT) helps improve a child's moods, anxiety, and behavior by examining confused or distorted patterns of thinking. Therapists teach children that thoughts cause feelings and moods that can influence behavior. A child learns to identify unrealistic thought patterns. The therapist then helps the child replace this thinking with ideas that result in more appropriate feelings and behaviors. Research shows that CBT can be effective in treating a variety of conditions, including depression and anxiety.

- Dialectical behavior therapy (DBT) can be used to treat older adolescents who have chronic suicidal feelings/thoughts, engage in intentionally self-harmful behaviors, or have a borderline personality disorder. DBT emphasizes taking responsibility for one's problems and actions and helps adolescents examine how they deal with conflict and intense negative emotions. This often involves a combination of group and individual sessions.

- Exposure response therapy (ERT) is a targeted type of behavioral therapy that enables a youngster to become desensitized to an anxiety provoking stimulus by repeated exposure to it and repeated practice of substitute responses.

Group, Family, and Psychosocial Therapies

Children with emotional and social issues can be treated with other members of their families present, or as part of a group with same-age children.

- Group therapy is a form of psychotherapy where there are multiple (unrelated) patients led by one or more therapists. It uses the power of group dynamics and peer interactions to increase understanding of mental illness and/or improve social skills. There are different types of group therapy, such as psychodynamic, social skills, substance abuse, multi-family, desensitization, and parent support.

- Family therapy focuses on helping a family function in more positive and constructive ways by exploring patterns of communication and by providing support and education. Family therapy sessions can include a youngster identified as the patient along with parents, siblings, and even grandparents. It is the subject of Chapter 21.

- Psychosocial therapy is an educational approach that teaches children and adolescents problem-solving skills, anger management, social skills, and how to handle emotional or social problems a youngster is experiencing. Parent Effectiveness Training (PET) teaches child and adolescent management skills to parents with an emphasis on handling problem behaviors. It is particularly effective when a parent is dealing with a child with an oppositional defiant disorder.

At times, a combination of different individual psychotherapy approaches may be most helpful. In some cases, a combination of medication and psychotherapy may be needed. Child and adolescent psychiatrists are trained in different forms of psychotherapy and are able to combine these forms of treatment with medications.

FIELD STUDY

An Ohio State University meta-analysis of 42 studies assessed the relative effectiveness of family therapy, individual child/adolescent, and a combination of both. It found that the combination of individual psychotherapy and family therapy produced moderately better treatment outcomes for child and adolescent patients compared to only individual or only family therapy.

Does Psychotherapy Work?

In a word, yes. Unlike most medical conditions, a mental or emotional problem, also known as a psychopathology, manifests in behavioral changes. A depressed child often is lethargic and may sleep more than usual. An emotionally disturbed adolescent may pull out her hair and refuse to eat. These symptoms have physiological aspects but are primarily behavioral in nature. Research on psychotherapy is facilitated when objective evidence for the alleviation of behavioral manifestations that brought the patient to therapy can be demonstrated in addition to subjective changes.

An assessment of outcome research for child and adolescent therapy was reported in *The Handbook of Psychotherapies with Children and Families.* From the early 1960s to 1997, there were an estimated 1,175 studies assessing outcomes for child and adolescent patients receiving individual or group therapy. To qualify for this classification, these studies included a "control group"—a separate population comparable to the study participants except that they did not receive the treatment being studied. Another 700 studies used "single subject designs" without control groups.

Meta-analyses of these control group and single subject studies have been impressive. Child and adolescent psychotherapy clearly is effective. Virtually all types of symptoms that brought patients into therapy responded positively to therapy, although the amount of research done on different diagnostic categories has varied:

- One study found that 60 percent of treated patients' behavior returned to a normal range after treatment; and 64 percent no longer met criteria for the diagnosis they had when they entered treatment.

- Another study of psychological treatment of a high-risk adolescent group found 50 percent fewer arrests among those who received treatment compared to those in a control group who hadn't.

There are two general categories of psychological problems for which the most outcome research has been done:

- **Externalizing behaviors**—A child "acts out" using aggression, noncompliance, or classroom disruption. These are the most studied.

- **Internalizing behaviors**—A child emotionally withdraws or exhibits phobias or depression. These have been studied less frequently.

For both categories, and especially for externalizing problems, behavioral and cognitive behavioral therapy approaches have proven most effective when compared to non-behavioral approaches to the same problems. A caveat is that the outcomes of psychodynamic treatment have been less frequently studied. Another issue is the lack of diversity among the populations served by either approach. Low-income families and members of different ethnic and cultural minority groups frequently do not receive the psychological services they need. It is likely that most children and adolescents who need psychotherapy do not receive it.

The Least You Need to Know

- Psychotherapy with children and adolescents adapts the processes of adult psychotherapy to fit different developmental levels and abilities.
- Psychotherapy with children and adolescents takes place in a variety of forms that focus more or less on insight, corrective emotional experiences, education, and monitoring behavior.
- A therapist is not a friend; she is someone a youngster can work with on real problems, even if those problems are not recognized by the youngster.
- Fantasy play can reveal hidden internal conflicts and emotions and provide a means to resolve a youngster's negative feelings.
- Evidence-based outcome research shows that child and adolescent psychotherapy are effective.

Family Therapy

In This Chapter

- When a child's problem is the tip of an iceberg
- How individual and family life cycles match or clash
- How to decode the scripts and triangles in family dramas
- Why adding or subtracting a family member = stress

In this book, family refers to a two-generation unit. As each of us knows from personal experience, families are complicated, powerful, and sometimes fragile. A family can be a force working for or against its members, but each family is only as strong as its weakest link. Because of this interconnectedness, psychologists have found that treating a family is often an effective way to help an individual child confront and resolve a symptom, such as school failure or emotional withdrawal. There's another factor frequently at work in family disruptions called "the iceberg effect." Just as 90 percent of an iceberg lies under the surface of the water, a child's symptom often is only a small but visible piece of a larger problematic family dynamic. This chapter discovers what psychologists have learned about helping families with children cope and thrive.

Stages of Family Life

Researchers looking at families have identified six typical stages for the average married two-parent family. Similar principles apply to one-parent and cohabiting families. Each stage requires adjustments which, if not made successfully, could bring a family into therapy. Here are the typical stages of family growth and problems that may arise within that stage.

1. Single young adults leaving home:

    - A weak personal identity

    - An inability to emotionally separate from one's family of origin

    - A lack of social and relationship skills needed to develop an intimate relationship with a potential partner

    - A lack of opportunity or desire to find a suitable partner

2. The new couple:

    - Inability to adjust to living as a couple

    - Difficulty with in-laws

    - The question of whether or not to have children

3. Families with young children:

    - Negative impact of children on marital relationship

    - Difficulty establishing limits for a young child

4. Families with adolescents:

    - Conflicts between parents and teenagers, such as setting limits and dealing with individual differences

    - Changes in the marital relationship causing disappointment or detachment

    - Pressures for parents to care for their aging parents and children ("the sandwich generation")

5. Families launching children and moving on:

    - Parents' sense of loss ("the empty nest")

    - Conflict when older child does not become independent

    - Frustration over marital relationship or perceived/actual career failure

6. Families in later life:

   • A lack of meaning or fulfillment

   • An inability to form solid relationships with grown children, grand-children, or in-laws

INSIGHT

Which period of family life poses the most challenges for its members? Families with young children and adolescents report the highest levels of stress. Greater levels of well-being are reported by younger couples without children and older couples whose children have left home. The obvious conclusion is that families with children have difficulty in our individualistic society. If this was more openly recognized, more might be done to help parents and families cope.

Interacting Stages

Another way of looking at the stages of family life is as the interaction between the individual life stages of parents and their children. To understand how individual and family stages intersect, we draw on Erik Erikson's eight stages of psychosocial *development*. This framework for understanding the age-related crises each child needs to resolve for healthy personal growth can help us see the issues and conflicts that parents must resolve as their children mature.

DEFINITION

The term **development** used throughout this book has a special meaning in a family therapy context. Here it refers to predictable physical, mental, and social changes that occur during the life of an individual and a family with one shaping the other. This process of individual and family growth is uneven with times of growth and regression.

The Developmental Stages of Parenthood

The parents in a young family, usually two individuals between the ages of 20 and 34, are at the time of life Erikson calls the fifth stage of developing relationships—a time to experience intimacy (versus isolation). At this point, parents have presumably formed their own individual identities and must now learn how to be intimate and nurturing with a partner. If they have children, they then extend this new capacity for nurturance to a child who comes to them by way of birth, adoption, or as a stepparent entering a blended family.

As parents progress into middle age, from 35 to 65, they enter the sixth stage of life which Erikson calls "generative." This is when parents need to guide their children into adolescence and simultaneously begin the process of letting go. This is a delicate stage, because, as you've seen in earlier chapters, adolescence has elements of returning to early childhood.

Helpful and Hurtful Matches

If it's a good match—for example, when a mature adult in the nurturing, generative stage parents an adolescent successfully forming his identity—the two have a better chance of aiding each other's growth. If a parent has not yet moved from the intimacy stage into the generative, she may not be able to offer much help to the same adolescent, because she's more focused on her marital role (intimacy) rather than her parental role.

Each of these stages presents challenges to individual family members. If one family member hasn't successfully navigated an earlier stage, that lack of resolution impacts others. For example, a 14-year-old who's struggling with a diffused identity—unable to figure out who he is—may act out aggressively against his 8-year-old brother. This then may cause the younger child to have feelings of inferiority and interfere with his struggle to attain a sense of personal competence—the challenge of his developmental stage. When such problems become too much for families to solve on their own, they may involve a family therapist.

Ancient Art, New Science

Clan and family members advising and helping each other sort out conflicts and problems is nothing new. There are prehistoric records verifying this—written accounts from 2,000 years ago describing systematic processes for families designed to help individual family members exhibiting problematic behavior. Beginning in the 1940s, largely as an outgrowth of marriage counseling, psychologists and other mental health practitioners began to formally treat families. The field of family therapy was recognized by the National Institute of Mental Health in the 1950s when it began to sponsor counseling sessions with family members of schizophrenic patients. From there, family therapy theory and practice grew in earnest, gaining credibility and acceptance as a therapeutic option for troubled families and as an adjunct to individual therapy for children.

Who Practices Family Therapy?

Among the types of professionals who are trained to offer family therapy are …

- Child psychologists, represented by the American Psychological Association (APA).

- Child psychiatrists, represented by the American Academy of Child and Adolescent Psychiatrists (AACAP).

- Marriage and family therapists, often using the assignation "MFT," represented by the American Association of Marriage and Family Therapists (AAMFT).

- Social workers, represented by the National Association of Social Workers (NASW).

- Counselors, represented by the American Counseling Association (ACA).

Why Family Therapy?

The goal of family therapy is to identify and resolve issues and interactions in a family so that it can more adequately meet the needs of its members and function effectively in its surrounding world. There are advantages for a therapist to work with an entire family when one child is seen as having a problem, rather than treating the child as an individual:

- Family therapy allows therapists to see the cause of a problem in a cross-sectional as well as a linear view. This is helpful when dealing with a complicated problem such as an adolescent's anorexia, which may in fact reflect other stresses in the family as well as stresses within the child.

- Family therapy allows interactions between family members to be seen with an objective mediator present who can point out problematic dynamics between individuals.

- Family therapy can eliminate secrets and covert alliances within a family by challenging family members to work together to face a problem.

- Family therapy usually takes less time than individual counseling.

Because of these advantages and efficiencies, family therapy often is more likely to offer a practical solution to a family or individual problem than individual psychotherapy.

INSIGHT

In a national poll taken in 1996, 97 percent of clients said that the services they received from marriage and family therapists helped them deal with a problem in their family more effectively.

The Family System

Every family—whether it has one or two parents, one child or six—is a system with its own rules and dynamics. Each member of a family also is her own subsystem, because she maintains separate relationships with every other family member: parents, siblings, and everyone in her extended family. What happens when a 13-year-old girl in a family of four wins a statewide ice skating tournament, while, in the same week, her twin brother fails the eighth grade? Many happy, sad, proud, and disappointed feelings co-exist in parents and children alike. To put it in interactional terms, when one member of a family goes through a change, the effects of that change are felt by every other family member in a chain reaction called a feedback loop. The term *cybernetics* refers to this way of understanding the relationships between systems and subsystems in any context.

DEFINITION

In the context of family therapy, **cybernetics** lends insights into the developmental and dynamic nuances of family life. It illuminates the positive and negative feedback loops between family members that reinforce and deter the behavior of individuals.

Changes in a family can originate internally, such as an illness or misbehavior, or externally, such as graduating from high school or losing a job. Every change causes a family system to expand or contract its range of behaviors to deal with the ramifications of that change. And every family is constantly changing, expanding, or contracting its activity level to achieve stability. What types of behavior cause an expansion in activity level? Here are two examples, which you'll see require that you remove the value judgments "good" or "bad" and simply view the behaviors as descriptors of a family's interactions.

Feedback Loops in Action

Example A:

1. Change/action: A teenager violates curfew.

2. Parental response: Teenager is grounded for a week creating a negative feedback loop with a contraction of activity/behavior.

3. Teenager response: Teenager is less likely to violate curfew.

Example B:

1. Change/action: A child throws a tantrum in a supermarket.

2. Parent response: Child is not disciplined.

3. Child response: Child throws more tantrums, which then create a positive feedback loop amplifying the activity/behavior of throwing tantrums and parental frustration.

Because change-provoking events are inevitable, every family must learn how to cope constructively with change. This means being cognizant of the need to follow periods of expansion with activities to promote contraction and thus a return to equilibrium (homoeostasis).

Boundaries in a Family System

Healthy families have clear roles and boundaries between their members. Subsystems in a family, such as siblings who are close in age or the parents, need boundaries—physical and psychological lines of demarcation—between them and other subsystems to grow and thrive. When one family member steps out of bounds, for example when a child doesn't do his chore of taking out the trash, other family members or subsystems (parents) will bring him into line. The goal is to resist disruption of equilibrium in the family.

Barriers to healthy family boundaries include the existence in a family of stereotyped roles acted out by different family members in relationship to each other. Examples of these roles are victim, martyr, hero, tyrant, scapegoat, saint, rebel, fool, and genius. When one of these roles is played out by a family member it often is an unconscious action. In psychological terms, the child or adult is said to be operating from a "ritualized script." When siblings or parents and children base their behavior with each other on such scripts, they can form destructive patterns. For example, a child who always plays the martyr in relationship to an older sibling who plays the tyrant is unlikely to fulfill his potential. Family therapy can create awareness of these counterproductive scripts and roles through confrontation, interpretation, playfulness, and humor to support family members in legitimate family roles.

It's All Stress

Stress is part of every family's life, and, as you have seen, family stress levels are higher when children are young or in their teenage years. No surprises there. But all stressors are not alike. Winning the lottery can be stressful as well as unexpected and positive. Certainly a teenage pregnancy and a sudden illness are unexpected negative stressors. Some stressors are predictable and can be planned for, such as an empty nest. It's the stressors that cannot be anticipated that throw a family into crisis and lead to treatment by a family therapist. However, even predictable stressors may provoke unanticipated emotional reactions.

Vertical Stressors

These are the stressors that can be called historical. You can't control vertical stressors; they constitute the "hand you were dealt." Genetic inheritances can be considered in this category. They are your family legacies, including attitudes, culture, and any family secrets lurking in closets. Sometimes these stressors jump from the background to the foreground, for example when a young person's choice to marry outside the family's traditional faith upsets his elders. Societal factors, such as racism or homophobia, fall into this category as well.

Horizontal Stressors

These stressors can be expected (life stage transition points) or unexpected (surprises or traumatic events). Either precipitates change and can produce strong positive or negative emotions and are, thus, stressful.

It's been found that families recognize and deal more constructively with vertical stressors than horizontal stresses, whether these are expected or not. Whenever anyone enters or exits a family system, other family members become unsettled and experience higher stress levels until individual and collective adjustments are made.

FIELD STUDY

Researchers identified 43 life-stress situations from job loss to natural disasters. Of the top 14 situations causing the most stress, 10 involved gaining or losing a family member.

Family Therapy Theory and Practice

The theory and practice of family therapy has been built on the foundation of the fields of psychology and psychiatry. For this reason, in this section you will find some of the same thinkers and researchers who were pioneers in these fields. Family therapy evolved from marital couple therapy and from attempts to create more supportive family structures for mentally ill patients. Along the way, it integrated the therapeutic concepts and tools of other forms of individual and group psychotherapy. It also created some of its own, custom-made for families.

The theories and practices of family therapy tend to focus on three areas:

- **Past family patterns**—The family therapist primarily examines individual behavior in the context of past family patterns, which may be based on conscious or unconscious motives. This category encompasses psychodynamic theory and its off-shoots. Theorists include Nathan Ackerman, Murray Bowen, Ivan Boszormenyi-Nagy, and Ross Speck.

- **Present family interactions**—Families are understood by seeing and hearing how they interact in the present. This experiential school includes the theories of Virginia Satir, Carl Whitaker, and August Napier.

- **Changing family behavior**—The third category takes a behavioral or cognitive behavioral approach, focusing more on behavior and thoughts and less on causes. Theorists include B. F. Skinner, Albert Bandura, and John Gottman.

These foci overlap, but you'll look at each to identify the primary theoretical contributions and practices which they produced.

Family Therapy with an Eye on the Past

Schools of family therapy theory that focus on established family patterns include the psychodynamic and Bowen approaches. The latter refers to a group of practitioners that adapted Freudian principles to their work with families beginning in the 1950s.

Psychodynamic Family Therapy

This school draws on Freud's understanding of individual unconscious drives and conflicts and puts it in the family context. Nathan Ackerman (1908–1971) advanced this perspective by encouraging psychotherapists to treat families and individuals together as a single system. Key ideas include the following:

- A "layer of intra-psychic conflict," also called a family's "interlocking pathology," divides family members into factions. It's seen as an unconscious process that keeps family members repeating the same, often dysfunctional, patterns.

- The "double bind" in a family system is a covert or hidden family relationship in which one person has power over the other who cannot escape.

A double bind has two important components:

First, the less powerful member of the two is given conflicting messages by the more powerful member. These can be given either through impossible demands, such as "be spontaneous" or through contradictory verbal and nonverbal messages, such as when a parent says "don't worry about me" in an anxious tone of voice.

The second component occurs over time in which the mixed messages lead to repetitive behavior patterns. For example, a mother criticizes her silent daughter and encourages her to express her feelings. When she does, the mother breaks into tears with, "How can you feel that way after all I have done for you?" Then the daughter becomes silent, eliciting her mother's criticism again, because she is not speaking.

Object Relations Theory

A more recent theoretical focus of psychodynamic family therapy is "object relations theory." An object is someone who is loved. Relations between two people in the present are shaped by residues of strong relationships with past objects (persons) that have been internalized by each person in the form of "internal objects."

As they grow up, children internalize "good" and "bad" aspects of their objects of attachment (usually their parents) and take them on as their own "internal objects." These "internal objects" then form the basis of how a person perceives and forms close relationships, such as to a wife or husband, but the perceptions and process also can extend to parent-child relationships and even friendships. The expectation of this theory is that, if the characteristics of these "internal objects" are not made conscious, there is a tendency to be attracted to the sort of person who resembles an "internal object." You then may perceive that person as having the "good" or "bad" characteristics of your own "internal object." The result is a projection of inappropriate "good" or "bad" qualities onto the other person.

The importance of object relations in family therapy is that it enables psychodynamic family therapists to understand intergenerational relationships and marital choices. It stresses the importance of working with unconscious forces in addressing dysfunctional family patterns.

In practical terms, if a wife unconsciously projects qualities of an "internal object," such as her father's tendency to make harsh criticisms of her on to her husband, she will tend to overreact to her husband's words and actions and create a dysfunctional pattern between them. When these patterns are uncovered, psychodynamic theory says, new more productive ways of relating can be tried.

Bowen Family Therapy

Murray Bowen (1913–1990) also advanced a theory of family therapy emphasizing the importance of individuals rectifying relationship patterns from earlier generations, but Bowen characterized this cross-generation inheritance as rooted in anxiety carried from one generation to the next. Anxiety, he said, is common to all human beings, but it can be either high or low based on how well previous generations handled their own anxieties.

To address chronic anxiety in families—which manifests in emotional disturbances, such as aggressive acting out or withdrawal among adult and child members—Bowen emphasized concepts such as these:

- **Differentiation**—This describes a family's ability to allow each member to be him or herself. This ability is weakest, Bowen said, in emotionally fused families with high levels of intra-generational anxiety.

- **Triangles**—The most obvious triangle in a family is between two parents and a child, but there are other possible triangular relationships. Triangles often lead two family members to project negative traits onto a third person. Triangulation is characteristic of the "parental alienation syndrome" in which one divorced parent turns a child against the other parent.

- **Cutoffs**—A cutoff is when a member distances himself from his family to manage unresolved emotional issues. Although cutting off from one's family may temporarily reduce individual and family tensions, they may simply be latent and arise again at a later point.

Bowen family therapy promotes individual differentiation of family members encouraging stronger self-identities among individual members. It encourages "de-triangulation" so that individuals recognize their projections onto another family member and cease making that person a scapegoat for their own anxieties.

Family Therapy with an Eye on the Present

In the 1960s, the "here and now" approach grew out of Gestalt, psychodrama, and client-centered therapies in which the client did most of the talking. Now referred to as "experiential," this family therapy approach stresses present interactions between family members as a means of recognizing and rectifying problems of and between individuals.

This approach relies on attachment theory as the basis for positive or negative family interactions. Abstract ideas and unconscious motivations or conflicts are less important. Emotions matter most. Family members' conscious feelings may hide intense, underlying emotions, creating an atmosphere of deadness in a family. The purpose of experiential family therapy is to promote emotional sensitivity and feeling expression by gaining emotional self-awareness and learning better interpersonal skills.

Theorists who developed this school of family therapy tended to fall into one of two camps—those who relied on the strength of their personalities and used fewer techniques and those who favored structured therapy sessions using a variety of techniques.

Emotional Confrontations

As a major theorist in this school and a family psychiatrist, Carl Whitaker (1912–1995) relied on the strength of his personality, spontaneity, and creativity to leave a lasting mark in his field. Part of Whitaker's approach emphasized enlarging the pain of an individual family member so that other members couldn't deny its existence and would be less able to suppress it or their reactions to it. He also encouraged emotional confrontations within family therapy sessions. This school of family therapy also emphasized the importance of treating children as children and not as adult peers. Overall, in Whitaker's approach, the individual members mattered more than the structures or patterns within a family.

"I" Messages, Blamers, Distractors

Virginia Satir (1916–1998), a social worker, developed a variety of techniques to help families communicate as a way to break dysfunctional patterns. From better communication they would grow as individuals and as a family unit. Perhaps the best-known technique she advanced is the use of "I" messages, which focuses on taking responsibility for one's feelings when addressing another. For example, rather than "you are a slob," a parent might say, "I get very anxious when I have to walk through your messy room."

Identifying and disengaging from dysfunctional roles played by parents and children, Satir said, could improve family communication and bring greater family emotional health. For example, she described blamers ("Now look at what you made me do"), placaters ("That's fine," "Whatever"), and distractors (jokesters and subject changers) as common dysfunctional roles in families.

Virginia Satir created "sculpting" a technique for creating a 3-D family portrait so that family members could gain a clearer view of family dynamics. By physically moving family members to different positions in the room and sculpting their interactions she could expose outmoded family perceptions and patterns and help the family change them.

In the same vein, Satir created "family mapping," a technique to reconstruct a family's past by drawing a family tree charting three generations of its members along with key facts and events, such as a suicide or adoption. The purpose is to uncover facts dealing with the origins of distorted ideas, such as the belief that the experience of suffering is nobler than joy. A final step in family mapping involves a type of psychodrama where a group of people, not necessarily related, re-enact a historical family event that resonates with an individual's present emotional problem.

Family Therapy with an Eye on Changing Behavior

This school of family therapy is based on behavioral theory and social learning theory in child psychology, which stresses the modeling or demonstration of new behaviors to change dysfunctional ones in an individual. The thinking of Watson, Skinner, and Bandura figures largely in this approach, as do the concepts of operant conditioning, reinforcers, and rewards. A leading proponent is John Gottman.

Behavioral Parent Training

In this model, family therapists function as educators teaching parents new behaviors they can use to socialize and manage their children. They also help improve the self-esteem and well-being of parents. As a first step, problem behaviors of children and parents are identified. Lectures and role playing are used to train parents to use better parenting behaviors. This type of psychosocial parenting program has been shown to be particularly effective in helping families of low socioeconomic status.

CBT Family Therapy

Using techniques borrowed from individual and marital cognitive behavioral therapy, this approach combines education and problem-solving techniques. Their purpose is to reinforce desired behavior and discourage maladaptive behaviors.

Among the individual techniques used are …

- **Modifying beliefs**—Teaching families to think differently about what constitutes a "good" (effective) versus "bad" (ineffective) behavior or form of communication.

- **Contracting**—Specific agreements, tokens of reward, and penalties are used to change problem behaviors into desired ones.

- **Shaping**—The process of learning new behaviors in small, gradual steps.

- **Time-outs**—Removing children from an environment in response to their actions. For example, a child who hits his sibling during play is removed from the play area.

- **Charting**—A child or parent keeps a chart documenting occurrences of a problem behavior. After getting a baseline of the rate of occurrence, interventions are made to reduce this rate with subsequent results charted.

- **Modeling**—Role-playing is used to model new behaviors with feedback from the family therapist and other family members.

Behavioral and cognitive behavioral family therapies usually do not attempt to uncover root causes of problematic family dynamics. They can be effective in rapidly reducing family conflict stemming from specific behaviors.

More Grist for the Mill

Other theoretical approaches in treating family problems that have added valuable techniques and concepts to the field of family therapy include …

- **Structural family therapy**—Salvador Minuchin and his colleagues took a systems approach to family dynamics. Family members are given instructions and homework to do between sessions. Treatment focuses on removing symptoms by problem solving.

- **Strategic family therapy**—Milton Erikson (1901–1980) and later adherents to this school emphasize clarity about what needs to be changed in a family and then they address that single issue. It's also called "brief therapy" in that it is highly directive and goal-focused. Change doesn't require insights or consideration of family history. Problems are solved by revamping family rules and changing the family culture from a competitive stance to a cooperative one.

- **Solution-focused family therapy**—Drawn from the ideas and writings of Gregory Bateson (1904–1980) and Michel Foucault (1926–1984), solution-focused family therapy employs *externalization* to take into account the linguistic, social, and cultural context of a family because each of these factors influences which behaviors are considered normal and which are not. Internal causes within the family are not the focus. Families are encouraged to define their problems in their own terms and come up with their own solutions and to plan and make small, rapid changes.

DEFINITION

Externalization in the context of psychology means to separate a problem from the person who is experiencing it. For example, envy is not seen as a personal problem but as something causing negative effects on the family as a whole. Thus, no one person owns the problem that then can be more constructively solved by family members together.

- **Narrative family therapy**—Michael White (1948–2008) advanced this post-modern approach to family therapy where most issues have a social/cultural context and cause. Narrative family therapy focuses on having family members "re-author" their lives. By "changing their stories" families can externalize a specific problem—such as financial difficulties—and open up new possibilities to remedy it that will work better for them. If the family's current story is that their source of money can only be the father's work, the narrative can be changed to include or shift emphasis to a mother's potential financial contributions—especially when he's out of work. In treatment, the narrative family therapist is more of a collaborator than an expert, helping to shift a family from one form of thinking to another. Treatment ends when goals are achieved.

- **Parent education**—Parent-guidance materials are important adjuncts to family therapy of all types by helping parents understand and cope with a child's characteristics. Training in parenting skills also is useful. This is particularly needed in developing communications skills through listening, talking with children, and verbal problem solving as employed in Parent Effectiveness Training. Parent modeling of self-discipline, forgiveness, and a willingness to acknowledge mistakes promotes similar qualities in their children. More specific behavioral management techniques have been developed for children with mental disorders, such as hyperactivity, learning difficulties, conduct disorders, and autism.

Family therapists most often take an eclectic approach to treating families. They take techniques and concepts from these theoretical approaches and use whichever methods are appropriate for the problems presented by a family.

The single most important determinant of successful family therapy is finding the right therapist and techniques for a specific family. The family's life cycle, cultural background, size, and lifestyle are all important factors in making the most suitable match.

The Least You Need to Know

- The symptoms of a family in crisis often manifest in problem behavior exhibited by one of its children.
- Different approaches to family therapy emphasize past or present family interactions while others look strictly at desired behavioral changes.
- Family therapy combined with individual child psychotherapy has the best outcomes in resolving the psychological problems of children and adolescents.

Psychology of the Whole Child

In This Chapter

- Why attachment bonds between all parents and children matter to you
- A look inside the moral decline of today's teens
- How chaos/complexity theory explains social ills affecting children

The majority of this book has examined the components of child psychology. This final chapter expands the focus and provides a theoretical framework within which to view a child as part of a larger society. No child is an island apart.

Just as psychological problems and negative behavior in a child often reflect family dysfunctions, the ills affecting America's children can be seen as symptoms of our deeper unresolved issues as a society. A few of these most pressing issues are highlighted here and placed in the context of the psychological themes covered in previous chapters. Perspectives from thinkers who provide an *integrative* multi-systems approach to the study of children also are offered.

A Child Is Part of a Community

What's wrong with our children? It's a question often asked by parents, teachers, judges, legislators, and pundits. I suggest that the answer to this question needs to begin at home, but not remain there. It must move outward from the family unit in concentric circles to encompass our culture, laws, economics, and public policies regarding children and families.

> **DEFINITION**
>
> **Integrative** is an approach that views separate systems together as an interacting whole by bringing all component parts together.

A child's parents have the most impact—for better or worse and often both—on shaping the grown man or woman. Peers strongly influence young persons' interests, fashions, and behavior. However, the processes by which they develop character and morality have one thing in common: they require contact time between parents and their children. Competent parenthood rests upon attachment bonds between child and parent that promote self-respect, self-confidence, and resiliency in dealing with the vicissitudes of life. Parents must be physically present and emotionally, intellectually, and morally engaged with their children. When they aren't, the problems and deficiencies in a family quickly spill over into the surrounding community. Here are just a few of the ways in which these ills tear at our social fabric.

Schools in Trouble

When a child has not formed a solid attachment with his parent and his essential needs are not met at each stage of development, the first place his problems manifest is the classroom. A 2006 AP-AOL Learning Services Poll found that two thirds of the teachers surveyed said that student discipline and lack of interest in learning are major problems in their schools. A national survey of more than 3,500 kindergarten teachers in the late 1990s revealed that 46 percent said that at least half of the children in their classrooms were having problems following directions, some because of poor academic skills and others because of difficulties working in a group.

> **FIELD STUDY**
>
> The 2008 Ethics of American Youth Survey by the Josephson Institute of Ethics of 43,000 teens, 15 to 18, revealed that moral attitudes and behaviors are in decline:
>
> - Bullying: Nearly half (boys and girls) admit bullying someone, and 48 percent were victims of bullying in the past year.
> - Aggression: Around 37 percent of boys and 19 percent of girls say: "It's okay to hit someone who angers me."
> - Cheating: About 60 percent had cheated on a school test.

Darcia Narvaez, professor of psychology at the University of Notre Dame, pinned the moral decline of U.S. teens (as revealed in the Joshephson Institute survey) on an empathy gap formed early in life. She explained that when parents have less time for parenting, young children do not receive enough positive interaction with them. This missing affection and bonding brings about a lack of empathy and self-regulation in children and more aggression as those children become teens.

In a relatively affluent Madison (Wisconsin) Metropolitan School District survey of students and teachers, 13 percent of the students and 42 percent of the teachers felt that their parents were not involved in helping them succeed in school. Of students, 22 percent felt that they would not be in trouble at home if they breeched rules in school; 25 percent felt unsafe at school; 60 percent felt that their personal possessions were unsafe at school; 61 percent felt vulnerable to bullying; 54 percent felt vulnerable to sexual harassment; and 45 percent felt they could not talk with an adult at school about drugs, sex, or suicidal talk by other students.

Measures of Child Well-Being

In the 2010 The Programme for International Student Assessment, the United States ranked 18th of 21 Western countries in child well-being. It also ranked twenty-third in science, seventeenth in reading, and thirty-first in math achievement of 32 Organization of Economic Cooperation and Development countries, including Shanghai, China (first in all); South Korea (sixth, second, and fourth); Finland (first, second, and sixth); Canada (eighth, sixth, and tenth); Poland (nineteenth, fifteenth, and twenty-fifth); and Germany (thirteenth, twentieth, and sixteenth). Our children face the following challenges:

- Forty percent are born out of wedlock.

- Half do not live with their biological father at some time during their childhoods.

- Around 145,000 are born annually to school-age mothers; 6,000 to those 14 or younger.

- About 11 million have been substantiated as having been abused or neglected.

- One in five lives in a family with an income lower than the official poverty threshold.

- Almost half were assaulted at least once during the past year.

- The average age for the onset of menstruation has dropped to 12½.

- Only 15 percent in the high school graduating class of 2007 had a grade level predictive of college success or higher on an Advanced Placement Examination.

A Mental Health Crisis

When a child lacks proper parental support, and when symptoms of emotional and mental disturbances are not treated, milder disorders become more severe. In 2001, Surgeon General David Satcher released a National Action Agenda for Children's Mental Health in response to the nation's public health crisis in mental health care for babies, children, and adolescents. At that time 10 percent of children and adolescents suffered from severe mental illnesses, and only one in five received mental health services. In 2007, 20 percent of young people had a diagnosed psychiatric disorder by the age of 18.

The World Health Organization indicates that by the year 2020, childhood psychiatric disorders will rise by more than 50 percent to become one of the five most common causes of morbidity, mortality, and disability among children. The United States lacks a unified infrastructure to help these children, many of whom are falling through the cracks. Too often, children who are not identified as having mental health problems and those who are but do not receive services end up in jail and then in prison. Children and families are suffering because of missed opportunities for prevention and early identification, fragmented treatment services, and low priorities for family resources. Most adolescents do not have access to mental health and substance abuse services.

A Missing Model of Character

We cannot expect our children to prosper when our society does not model, and actually undermines, the development of character. The "good life" is portrayed in mass media and culture as gaining power, pleasure, and possessions by any means. There is little emphasis on the strength of character needed to control your impulses, to tolerate frustration, and to postpone gratification—essential qualities for life in a civilized society. Children are not born with these qualities.

They learn them from adults who model them. They learn them most indelibly from competent parents supported by a social environment that sets limits on behavior.

James Garbarino, professor of psychology at Loyola University Chicago, indicts our socially toxic environment for the larger number of children with serious problems than in the 1950s and 1960s. Social toxicity includes exposure to violence; economic pressures; disrupted family relationships; and behavior reflecting depression, paranoia, rudeness, and alienation. All these "social contaminants" demoralize families and communities.

Juvenile Ageism

We like to think that our society nurtures and protects our children, but the vulnerability of children and their natural inclinations to challenge authority make them prime targets for prejudice and discrimination when they place competitive demands upon adults for space, material resources, emotional involvement, and time or when they arouse anxiety in adults.

In the past, fathers held life and death power over their children, who were regarded as the property of their parents. With the passage of time, successive restrictions were placed on the rights of parents over their children as society became increasingly involved in the lives of children. During the last century, children have been accorded an increasing number of legal and civil rights. But prejudice and discrimination against children were not described as expressions of "childism," "adultism," or "juvenile ageism" until the 1970s by Chester Pierce, Jack Flasher, the Child Welfare League of America, and Jack Westman.

Juvenile ageism reflects the views that children are the property of their parents and are not citizens. It has the virulence of racism and the prevalence of sexism. It has contributed to the alienation of many young people from our society's values. It has resulted in the staggering costs of violence, habitual crime, and welfare dependency—the ultimate products of child neglect and abuse.

The concept of juvenile ageism has not taken hold in our society. Rhetoric about our devotion to children obscures their victimization. We decry ageism as it applies to the elderly and are beginning to see it with older persons in the workplace, but we do not recognize that prejudice and discrimination based on age can apply to the young as well. From our society's point of view, juvenile ageism is an even more serious problem than racism, sexism, and elder ageism because the future of our society depends upon the well-being of our children and our adolescents, and, most importantly, one in three are not doing well in some aspect of their lives.

Identifying and overcoming juvenile ageism requires a civil rights approach. This means recognizing children as citizens from birth and sensitizing people to the developmental requirements of childhood and adolescence. Beyond that is the need for class and individual advocacy for newborns, children, adolescents, and their families. Of greatest importance is respect for the responsibilities of, and the support of, parenthood.

If juvenile ageism in our society is not addressed, the next generation is in peril. The emphasis will continue to fall on parents to protect their children from the hostile, exploitative elements of our society, rather than on creating a benevolent society that protects its young.

A Holistic Philosophy of Children's Needs

Newborn babies are persons in every sense of the word. They analyze and respond to sounds. They stop eating to listen to something. When they hear other babies cry, they usually cry with them. They may stop crying on hearing a recording of their own voice—suggesting they recognize themselves. They gaze deeply into their mothers' eyes like lovers. They closely observe their mothers. They are upset when their mothers wear expressionless masks in experiments. They are upset when their mothers are depressed. They hunger for interaction with human beings who are motivated to bond with them and can fill their survival needs.

Building on the work of Charles Darwin, historians, archeologists, and anthropologists have defined the evolution of the human capacity for attachment bonding, cooperation, and altruism from early life. Animal research even suggests that bonding between mother and baby is encoded through altering genes rather than the usual memory process. This bonding process tempers individual-survival drives with species-survival drives. Higher brain centers evolved to permit species survival through the reproductive advantages of attachment bonding between parents and children and persons living in intimate groups.

It is neither correct nor helpful to view children as independent entities or opera-tors. It is accurate and constructive to view each child as interdependent on her family and on a social system that nurtures both families and children. Here are some forward-thinking theorists who've taken this integrative perspective and applied it to child development.

General Systems Theory

General systems theory has its roots in the concepts of positive and negative feedback systems developed in the 1940s by Norbert Weiner who called it "cybernetics." A feedback loop connects an action to its effects on surrounding conditions that in turn amplify or dampen that action.

This theory proposes that understanding living systems requires understanding the relationships between the components of a system and between that system and its environment. As developed by Ludwig von Bertalanffy in the 1960s and elaborated by James G. Miller, it requires thinking in terms of relationships in the context of evolving—integrated wholes whose properties cannot be reduced to their parts.

Ecological/Transactional Theory

The field of human ecology had its roots in deep ecology, a school of thought founded by Arne Naess. Deep ecology recognizes all living things as integral parts of their environments. This perspective was elaborated by Gregory Bateson and by Urie Bronfenbrenner, who proposed the "ecological/transactional theory" to explain human development in 1979. Since then this theory has been elaborated to incorporate child psychology; the family system; the individual and family within their neighborhood and community; and the individual, family, and com-munity within the larger societal and cultural fabric. In this theoretical model, each of these becomes a "system."

Bronfenbrenner described troubled young people, both affluent and disadvan-taged, who were negatively affected by social ills as suffering from a "syndrome of alienation." The primary symptoms of this syndrome Bronfenbrenner cited were the following:

- Inattentiveness and misbehavior in school

- Academic underachievement

- Smoking and drinking

- Sexual activity

- Alcohol and substance abuse

- Dropping out of school

- Aggression and violence, crime, or suicide

Although genetic predisposition, pregnancy and birth complications, malnutrition, disabilities, poverty, and racism all contribute to the vulnerability of children, whether or not children show this "syndrome of alienation" largely depends on how they were parented. In other words, when society doesn't meet its obligations to support children and families and when neighborhoods are unstable, engaged parents can and must provide a buffer from social ills. Every system is interdependent with the others.

Physically or emotionally absent parents are seen as the common denominator in the record numbers of young people diagnosed with psychiatric disorders, taking medications, becoming obese, and contracting sexually transmitted diseases. These problems cross class boundaries as indicated by the increasing numbers of affluent parents who turn to therapeutic schools and programs for their troubled offspring, such as the 110 represented by the National Association of Therapeutic Schools and Programs.

In recent decades, the education, health, safety, and economic status of our children has been insidiously eroded through eras of both economic prosperity and recession. The inescapable fact is that too many children are growing up in the United States under circumstances that prevent them from becoming responsible, productive citizens because they lack the abilities and the opportunities to learn essential social and work-related skills.

Chaos/Complexity Theory

Beginning with an individual child, her parents, community, and society, all the interdependent and interacting systems that make up our society evolve over time. This evolution of interacting interdependent systems is the focus of chaos/complexity theory.

Classical science has been puzzled by the irregular, seemingly unpredictable side of nature. Disorder in the atmosphere and the oceans, fluctuations in wildlife populations, bodily rhythm oscillations, and differing paths of child development have not had a coherent theoretical framework until the emergence of chaos/complexity theory. This theory links your experience to your interactions in the world in which you are immersed through a complex web of nonlinear, interacting networks from which new patterns of complex order emerge. It incorporates general systems theory and the reductionism of classical science. It helps you make predictions by understanding how initial conditions set the stage for evolving systems.

Implications for Children and Families

Chaos/complexity theory helps us understand how living systems work. Instead of breaking things down into their components, it builds upward from simple initial conditions to more complex things as feedback in a system. It then explains how feedback between systems affects the systems' behavior.

Chaos/complexity theory has enhanced our ability to understand how small initial events can have large repercussions on systems far away. Using the example of weather changes in remote locations (popularly known as the "butterfly effect"), you can see how small changes in temperature in an ocean at high risk of chaos can produce repetitious patterns in weather that become hurricanes under amplifying circumstances. This applies to child development as well.

Living systems, whether a human body, family, community, or society, are inherently unstable and are on the edge of chaos. They require the continuous inflow of energy to maintain themselves. The more complex a system, the more unstable it is. Social systems from the family to society are inherently unstable and vulnerable to break down into chaos. Constant effort is needed to keep these systems from breaking down, as anyone with a successful marriage knows.

Living on the edge of chaos with its inevitable uncertainty is difficult for most of us. It takes work to keep all the systems in which you live from becoming chaotic whether that system is your body, your family, your school, your community, or society. Unless you tend to the needs of your body and family, you jeopardize your personal well-being. Unless you strengthen and protect your family, social workers and courts must enter the lives of parents and children. Unless you have safe neighborhoods, your security will suffer. Being on the edge of chaos can provide strong motivation for constructive change.

In the United States, self-sacrificial parenthood is devalued in comparison with remunerated vocations. As the foundation of our society and the source of the next generation, parenthood requires more respect and support from our society at large. Because parents are preoccupied with raising our nation's children and children cannot speak for themselves, parents and children need advocates in our political system.

The Least You Need to Know

- Increased teen aggression and moral decline can be tied to a lack of solid parent-child attachments, especially through touching, in early childhood.
- Emotional problems of children and teens at home spill into the community and cause a decline in school academic performance and increased dropout rates, among many other issues of concern to educators and mental health professionals.
- Unrecognized juvenile ageism is a more serious problem than racism, sexism, and elder ageism because the future of our society depends on the well-being of our children and our adolescents.
- Ecological/transactional theory and chaos/complexity theory provide a philosophical framework for understanding how the actions of one parent and one child then impact all the systems to which they are connected: school, community, courts, and the economic life of the nation.

Glossary

affect   Feelings; observable aspects of an emotional state, such as sadness, anger, or euphoria.

aggression   Forceful action against another person which may be physical, verbal, or symbolic, and is meant to cause pain.

altruism   Helping others without direct benefit to oneself.

amygdala   Part of the brain's limbic system that is considered the seat of emotions.

antidepressant   Medication used to treat depression.

anxiety   A feeling of nervousness, apprehension, fear, or dread.

Asperger's syndrome   A disorder of development characterized by seriously impaired social interactions and repetitive behaviors, interests, and activities.

attachment research   The study of how relationships shape mental processes.

attention-deficit/hyperactivity disorder (ADHD)   A disorder characterized by impulsivity, distractability, inattention, and excessive activity.

autism   A pervasive disorder of development that affects speech, social interactions, and thinking and includes ritualistic behaviors.

behavioral   Relating to how a person acts.

behavioral modification   A method of treatment used to help children change behaviors by rewarding desired behaviors and establishing consequences for undesirable ones.

bipolar mood disorder   A mood disorder characterized by alternating cycles of depression and mania (excitement and grandiose ideas).

bonding   A sense of connection (attachment) between parents and babies that forms the foundation of the parent-child relationship.

child psychiatrist   A physician whose education after medical school includes at least three years of specialty training in psychiatry plus two additional years of advanced training with children, adolescents, and families.

cognition   A process of thinking characterized by awareness with perception, reasoning, judgment, intuition, and memory.

cognitive therapy   A method of psychotherapy used to decrease symptoms of depression and anxiety by examining negative thoughts and ideas associated with these feelings.

conduct disorders   A disorder in which behavior exceeds normal range of aggression and is socially destructive, such as fighting, stealing, lying, arson, truancy, running away from home, or aggression.

cortisol   A hormone secreted by the adrenal gland in times of stress.

declarative memory   Also referred to as explicit memory, it refers to memories that can be consciously recalled, such as facts and events.

defense mechanism   A mental process of self-deception that reduces an individual's awareness of anxiety-provoking thoughts, wishes, or memories. Defense mechanisms include humor, denial, avoidance, and repression of memories and emotions.

depression   An emotional state or mood characterized by sadness, despair, and loss of interest in usual activities.

diagnosis   The name of a disease, disorder, or syndrome.

dissociative disorder   A psychological disorder characterized by a disturbance in the integration of identity, memory, or consciousness, such as with multiple personalities.

dysfunction   Inadequate, impaired, or abnormal function.

dyslexia   A reading learning disability.

dysthymia   A psychological disorder in which the feelings of depression are less severe than those in major depression but last for an extended period of time.

eating disorder   A psychological disorder where a person develops a pathological relationship with food, using it to meet needs other than physical hunger.

ego   Freud's term for the part of your personality that focuses on self-preservation and the appropriate channeling of basic instincts. It includes self-identity.

emotional intelligence   The ability to successfully understand and use emotions.

empathy   Perceiving and understanding how others feel.

explicit memory   The ability to retain information that required a substantial effort to learn.

gender dysphoria   A clinical disorder characterized by a desire to be, or an insistence that one is, of the opposite sex.

gender identity   Perception of one's self as male or female.

genetic   Relating to heredity.

habituation   The process by which a person becomes so accustomed to a stimulus that he ignores it and attends to less familiar stimuli.

hallucination   Visual, auditory (hearing), olfactory (smell), or tactile (touch) perceptions without external stimulation, such as hearing voices when no one is present.

heredity   Characteristics passed from parent to child through genes.

hippocampus   The part of the brain responsible for short-term memory.

hormones   Substances that regulate and control behavior and functions. Not all hormones are directly involved in sexual function, but many are.

hypoxia   Inadequate oxygen supply to the tissues of the body.

id   Freud's term for innate drives and the uninhibited pleasure-seeker in one's personality.

identification   The unconscious internalization of a mental model of another person in the development of personality.

implicit memory   The ability to remember information you haven't deliberately tried to remember.

learning disorders   Disorders characterized by difficulty in processing, learning, or expressing concepts and information, resulting in academic achievement below expected performance levels for age, schooling, and intellectual abilities.

major depression   A mood disorder characterized by persistently depressed mood for at least two weeks accompanied by other related symptoms.

menstrual cycle   The hormonally controlled monthly cycle of ovulation, egg development, and sloughing off of the uterine lining that causes blood and tissue to be expelled from the uterus through the vagina.

menstruation   The discharge of blood and tissue from the lining of the uterus during a female's menstrual periods.

nerve   A bundle of sensory or motor neuron axons that exists anywhere outside the central nervous system. Humans have 43 pairs of them—12 pairs from the brain and 31 pairs from the spinal cord.

neuron   A nerve cell in the brain that specializes in information processing. It consists of a cell body, axons, and dendrites.

neuroscience   The study of how the brain (central nervous system) gives rise to mental processes.

neurotransmitter   A biochemical substance that neurons secrete in a synapse to stimulate other neurons.

norepinephrine   A neurotransmitter central to the brain's emergency response that activates the fight or flight system under stress and puts the body on alert.

object permanence   The mental capacity, attained by most children around 7 months, to comprehend that an object still exists even when it is out of sight.

obsessive-compulsive disorder (OCD)   A disorder characterized by intrusive thoughts (obsessions) and repeated, ritualized behaviors.

oxytocin   A hormone important to maternal behavior. It also bonds lovers to each other and parents to children. It reduces anxiety, allowing for relaxation, growth, and healing.

parallel play   A pattern of play where babies and toddlers play alongside each other with little interaction.

personality Mental traits, characteristics, and styles of behavior that are stable over time.

play therapy A form of psychotherapy in which a child enacts experiences or emotions through play with dolls, clay, drawings, sand, or other toys.

psychiatric social worker A person with a Master's degree in social work (M.S.W.) or state certification as a licensed clinical social worker (L.C.S.W.). Both accreditations qualify a practitioner for counseling and/or psychotherapy in most states.

psychologist A person who has a Master's, Ed.D., Psy.D., or Ph.D. degree in clinical, school, counseling, experimental, or educational psychology.

psychopharmacology A medical specialty concerned with the use of psychoactive medications to alleviate the symptoms of emotional, mental, or behavioral disorders.

psychosis A severely disturbed mental state characterized by loss of contact with reality that may include disorganized speech or behavior, delusions, and/or hallucinations.

psychotherapist A person who uses various psychological principles to help a patient improve his behavior, feelings, thinking, or social interactions.

reflex An involuntary neurological response to stimulus.

regression A return to an earlier pattern of thinking or behavior.

repression The unconscious forgetting of a memory or emotion.

self-regulation Regular patterns of sleep, alertness, and feeding that most newborns develop for themselves, unless prevented by environmental changes.

serotonin A neurotransmitter that is a natural antidepressant and mood elevator.

social referencing A process by which a child looks to others, usually a parent, for cues on how to respond to a new or perplexing situation.

superego Freud's term for an individual's social conscience.

systematic desensitization Behavioral therapy where the patient is presented with a graduated hierarchy of anxiety-provoking stimuli; a treatment for phobias and social anxiety.

theory   A set of assumptions about a question.

trait   A stable characteristic that influences a person's thoughts, feelings, and behavior.

vasopressin   A peptide hormone secreted by the brain that enhances memory, cognition, and alertness. It facilitates testosterone assertive/aggressive behavior and discourages emotional and sexual extremes. It increases arousal and returns to normal prior to ejaculation.

Resources

The following websites and organizations are good places to find specific guidance on fostering children's development and mental health. Some offer helpful information on recognizing and treating specific mental disorders affecting children and teenagers.

Federal Mental Health Information

National Institute on Drug Abuse
http://drugabuse.gov/nidahome.html

National Institutes of Health
U.S. National Library of Medicine
www.pubmed.gov

National Institute of Mental Health
www.nimh.nih.gov/index.shtml

Professional Associations

American Academy of Child & Adolescent Psychiatry
3615 Wisconsin Avenue
NW Washington, DC 20016-3007
Phone: 202-966-7300
www.aacap.org/

American Association for Marriage and Family Therapy
112 South Alfred Street
Alexandria, VA 22314-3061
Phone: 703-838-9808
www.aamft.org

American Psychiatric Association
1000 Wilson Boulevard, Suite 1825
Arlington, VA 22209
Phone: 1-888-35-PSYCH
www.psych.org/
www.healthyminds.org/
www.healthyminds.org/More-Info-For/Children.aspx

American Psychological Association
750 First Street, NE
Washington, DC 20002-4242
Phone: 1-800-374-2721 or 202-336-5500
www.apa.org

National Association of Social Workers
750 First Street
NE Washington, DC 20002-4241
www.socialworkers.org
www.helpstartshere.org

Advocacy Organizations

Child Welfare League of America
1726 M Street NW, Suite 500
Washington, DC 20036
Phone: 202-688-4200
www.cwla.org/childwelfare/familyguide.htm

Mental Health America/National Mental Health Association
2000 N. Beauregard Street, 6th Floor
Alexandria, VA 22311
Phone: 1-800-969-6642 or 703-684-7722
www.nmha.org

There is also a MHA in every state and in many large cities. Chapter contact information is on their website.

National Alliance on Mental Illness
3803 North Fairfax Drive, Suite 100
Arlington, VA 22203
Phone: 703-524-7600
www.nami.org

Online Resources/Communities

Community of Mental Health Blogs
www.mentalhealthblog.com/

Healthy Place
www.healthyplace.com

Psych Central
www.psychcentral.com

Psychology Today
www.PsychologyToday.com

Resources for Specific Disorders

Alcoholics Anonymous
www.alcoholics-anonymous.org

Anxiety Disorders Association of America
11900 Parklawn Drive, Suite 1200
Rockville, MD 20852
www.adaa.org

Attention Deficit Information Network
475 Hillside Avenue
Needham, MA 02194
Phone: 617-455-9895
www.addinfonetwork.com

Autism Speaks
1 East 33rd Street
4th Floor
New York, NY 10016
Phone: 212-252-8584
www.autismspeaks.org

Children and Adults with Attention-Deficit/Hyperactivity Disorder
8181 Professional Place, Suite 150
Landover, MD 20785
Phone: 301-306-7070
www.chadd.org

CollegeBoard: Services for Students with Disabilities
PO Box 6226
Princeton, NJ 08541-6226
Phone: 609-771-7137
www.collegeboard.com

Depressive and Bipolar Support Alliance
730 North Franklin Street, Suite 501
Chicago, IL 60610-3526
Phone: 1-800-826-3632
www.dbsalliance.org

The International Dyslexia Association
40 York Road, 4th floor
Baltimore, MD 21204
www.interdys.org

Learning Disabilities Association of America
4156 Library Road
Pittsburg, PA 15234-1349
www.Idanatl.org

National Association of Anorexia Nervosa and Associated Disorders
www.anad.org

Schizophrenia Information/Community
www.schizophrenia.com

Parent Resources

American Camp Association (Special Needs Camps)
Phone: 1-800-828-CAMP
www.ACAcamps.org

Center for the Improvement of Child Caring/Trained Parenting Instructors
6260 Laurel Canyon Boulevard, Suite 304
North Hollywood, CA 91606
Phone: 1-800-325-CICC

National Head Start Association
http://nhsaresourceguide.com/

Parent Effectiveness Training
www.parenteffectivenesstraining.blogspot.com/

ParentFurther—Search Institute
615 First Avenue NE, Suite 125
Minneapolis, MN 55413
www.parentfurther.com

Parents Helping Parents
Sobrato Center for Nonprofits
1400 Parkmoor Avenue, Suite 100
San Jose, CA 95126
www.php.com

Parents **Magazine**
www.parents.com

The Parents Zone Community
www.theparentszone.com/

Questions About Psychiatric Medications

Parents Med Guide (Guidance for parents about medications for mental disorders)
www.parentsmedguide.org

Suggested Background Readings

Alvy, Kerby T., Ph.D. *The Positive Parent: Raising Healthy, Happy, and Successful Children, Birth-Adolescence.* Teachers College Press, 2008.

Brazelton, T. Berry, and Stanley I. Greenspan. *The Irreducible Needs of Children: What Every Child Must Have to Grow, Learn, and Flourish.* Da Capo Press, 2000.

Damon, William, and Richard M. Lerner, eds. *Handbook of Child Psychology* (6th Edition). John Wiley & Sons, 2006.

Despres, Renee, Lynn Reeves Griffin, Robert N. Golden, M.D., and Fred L. Peterson, Ph.D. *The Truth About Family Life.* Infobase Publishing, 2011.

Freund, Alexandra M., and Michael E. Lamb. *The Handbook of Life-Span Development.* Wiley On-Line Library, 2010.

Garbarino, James, and Claire Bedard. *Parents Under Seige: Why You Are the Solution, Not the Problem, in Your Child's Life.* Free Press, 2001.

Meyers, Karen H., Ph.D., Robert N. Golden, M.D., and Fred L. Peterson, Ph.D. *The Truth About ADHD and Other Neurobiological Disorders.* Infobase Publishing, 2010.

Thelen, Esther, and Linda B. Smith. *A Dynamic Systems Approach to the Development of Cognition and Action.* MIT Press, 1994.

Index

J-K

L

training, behavioral
change, 338
working mothers, 65
Parent Effectiveness
Training, 321
parent-child relationship, 71
attachment parenting,
71-73
communication, 80
corporal punishment, 72
culture, 79
divorce, 82-84
family as a social system,
78
good-enough parent,
76-77
leader and follower roles,
74
modified birth certificate,
78
needs of children, 79-80
nontraditional families,
85
only children, 81
outcomes-based evidence,
72
parental competency,
74-75
parental incompetency, 75
parenthood certification,
77
Parenthood Planning
Counseling, 77
purifier of rebellion, 72
siblings, 80-81
struggle, 74
parenting
attachment, 71-74
competent, 344
indifferent, 61
inductive, 126
interacting stages, 327
self-sacrificial, 352

strictness, 71
television family, 285
PDD. *See* pervasive
developmental disorders
pedophiles, 290
pendulum problem, 230
perfect idiot, 120
performance subscale, 224
personal fable, 231
personality, 7, 43
pervasive developmental
disorders (PDD), 259
PET. *See* positron emission
tomography
phobias, 253, 313
phoneme, 268
phonological disorder, 269
physical abuse. *See* abuse or
neglect
Piaget, Jean, 6, 135
accommodation, 14
cognitive development,
13, 317
concrete operational
thought, 213
conservation, 15, 41
criticism, 138
egocentrism, 15
formal operational
thought, 229
intuitive reasoning, 15
personal fable, 231
preoperational stage, 186,
203
toddler years, 187
pioneers, 3
Bandura, Albert, 12
behavioral learning, 11
birth of psychology, 4-5
building on foundation
created by, 16-17

cognitive development
theory
accommodation, 14
ages and stages, 14
assimilation, 13
cognitive structure, 13
concrete operations, 15
disequilibrium, 13
egocentrism, 15
evolution, 13
formal operations, 16
major precepts, 13
preoperational stage,
15
scheme, 13
sensorimotor stage, 14
theory in action, 14
developmental
psychology, 3
Erickson, Erik, 6, 8
adolescence, 228
central conflict, 9
generative stage, 328
identity crisis, 9
mastery, 202
psychosocial
development, 327
self-identity, 214
stages of psychosocial
development, 9
struggle to trust, 9
toddler years, 185
trial and error, 201
trust, 180
first child psychologists,
5-6
Freud, Sigmund, 3
anal stage, 7
Electra complex, 8
emotional maturation
stages, 7
free association, 315